NEW YORK
& NEW JERSEY

GETTING STARTED GARDEN GUIDE

Grow the Best Flowers, Shrubs, Trees, Vines & Groundcovers

Vincent A. Simeone

**COOL
SPRINGS
PRESS**
Home and Garden Experts™

MINNEAPOLIS, MINNESOTA

DEDICATION AND ACKNOWLEDGMENTS

This book is dedicated to my wife, Gloria, who deserves a great deal of credit for my successes. Thank you for your patience, support, and understanding through the long nights, holidays, and weekends. Life's garden path is full of surprises and we keep growing together every day.

I am so thankful for all of the professional staff at Cornell University, Cornell University Cooperative Extension, Rutgers University, and beyond. These gifted people share their talent with the rest of us every day, unconditionally. Mark Bridgen, Nora Catlin, Scott Clark, Bruce Crawford, Patrick Cullina, Margery Daughtrey, Vinnie Drzewucki, Dan Gilrein, Dr. Bruce Hamilton, Rich and Heidi Hesselein, Dr. George Hudler, Ken Karamichael, Caroline Kiang, Bonnie Klein, Tom Kowalsick, Steve Kristoph, Donna Moramarco, Dr. Elwin Orton, Don Rakow, Andy Senesac, the late Hank Schannen, Fred Spicer, Ralph Tuthill, Mina Vescera, Richard Weir, and Tamsen Yeh have all contributed to this book in some way.

I continue to participate in programs and projects with so many wonderful organizations doing meaningful work, including the American Public Garden Association, American Rhododendron Society-LI Chapter, Holly Society of America, Long Island Arboricultural Association, Long Island Daylily Society, Long Island Gold Medal Plant Award Committee, Long Island Horticultural Society, Long Island Nursery and Landscape Association, Mid Island Dahlia Society, Nassau Suffolk Landscape Gardeners Association, New Jersey Nursery and Landscape Association, New York Hortus Club, New York State Arborists-ISA Chapter, and the North American Rock Garden Society-LI and Watnong Chapters. And to Planting Fields Arboretum, for which the sun rises and sets for me—thank you.

I especially want to acknowledge John Bieber and Steve Nowotarski, two exceptional people whose spirit lives through their love for gardening.

My family and friends make me who I am and this book is a reflection of their untiring devotion to my career goals. Thanks for always being there.

I want to thank Billie Brownell and the staff at Cool Springs Press for giving me a great opportunity and for making this such a worthwhile project. Your talent, professionalism, and attention to detail are greatly appreciated.

Through all of the teaching, writing, lecturing, photography, garden travel, and public garden management, life continues to be a complex journey, rich with opportunities. Live each day to its fullest, appreciate what the garden has to offer, and always keep things in perspective.

CONTENTS

WELCOME TO GARDENING

IN NEW YORK AND NEW JERSEY

I have lived in New York my whole life and have travelled throughout most of the state. New York is a large and diverse state with a thriving gardening community that dates back hundreds of years. Growing up on Long Island afforded me many opportunities to grow a wide variety of plants while also learning from some of the best green industry professionals that horticulture has to offer. I started my career as a student at Farmingdale State College, where I first studied and taught horticulture and began my love for plants. Although Long Island is rich in horticulture, so much of the surrounding areas of New York and New Jersey support a wealth of knowledge, expertise and passion for gardening. New York and New Jersey are blessed with two of the most prestigious land grant colleges in the country in Cornell University and Rutgers University. Both states are havens for many horticultural experts including nursery professionals, growers, arborists, landscape designers, agricultural Extension agents, landscape gardeners, Master Gardeners, agronomists, and the like. Much of the information in this book is a result of years of gained knowledge and expertise that I have acquired from the many talented individuals within these organizations.

Although I am not from New Jersey, I have an intimate knowledge and fondness for the Garden State! Many garden friends and some of my closest relatives enjoy the rich soils, diverse landscapes, and thriving agriculture that New Jersey has to offer. Like New York, New Jersey offers a diversity of parks, public gardens, nurseries, and a great horticultural gem: Rutgers Gardens within the Rutgers University campus. The gardens and the university continue to enjoy a successful outreach and education program that promote horticulture, agronomy, and agriculture that are among the best in the country.

New York and New Jersey have much to offer gardeners who truly love to cultivate the earth, and each state is also fortunate to have well-educated, horticulturally savvy communities. The passion and camaraderie of gardeners eager to share information and craving the next great garden plant or gardening trend continues to amaze me. New York and New Jersey have incredibly diverse environments and eco-systems and enjoy an exceptional climate for growing a wide variety of plants.

Muscari, Betula, Tuilpa 'May Wonder', *Tulipa* 'Ile de France'

Although I travel all over the country and the world, it's great to come home and appreciate all of the virtues of gardening in the northeast. Gardening is an international language and the one common denominator that we all can relate to is our insatiable love for plants.

New York & New Jersey Getting Started Garden Guide offers readers an opportunity to learn about a wide variety of plants and useful information that can be applied to your own garden. Many residential landscapes offer us vast opportunities and challenges that require us to be well informed and prepared. Before you get started, it is important to accept the fact that gardening will have its ups and downs, its victories and defeats. The key to success is never to be discouraged and to always try, try again. All of us as gardeners have had a favorite plant die, even two or three times. But our love for gardening and passion to cultivate the land keeps us coming back for more. I hope this gardening guide provides the information you need to be successful gardeners and keeps *you* coming back for more!

A Few Gardening Rules to Follow

The best gardening advice I can offer is to have a plan before developing or renovating your garden. So many times we find a plant we like at a nursery and don't really pay much attention to the growing conditions the plant requires or where that plant will perform best, how big it will get, how it will look and function in your existing garden, and so forth. All too often, new plants are placed where we have room or where we think they will look best. Well, designing and caring for a garden is not that simple and requires a lot of thought and preparation. Great gardens are built on sound principles and a plan that takes all of these considerations into account. Some of the best gardens I have seen throughout the world are ones that have a well-thought-out plan with

A well-designed garden offers multiple seasons of interest.

Flowers will provide beauty and attract pollinators.

good gardening practices from gardeners who are well informed and patient. After all, patience is a virtue in the gardening world. But as challenging as a garden can be, it can also be—and usually is—a very rewarding experience. By implementing these basic steps, the exciting world of gardening will keep you on your toes and engaged every single day.

It Starts with Soil

The first fundamental rule besides having a good plan is having an intimate knowledge of your growing conditions. Plants are doomed for failure if you ignore these needs. Soil is the lifeline of all plants, and their survival starts in the soil. Soil is a very complex biological, living system that is sensitive and dynamic. Fortunately, compared to other areas of the country, New York and New Jersey have relatively good soils to offer, although they can vary greatly from one county to the next. The more time and effort you spend on supporting and enhancing the soil environment in the garden, the better your garden will perform. Take a soil sample annually or at least every few years, and compost regularly. The replenishment of organic matter on a regular basis is exactly what happens in nature and is a great model to follow.

The Right Plant for the Right Place

Gardening successfully is all about using common sense and employing sound practices. Of all of the miscues I see on a regular basis in the landscape, none is more prevalent or frustrating than seeing a plant sited in the wrong location. It is not uncommon to find a plant growing (or struggling to) in conditions that it is not adapted to. In fact, the norm is to find plants growing in less-than-optimum growing conditions because gardeners paid little attention to the soil and light requirements of the plant. How many times have we planted a new tree, shrub, or perennial where *we* wanted it, rather than where it would thrive or have enough room to grow? While it seems logical that both criteria should be considered before purchasing new plants, all too often where the plant will look the best or where it will "fit" in the landscape is the priority. But that goes against the fundamentals of good gardening practices and plants will fail as a result.

Colorful begonia, ipomoea, and petunia flower planter on a patio.

For example, putting your prized rhododendrons in full sun and dry soils when they are meant to grow in partial shade and moist, organic soils is only going to lead to poorly developed, weak plants that will likely succumb to an insect or disease infestation or die from drought. Or growing plants that prefer acidic soils in neutral or high pH soils, which turns them a sickly yellow color.

The same is true for plants that are growing in the right environmental conditions but are not given adequate space to grow, leading to regular and often too much pruning. This creates plants that are never able to develop into their natural form, where they are most productive and aesthetically pleasing. Remember that a happy plant is typically a healthy and productive plant. Plants that are growing in the proper growing conditions and given a large enough space to grow require less maintenance or intense care and perform at their best.

Sustainable Gardening

Over the past few years, the debate over climate change has become a major global issue. Many communities have initiated programs to reduce the negative effects of human activity as scientific evidence supports the idea that global climate change and human activity are linked. Many experts believe that more fluctuations in weather patterns will be an ongoing trend for years to come. This includes extremes in weather patterns and temperatures. Programs such as recycling, water conservation, pesticide reduction, and energy efficiency are just some of the ways humans can reduce their impact on the environment. The practice of living a more sustainable, eco-friendly lifestyle is becoming more the norm than ever before. Sustainable gardening is a no-brainer these days and the plant recommendations and gardening practices presented in this book support these ideals.

Climate Change

Within the context of gardening, climate change or, more specifically, the idea of global warming, can be looked at several ways. Some gardeners will view climate change as an opportunity to grow plants that they never could before. For example, thirty years ago I would have *never* imagined that I could grow crape myrtle (*Lagerstroemia indica*) on Long Island in southern New York. But since the mid-1990s, these flowering shrubs, typically found in the southeastern United States, have thrived. Is this a result of a warming trend or are plant breeders just selecting more cold-hardy, vigorous plants? I do not deny the reality of climate change but I suspect the plants being developed are far more adaptable than they were thirty years ago as well. Of course, others view climate change as part of the bigger picture and look at the long-term effects these changes have on the health of our air, water quality, soil environment, and so forth. My personal view on this subject is that climate change is a serious and real issue that we need to address for decades to come. We should all do our part to live a more sustainable and healthy lifestyle, especially in the garden. But as gardeners, we should also not be afraid to try new plants, even if they may not be considered hardy in the climate we garden in. For me, the appeal of gardening is the excitement of trying new plants and having the newest and most unusual varieties and species that the horticultural community has to offer. This comes with inherent risks and sometimes plants may be lost, but the successes and challenges of gardening are a constant dynamic that gardeners must navigate through. With good horticultural practices, proper planning, and some research, it is inevitable that the joy of your gardening successes will far outweigh the disappointments.

Visiting botanical gardens is great inspiration for home gardeners.

Stay Informed for Gardening Ups and Downs

The reality is that gardening has its successes and failures, and not all plants will thrive all the time. The best way to be successful in the garden is to keep yourself well informed on issues relating to climate change, on eco-friendly gardening trends, and especially on new and improved plant varieties. With so much happening in the gardening industry and in plant breeding, the possibilities are endless for the enthusiastic gardener willing to think outside the box. Besides, who wants to plant the same old boring annuals or shrubs year after year? Gardening is an ever-changing, exciting journey that is meant to be enjoyed and shared.

Microclimates

Microclimates can be naturally occurring or man-made areas of the garden that are slightly different culturally (usually with regard to temperature) from surrounding areas. Warmer microclimates will support plant growth and better performance of plants with limited hardiness or other specific cultural requirements. Because bodies of water are "heat sinks," areas near streams, ponds, and lakes or even areas protected by natural vegetation can create microclimates, which can result in later frost dates and more moderate temperatures. For example, the growing environments along maritime areas of New York and New Jersey are much more moderate than inland areas. In a garden setting, creating a windbreak with a tall, growing evergreen can protect cold-sensitive plants from damaging winter winds. Heat-loving plants should be grown near the foundation of the house or close to brick walkways or walls. These plants will take advantage of the warmth coming off these surfaces in the spring, summer, and fall

A bed of *Sedum*.

A bed of large hostas in bloom.

seasons. But remember, microclimates can go both ways. Valleys or low areas of the garden that are more exposed can actually create frost pockets because cold air sinks, so avoid putting cold-sensitive plants in these areas, choosing instead plants that like cooler conditions. Adding mulch is another great way to create a microclimate around your plants. Mulch acts as an insulator, moderating soil temperature and moisture, reducing the chance for major fluctuations in both. The virtues of mulch are discussed in more detail under plant maintenance on page 176.

Hardiness

The main way gardeners can learn which plants will grow successfully where they live is by using the hardiness zone map. Developed by the United States Department of Agriculture, this map is divided into various color-coded zones. These zones are further divided by a designation of "a" and "b" with "a" representing the colder parts of the zone and "b" representing the warmer parts. These zones were developed from data recorded of the average temperatures within a given zone. The coldest zone in New York is 3a and the warmest is 7b. In New Jersey, the coldest zone is 6a and the warmest is 7b. So, if you live Albany, New York, your hardiness zone is 5a, which is considerably colder than zone 7b, in Queens, New York. Before you purchase new flowering perennials, shrubs, trees, and so forth, it is important to find out what zone or zone range a plant is best suited for. What makes the hardiness issue a bit more complicated is the notion that heat and humidity also affects plant growth and survival. (Zones don't matter for annuals, because they live their life in one season.)

The American Horticultural Society has also developed a heat zone map to help gardeners determine the level of heat and humidity in your area. The heat zone map works similarly to the hardiness zone map but it focuses on relative heat and humidity for a given area. For example, even though Westchester County, New York, and Princeton, New Jersey, may both be within hardiness Zone 6a, their heat and humidity levels may in fact be very different. So perhaps certain plants might perform better in one area over another. Or growing certain tropical annuals outdoors in the summer may not be as successful in Niagara, New York, as it might be in Central Park in New York City due to heat and humidity requirements. It's important to know the details of your growing conditions and match that with the requirements of the plants you want to grow.

A close-up view of heuchera foliage reveals beautiful colors and textures.

Garden Design: Plan Your Garden

The proper planning of your garden is the first step and probably the most important thing you can do to ensure success. A good plan affects all of the other aspects of gardening discussed in this book, such as the proper selection, siting, and care of plants. The impulse to buy a plant you like and place it where it fits, rather than where it will perform its best, should be avoided. I have seen many beautiful gardens in my travels and they all have the same qualities: good design with specific attention paid to plant culture and ornamental qualities that work together. Proper landscape design techniques will inevitably result in a healthy garden with multiple seasons of interest. If designed properly, this multifaceted landscape will also require less maintenance and become more sustainable over time.

Newer coleus introductions have spectacular color.

As described in the popular and well-written book by David L. Culp, *The Layered Garden*, this design technique of layering the garden entails interplanting a wide variety of plants in the garden so that as one plant or group of plants pass their peak season, others take over and shine in the landscape. The result of this "layering" is a continuous display of color and texture that can extend from late winter to late fall and beyond. Early spring bulbs, spring-blooming perennials and shrubs, summer-blooming annuals, and fall foliage and fruit displays can be staged to create a concert of interest throughout the year.

The other aspect of a well-designed landsape is observing and implementing the fundamentals of nature that are all around us. Whether your garden is a naturalistic landscape or one that is more cultivated, we need to learn from the lessons taught by nature every day. That includes paying close attention to where and how plant species grow in their natural habitat, what plants grow together well, how composting and recycling occur in nature, and how wildlife plays a role in the environment. We are all connected to nature and the success of the garden directly relates to the world around us. For example, by selecting the right plants and maintaining them properly, you will create the right habitat for beneficial insects, birds, turtles, snakes, and other creatures that will help reduce the population of harmful pests in the garden.

There is Always Next Year . . .

Gardening can be a humbling experience, with even the best-laid plans falling short of expectations. But we do not live in a perfect world and with so many factors that influence plant growth, it's hard to imagine 100 percent success. The beauty of gardening is that tomorrow is another day. We can learn from past failures to improve and try again next year. A wise man once told me that gardening is not a race but a journey. If you accidently kill a plant or it dies on its own, try, try again. After the third time you might want to try something different, but don't be discouraged. There is always next year.

Close-up of stewartia bark.

How to Use This Book

Under each plant description, important information on plant characteristics, cultural requirements, and my personal experiences and opinions are offered. All of the information presented is designed to assist you in your gardening endeavors and to maximize the potential of a wide variety of landscape plants. You will find beneficial information on each plant or plant group such as ultimate plant size; ornamental qualities and seasonal interest; light, water, and soil requirements; and potential pests or maintenance considerations. It is important to understand and follow this information in an effort to be well informed before selecting and using these plants in the garden.

Sun Requirements

In each plant description, different symbols represent a range of appropriate levels of sunlight for each plant. Full sun means eight or more hours of sunlight, part shade/part sun represents four to six hours of sun but generally not during midday, and shade means four hours or less of sun, and in some cases, no direct sun any part of the day. Many plants in this book will grow in a range of light levels so you will see several symbols in those cases.

Full Sun   Part Sun/Part Shade   Shade

Added Benefits

Other icons that you will find with the plant descriptions include features such as native, drought tolerance, deer resistance, attractive to pollinators, attractive to birds, and exceptional fall color.

 Native plant to the United States

 Attracts beneficial insects, such as butterflies and bees

 Drought tolerant

 Critter resistant, primarily to deer, rabbits, and rodents

 Attracts hummingbirds

 Fall color

Companion Planting and Design

This section is used to offer suggestions on unique and effective ways to use these plants in the landscape as well as using plants in combination with other species and cultivated varieties to create pleasing displays. This allows gardeners to be creative and think outside the box.

Try These

This is one of my favorite sections of the plant descriptions, as it discusses specific cultivated varieties and species that you should try. These superior, often exciting and new selections are a must have in the garden with the right growing conditions.

USDA Hardiness Zone Maps

Plants offered in this book should be considered hardy throughout the states unless otherwise noted. If a plant is not hardy everywhere in New York and New Jersey, or has specific hardiness limitations, the coldest zones they specifically will grow in will be stated. For example, the coldest hardiness zone in New York is Zone 3. If a featured plant is only hardy to Zone 4, that will be noted in the text.

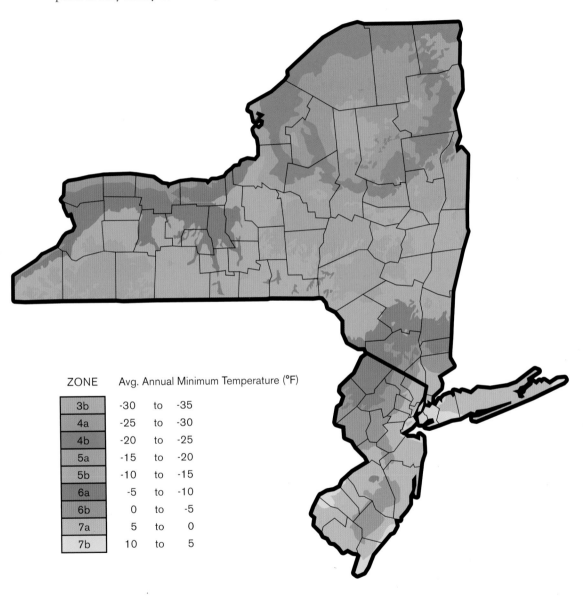

ZONE	Avg. Annual Minimum Temperature (°F)		
3b	-30	to	-35
4a	-25	to	-30
4b	-20	to	-25
5a	-15	to	-20
5b	-10	to	-15
6a	-5	to	-10
6b	0	to	-5
7a	5	to	0
7b	10	to	5

USDA Plant Hardiness Zone Map, 2012. Agricultural Research Service, U.S. Department of Agriculture. Accessed from www.planthardiness.ars.usda.gov.

ANNUALS

FOR NEW YORK & NEW JERSEY

Annuals are among the most treasured plants in the gardening world because they provide color, color, and more color in the garden. Annuals add a certain pizzazz to any landscape and complement perennials, bulbs, shrubs, and trees in the landscape. Whether in pots, hanging baskets, or in the ground, these versatile plants are purchased and planted by the millions each year all across American gardens.

Technically speaking, annuals are plants that complete their life cycle in one growing season and cannot survive our cold winters. While annuals are typically replanted each year, gardeners can move some of their favorite annuals indoors in pots in order to take cuttings (to propagate them) for the following year. But unless you have an area with a sufficient amount of light and proper growing conditions, it is usually wise to purchase new plants each year.

Selecting Annuals

Annuals can be grown from seed or young plants that are grown in a nursery. Starting annuals from seed gives you more control of what you select and is more economical, but you must have the proper growing conditions to do so. Some gardeners install

Calibrachoa planted in a graceful urn.

small greenhouses or convert their heated garages or basements, outfitted with artificial lighting, to start plants before spring. The majority of gardeners purchase annuals in small pots or cell packs because it is easier, and plants are ready to be planted. When selecting annuals, always buy from a reliable source with a good reputation. With annuals, you get what you pay for and saving a few pennies will cost you more in the long run. Quality plant material should be free of insects and disease and look healthy and vigorous. Annuals that have been hanging around the nursery for too long or improperly cared for are often weak and will suffer from transplant shock, requiring a longer time to recover and grow.

Annuals add curbside appeal and color.

General Care and Maintenance of Annuals

Remember that annuals are tender and need specific handling in order to thrive. In spring, you need to acclimate your annuals to life on the "outside." Whether coming from a warm greenhouse or your home, your annuals need time to gradually adjust to the outdoors. This process is called "hardening off" and can be accomplished in several easy steps. First, place your annuals in partial shade in a sheltered location and over several weeks, slowly give plants more light. In addition, keep plants on the drier side between waterings and do not fertilize until they are planted in the ground or in containers.

The most important thing you can do to ensure your annuals will thrive in the garden is to pay special attention to soil preparation. A soil test to check soil type, soil fertility, and pH will prove invaluable. Your local nursery professional or agricultural Extension agent can complete these tests. When planting, be sure to loosen your soil so it is light and fluffy. Gently slide plants out of their containers and lightly tease the roots to encourage them to grow into the soil. Plant your annuals at the same level in the soil that they were growing at in the container. Gently firm the soil around the plants to remove air pockets.

Once planted, your annuals should be watered thoroughly several times a week until established and then as needed after that. Watering intervals will depend on the type of soil you are gardening in. A light layer of mulch such as wood chips, shredded leaves, or pine straw will keep plants evenly moist and reduce weeds. A slow-release, low-nitrogen fertilizer at time of planting will get plants off to a good start. After they've established a general-purpose liquid fertilizer every few weeks will keep plants lush and beautiful.

Successfully growing annuals requires planning, proper planting and site selection, and regular aftercare. There is no doubt that properly placed annuals will brighten up the landscape for months of enjoyment.

Angelonia

Angelonia angustifolia

Botanical Pronunciation
an-jel-OH-nee-ah an-gus-tih-FOE-lee-ah

Other Name Summer snapdragon

Bloom Period and Seasonal Color
White, pink, lavender, and purple blooms from early summer until fall

Mature Height × Spread
12 to 18 inches × 8 to 12 inches

Angelonia is an attractive and rather carefree annual that is gaining in popularity. The sudden surge in interest of this plant is largely due to the introduction of new varieties that have been promoted in recent years. Now more than ever, angelonia is offered in a wide variety of colors including white, pink, lavender, and purple. Whenever I see angelonia it seems to stand out with its bright colors and upright floral heads. Angelonia offers dark green, fine foliage and spikes of showy flowers that resemble salvia and snapdragons. The foliage is slightly fragrant and this plant is known to be deer resistant. Angelonia is a great complement to a wide range of other annuals and perennials and it is very versatile in the landscape.

When, Where, and How to Plant

For best performance, angelonia should be planted in late spring in an area of the garden that receives full sun and has moist, well-drained soil. Angelonia is remarkably tolerant of heat and humidity and—once established—is quite drought tolerant. For maximum results angelonia should be planted in soil that is rich in organic material. New plantings should receive a thin layer of mulch to keep roots cool in the heat of the summer. Plants in containers and flats can be purchased locally in spring and should be spaced 6 to 12 inches apart. Angelonia can also be grown from seed with a wide selection of seed mixes currently being offered in garden catalogues.

Growing Tips

Plants should be fertilized with a moderate dosage of liquid fertilizer monthly. But be careful not to overdo it, as plants will tend to produce more leaves and fewer flowers. New plantings should be watered regularly to establish quickly. Once established, angelonia will require little to no maintenance.

Regional Advice and Care

Although often problem free, angelonia can sometimes develop disease and insect problems such as powdery mildew or aphid infestations. Monitor plants closely as early detection is the key to remedy problems. Occasional pruning of flower spikes that grow too tall is sometimes needed to prevent the spikes from leaning or toppling over.

Companion Planting and Design

Angelonia works well in containers or flowerbeds and can be used in mixed plantings or as a standalone plant. I have seen angelonia used very effectively in containers with petunias, ornamental grasses, sweet potato vine, and other colorful plants as well as single mass plantings in hanging baskets.

Try These

The Serena®, Serenita®, and Sungelonia® series are all good compact varieties growing between 12 inches to 14 inches tall while the AngelFace® and Statuesque™ series will grow to 18 inches tall. 'Archangel™ Dark Rose' offers rich, rose-colored flowers and an upright habit. With new varieties seemingly being developed overnight, the best seem to be heat and drought tolerant, performing most of the gardening season.

Coleus

Solenostemon scutellarioides

Botanical Pronunciation
sol-en-oh-STEM-on

Bloom Period and Seasonal Color
A wide selection of foliage colors from spring to the first frost in fall

Mature Height × Spread
12 to 36 inches × 12 to 24 inches, depending on variety

Coleus is, without question, one of the most popular and diverse groups of annuals in the gardening world. It's hard to go anywhere these days without running into coleus in the garden. The seemingly endless combinations of solid and multi-colored leaves splashed with green, gold, burgundy, and more make coleus very versatile. Coleus are great as standalone plants, but they can also be used in combination with other annuals, tropicals, perennials, and shrubs, offering gardeners many options in the landscape. Although originally considered a shade-loving plant, many new selections have yielded sun-loving types as well. Several series including the Solar® series, Sunlover® series, and Duckfoot® series are all garden worthy.

When, Where, and How to Plant

Coleus is a colorful annual that thrives in the warm temperatures of summer and is quite sensitive to cool temperatures. Be sure to plant after the chance of frost in your area has passed, which is typically mid- to late May. Depending on variety, coleus thrives in full sun and partial shade. For example, the Sunlover series are adapted to grow in full sun. Coleus can be purchased in small pots or cell packs and can also be grown from seed. When starting from seed, read the instructions and start indoors in bright light about eight weeks before planting time. When planting, provide plenty of compost to the soil, especially sandy or heavy clay soils. While it depends on the variety, coleus should be planted 10 to 18 inches apart.

Growing Tips

Coleus requires well-drained soils and prefers even moisture. Plants should be kept well watered during a drought. To encourage lush, rapid growth, fertilize plants every few weeks with a water-soluble plant food.

Regional Advice and Care

Coleus develops spikes of pinkish purple flowers, which should be pinched off regularly. Pinching off flowers and new growth results in vigorous, bushy plants. While coleus are relatively carefree, spider mites and whiteflies can be problematic. Spraying plants with a stream of water regularly to knock pests off and/or using horticultural soap are two eco-friendly ways to control these harmful pests. When applying pesticides, read the label carefully and apply the correct dosage at the right time.

Companion Planting and Design

In addition to a myriad of foliage colors, coleus comes in many sizes from ground-huggers to large, upright plants reaching several feet tall and wide. For these reasons, coleus can be used in mixed borders, as an edging plant, or in containers. Some coleus can even be used in hanging baskets.

Try These

The Fairway series offers a wide variety of foliage colors and a compact habit. The Kong® series is also impressive, offering unusually large, colorful leaves and is well adapted for shade. My favorites include 'Alabama Sunset', 'Inky Fingers', 'Patent Leather', 'Penny', and 'Red Trailing Queen'.

Cosmos

Cosmos bipinnatus

Botanical Pronunciation
KOZ-mos bye-pin-ATE-us

Bloom Period and Seasonal Color
White, pink, and red flowers from early summer until frost

Mature Height × Spread
Size depends on variety but typically 3 to 4 feet × 1 to 3 feet

Cosmos has long been a beloved flower in American gardens, gaining popularity during the early part of the 20th century when breeding on the plant began. Cosmos is known as an easy, reliable performer with large, showy rounded flowers ranging in color from white to pink to red. The upright, open habit and soft, fernlike foliage also make this plant a desirable addition to any garden. Although not a native, cosmos has the appearance of a wildflower with an informal, wispy look. Cosmos is a favorite of pollinators and is often visited by bees and butterflies. More recent breeding has yielded a wider variety of colors and flower types as well as more compact plants. Cosmos is most effective in mixed borders, containers, and as a cut flower.

When, Where, and How to Plant

Cosmos is not too picky, preferring moist, well-drained soil and full sun but it is adaptable to drier areas as well. Cosmos can be grown from seed or planted as young plants from pots. Cosmos are especially easy to grow from seed and seed can be sown indoors six to eight weeks before the last frost date in your area. Seed can also be sown directly in the ground, which can be done just before the last frost date in mid-spring. Cosmos can get large, so spacing should be done at 18 to 24 inches with plants being arranged in groupings. This will help taller plants support one another, reducing the chance of plants toppling over.

Growing Tips

Cosmos is adaptable and does not require very fertile soil to survive. Plants prefer even moisture but tolerate dry conditions once established. Incorporating well-aged compost to the soil at the time of planting should sustain plants for the season. Occasional light fertilizer applications during summer are acceptable but overfertilizing may result in decreased flower production.

Regional Advice and Care

Although it's a tough plant, cosmos may be bothered by powdery mildew, gray mold, root rot, or aphids. Keep a close eye of your plants, as early detection is important. Deadheading to remove spent flowers will keep plants reblooming.

Companion Planting and Design

Cosmos, like spider flower and other tall annuals, have sort of a wild look in the garden and should be used in informal plantings. They work well in groupings and containers along with annuals and perennials in a mixed border, cottage garden, or cutting garden.

Try These

'Sensation Mix' are big, bold plants with a range of exciting colorful flowers while the 'Sonata' series provides a much different look with compact plants only growing to 1 to 2 feet in height. The unique 'Sea Shells' series offers flowers with quilled petals.

Geranium

Pelargonium spp.

Botanical Pronunciation
pell-are-GOE-nee-um

Bloom Period and Seasonal Color
White, pink, red, orange, and purple flowers from spring until a hard frost

Mature Height × Spread
12 to 24 inches × 18 to 24 inches, depending on the species

Annual geraniums are popular, old-fashioned plants that have been cultivated in American gardens since the 18th century. These colorful annuals (*Pelargonium* spp.) should not be confused with the perennial species (*Geranium* spp.), which are much different plants featured under the Perennials chapter in this book. The two main types of annual geranium, which can be used in containers, window boxes, hanging baskets, and flowerbeds, are zonal geranium (*Pelargonium × hortorum*) and ivy geranium (*Pelargonium peltatum*). They both offer large, rounded showy flowers ranging in color from white, pink, purple, orange, and red. The main difference is that zonal geraniums tend to be upright and bushy while ivy geraniums are more mounded and spreading like a vine or groundcover. In addition, zonal geraniums have red, circular patterns in their round, aromatic leaves. Recently some exciting new hybrids between the two species have emerged with the best attributes of both types represented.

When, Where, and How to Plant
In general, geranium prefers well-drained, organic rich soil and full sun or partial shade. Zonal geraniums should be planted 12 to 24 inches apart to give them some breathing room, while ivy geraniums can be planted 18 to 36 inches because they can spread quite a bit. Although geraniums can be grown from seed, new plants are most often purchased in small pots in spring at a local nursery or garden center.

Growing Tips
In spring, incorporate well-aged compost into the soil before planting. Adding a slow-release fertilizer can also help plants get established. An additional light application of granular fertilizer in summer will help keep plants vigorous. Geraniums can also be fertilized with a balanced, liquid fertilizer once every few weeks, but be sure not to overdo it as fertilizer salts can build up over time. Plants prefer evenly moist soil and should not be allowed to dry out.

Regional Advice and Care
Geraniums benefit from being deadheaded, removing spent flowers every few days. In addition, pinching back leggy plants will encourage more compact, dense plants. Ivy geraniums can be pruned to control where and how far they spread in the garden. Sometimes a fungus will attack plants, starting with the flowers, so if you see the disease, remove the affected areas of the plant *immediately*.

Companion Planting and Design
Geraniums work as standalone plants in containers or baskets or as companions to other annuals. They can also be used along the edges of flowerbeds and borders.

Try These
The Calliope® and Caliente® are two good hybrid geraniums that offer the best of both species. Calliope types have deep red flowers, rich, green foliage, and a compact, semi-trailing growth habit to 10 to 12 inches. Caliente types also have rich, dark green foliage and a mounded, semi-spreading habit but come in pink, coral, rose, and red and grow to 12 to 18 inches tall. The hot colors and exceptional foliage make these plants a must-have in any garden.

Lantana

Lantana camara

Botanical Pronunciation
lan-TAY-nuh kuh-MAR-uh

Other Name Shrub verbena

Bloom Period and Seasonal Color
Yellow, orange, pink, and bicolor flowers from spring to fall

Mature Height × Spread
12 inches to 4 feet × 24 inches to 4 feet

Lantana is one of the more popular annuals in American gardens with new varieties emerging steadily each year. The rounded, colorful flowers offer a wide range of colors from yellow to orange to pink and even bicolor types with combinations of yellow and orange or yellow and pink. Lantana is a very practical, nonstop bloomer growing in less than ideal conditions while displaying color all summer long. From groundcovers to large shrubs, lantana rarely disappoints and often amazes with its versatility and landscape function. Lantana is a pollinator-friendly plant attracting bees and butterflies and is also deer resistant. But gardeners should keep lantana at a distance from children and pets as the fruit can be poisonous and the aromatic leaves can cause skin irritation to sensitive skin.

When, Where, and How to Plant

Lantana come in many shapes and sizes so spacing will depend on the variety you have chosen. In general, lantana should be spaced between 12 to 24 inches apart with the idea that they will eventually grow together, making a dense planting. Lantana is remarkably adaptable and will thrive in clay, sandy, and loam soils and in full sun or partial shade. Keep plants away from dark, damp conditions and soggy soil. Although lantana will tolerate partial shade and perform respectably, they are more productive in full sun and are quite adaptable to dry, exposed sites once established.

Growing Tips

Lantana are not too fussy with fertilizer and it is best to incorporate a well-aged compost and a slow-release granular fertilizer at time of planting to get plants off on the right foot. Plants can be lightly mulched (1 to 2 inches) and should be watered regularly until they're established.

Regional Advice and Care

Some lantana varieties can get quite large and occasional pruning to keep plants from growing into walkways and on patios is wise. Removing spent flowers will help keep plants reblooming. Although rather pest free, lantana can sometimes be bothered by whiteflies and powdery mildew.

Companion Planting and Design

Lantana looks good with other lantana or with flowering shrubs and perennials. The low-growing, spreading types work well in hanging baskets, containers, or along the edge of a pathway in front of larger plants.

Try These

The Bandana® series is compact and comes in a wide variety of colors from red to pink to yellow and even white. 'New Gold' is an excellent groundcover with dark green foliage and rich golden flowers. 'Miss Huff' is a large, shrubby grower with tri-color flowers of pink, yellow, and orange. What is most impressive is that it is a variety that has been known to be hardy in Zone 7 and although killed to the ground in the winter, it will regenerate from its roots and flower the same season. Wow!

Marigold

Tagetes spp.

Botanical Pronunciation
tuh-JEE-teez

Bloom Period and Seasonal Color
Bright orange, red, maroon, yellow, cream, and bicolor flowers from spring until frost

Mature Height × Spread
10 inches to 4 feet × 10 inches to 3 feet, depending on species and variety

It's hard to imagine a garden without the reliable, old-fashioned marigold. This is one of those annuals that bring back memories of our childhood with mounds of rounded flowers and aromatic, fernlike foliage. It has been a beloved garden favorite in the American landscape since colonial times. For centuries, marigolds have been used for their edible and medicinal properties as well as their ornamental value. While there are many, the three main species that are excellent for a wide variety of uses are the French marigold (*Tagetes patula*) growing from 6 to 16 inches tall; African marigold (*T. erecta*), reaching 1 to 4 feet tall; and my favorite, the Signet marigold (*T. tenuifolia*), which only grows 6 to 14 inches tall.

When, Where, and How to Plant
Marigold is among the easiest annuals to grow from seed. Seed can either be purchased or harvested from dried flowers on your plants. Marigold seeds can be started four to six weeks before the last frost or directly sown in the ground after danger of frost has passed. Marigolds can also be purchased in cell packs from local nurseries or garden centers. Marigolds prefer sun and moist, well-drained soil but are adaptable as long as soil is not too wet or the area is not in dense shade. Marigolds perform best in rich, organic soil that is well drained so incorporating some compost at the time of planting is a good idea. Spacing marigolds depends on the species and varieties chosen. The popular French marigold should be spaced 8 to 12 inches while the African marigold and its hybrids should be spaced

1 to 2 feet apart. The delicate Signet marigolds can be spaced 6 to 10 inches apart.

Growing Tips
An initial granular fertilizer incorporated into the soil when planting is done will get plants off to a good start. Keep soil moist but marigolds are drought tolerant.

Regional Advice and Care
Marigolds are not high maintenance but deadheading and occasionally trimming back will keep plants blooming and dense so they do not become too top heavy and fall over. Marigolds are not without their pest issues so be on the lookout for aphids, spider mites, mold, and root rot. Avoiding overcrowding, keeping plants in areas with plenty of air circulation, and well-drained soil will reduce the likelihood of these problems.

Companion Planting and Design
Marigolds work well as bedding plants in mixed borders, as edging plants, in containers, and even as cut flowers. Many gardeners believe that using them in vegetable gardens will repel harmful pests.

Try These
There are just too many good varieties to mention so my advice would be to look in your favorite garden catalogue and choose what suits your garden the best. *T. tenuifolia* 'Lemon Gem', 'Red Gem', and 'Tangerine Gem' are three excellent varieties of the Signet marigold.

Million Bells

Calibrachoa hybrids

Botanical Pronunciation
kal-ih-brah-KOE-ah

Other Name Trailing petunia

Bloom Period and Seasonal Color
Summer until frost

Mature Height × Spread
6 to 12 inches × 12 to 15 inches

Million bells are closely related to petunias and look like them, but in miniature form. The petite, bell-shaped flowers and low, spreading habit make this plant desirable in containers, hanging baskets, or as a groundcover in a flowerbed. What is most attractive about million bells is the rainbow of flower colors that are available to gardeners. An amazing array of flower colors are available including peach, pink, purple, yellow, white, and red, and flowers can be striped or streaked with varying colors. Flowers can be single or double and will attract butterflies and hummingbirds. The trailing or mounding habit allows gardeners to put this plant in small crevices, edges, or pots, along rock walls, and in other tight spaces. This delicate but effective annual gives gardeners unlimited possibilities in small spaces.

When, Where, and How to Plant

Million bells prefer moist, well-drained soil with plenty of organic matter. Full sun is best for flowering; light shade is acceptable but may reduce flower production. In spring, set new plants out in a sheltered location and plant when the weather is warm and the threat of frost has passed. Million bells are rather heat and drought tolerant once established. Plants should be spaced about 12 to 15 inches apart to allow them to spread. Million bells can be grown from seed or purchased as small potted plants and the numbers of varieties available can be mind-boggling.

Growing Tips

You can incorporate a slow-release fertilizer at planting and then fertilize plants with a liquid fertilizer once a month with good results. Plants should be well watered before and after applying fertilizer. Once established, plants can be kept on the drier side but should not be allowed to dry out too much.

Regional Advice and Care

Million bells require little maintenance but during the heat of summer, if plants are looking tired or not performing up to your standards, lightly prune them; this will often stimulate growth and more flowers. Million bells are not prone to diseases and insects and will perform well in the garden as long as adequate light, moisture and drainage is provided. Avoid overwatering to reduce the chance of root rot.

Companion Planting and Design

Million bells are excellent companion plants to other low-growing or dwarf plants and are especially effective in containers and hanging baskets. They are effectively used as one solid color or by mixing several complementary colors together in groupings.

Try These

With so many varieties to choose from, it's hard to decide. Rarely can gardeners pick just one color and they often will choose several varieties for different areas of the garden. Among the best are Celebration® series, Conga™ series, MiniFamous™, and Superbells®. Although there are so many to choose from, Superbells® Lemon Slice is a quite attractive variety with white and bright yellow-striped flowers.

New Guinea Impatiens

Impatiens hawkeri

Botanical Pronunciation
imp-PAY-shens hawk-er-EYE

Bloom Period and Seasonal Color
Flowers range from white, pink, purple, orange, and red from spring until first hard frost

Mature Height × Spread
12 to 36 inches × 12 to 24 inches or more, depending on the variety

New Guinea impatiens are without question one of the most popular annuals on earth. The mounded habit and myriad flower colors including white, pink, purple, orange, and red make a striking statement in the landscape. A variety of foliage colors are also offered in green, bronze, and even variegated forms. New Guinea impatiens tolerate more sun than the shade-loving impatiens but they will also tolerate a partially shaded area. Recently a devastating disease called downy mildew has caused severe damage to the common impatiens (*Impatiens walleriana*). New Guinea impatiens is recommended as an alternative because it's highly resistant to this disease. With so many colors, sizes, and uses of New Guinea impatiens for sun, shade, and containers, it has become an even more desirable annual in the landscape.

When, Where, and How to Plant
New Guinea impatiens prefer moist, well-drained soil, and partial shade, but will tolerate full sun as long as they are well watered. Some varieties of New Guinea impatiens have been developed specifically for full sun exposure so be sure you know which one you have chosen. While plants *can* be started from seed, this can be somewhat difficult and most gardeners choose to buy impatiens transplants in small pots and plant in spring. New plants should be spaced 10 to 18 inches apart depending on the variety chosen.

Growing Tips
A general purpose, slow-release fertilizer should be incorporated into the soil when your New Guinea impatiens are planted outdoors in flowerbeds. It is also recommended that compost or well-aged manure be added to sandy or clay soils since New Guinea impatiens prefer rich soil with organic matter. In containers, New Guinea impatiens will need to be fertilized lightly every few weeks with a water-soluble fertilizer.

Regional Advice and Care
Although rather trouble free, New Guinea impatiens can be susceptible to root rots in poorly drained soil and to insects such as spider mites, aphids, mealybugs, and whiteflies. Plants in hot, exposed sites may experience sunscald on their leaves. If plants become tall and leggy in shade, pinch them back lightly to encourage a bushy plant.

Companion Planting and Design
New Guinea impatiens are very versatile and can be used in flower borders, groupings, mass plantings, containers, and hanging baskets. They work well with other annuals and perennials of similar size or they can work well as a standalone plant.

Try These
The 'Magnum' and Super Sonic® series offer vigorous plants with big and bold flowers. The SunPatiens® series gives gardeners the option to use New Guinea impatiens in full sun. The Bounce™ and Big Bounce™ series are hybrids that offer bold colors and vigorous plants that will bounce back from wilting quickly from a missed watering.

Petunia

Petunia spp.

Botanical Pronunciation
peh-TOON-yuh

Bloom Period and Seasonal Color
Colorful, trumpet-like blooms from mid-spring to fall ranging in color from white, pink, rose, purple, red, yellow, and bicolors

Mature Height × Spread
Up to 12 inches × 12 to 36 inches plus

Petunia has real lasting power and is a household name in the gardening community. These sun-loving annuals are known for their spreading and mounded habit and ability to adapt to a variety of situations. While there are many species and complex hybrids, among my favorites are the mounding or trailing types. These garden-friendly hybrids and species are known as "fillers" and "spillers." Some petunias are large-flowering (grandiflora), bushy types while others are smaller, profuse flowering (mulitifora), trailing types. Others are bred to offer large flowers in profusion (floribundas) and miniature petunias with continuous blooms (milliflora). The spreading types of petunias are probably the most popular and used by professionals and more novice gardeners alike.

When, Where, and How to Plant
Petunias can be grown from seed or bought in flats or small pots. They typically thrive in warmer weather so don't put them out in the garden too early. Petunias are adaptable to poor soils but thrive in well-drained soil with moderate moisture. Petunias prefer full sun or at least six hours a day to perform well. Spacing depends heavily on which series or specific variety you have chosen, but generally space plants 6 to 12 inches apart on the smaller varieties and 12 to 18 inches apart on the larger, spreading varieties.

Growing Tips
For plants that have been planted directly in the ground, fertilizing a few times during the spring until they are established will keep them growing. In containers and hanging baskets, a balanced, liquid fertilizer every few weeks for the summer is recommended. Maintain even soil moisture but they will tolerate drier conditions.

Regional Advice and Care
The old-fashioned grandiflora types tend to need deadheading to remove flowers. However, the newer varieties, which spread, do not need deadheading but will branch and become denser when occasionally pinched or pruned back. Overwatering or overcrowding can sometimes cause fungus to develop so be mindful of that.

Companion Planting and Design
Petunias work in all sunny areas of the garden in beds and along borders, in containers, flower boxes, and hanging baskets and can even be used as cut flowers. They work well in companion plantings with a wide variety of sun-loving annuals with similar needs such as coleus, morning glories, and geranium.

Try These
The Wave® series is still one of the most popular with bright colors and a vigorous, ground-hugging habit. Supertunia® are good performers with smaller but profuse flowering in a variety of colors and a dense, slightly mounded habit that also spreads. *Petunia integrifolia* is also worth mentioning as it is a species with rosy purple flowers and a free-flowing habit. 'Phantom' is a variety that rocked my world when I first saw it, showing off black and yellow bicolored flowers and a dense, mounded habit.

Salvia

Salvia spp.

Botanical Pronunciation
SAL-vee-uh

Other Name Sage

Bloom Period and Seasonal Color
Spring until fall with red, white, violet, or blue
flowers depending on the species and variety

Mature Height × Spread
12 to 36 inches × 10 to 18 inches

Salvia is another annual that has perennial counterparts as well. While the two groups are quite different in appearance, they all have spikey flowers and interesting foliage. Salvia in general is well known as a favorite to pollinators such as bees and butterflies and even hummingbirds. There are many species but the two noteworthy annual types covered here are *Salvia splendens*, scarlet sage, and *Salvia farinacea*, mealycup sage. Scarlet salvia does indeed have large spikes of scarlet red flowers but also comes in violet, white, and other color combinations. Mealycup salvia has tall spikes of lavender blue flowers and glossy green foliage. Salvia in general work well in a wide variety of landscape situations with a variety of plants in flowerbeds, containers, and window boxes.

When, Where, and How to Plant
Salvia can be grown from seed or purchased as small plants in individual pots or flats. Salvias enjoy rich, organic soils so add some well-aged manure or compost to the soil at planting. Seed of scarlet salvia should be sown six to eight weeks before last frost while mealycup salvia will need twelve weeks. Salvias prefer moist, well-drained soils and full sun but are remarkably adaptable to less-than-ideal soils and partially shaded areas of the garden. Space plants 8 to 12 inches and they will eventually grow into one large mass planting.

Growing Tips
New plantings also benefit from a light layer (1 to 2 inches) of mulch to keep their roots cool in the heat of the summer. A general-purpose, slow-release granular fertilizer should be sufficient to get plants off to a good start. Salvias in containers will likely need regular liquid fertilizer to keep them vigorous and productive. Be sure plants do not dry out, especially in containers.

Regional Advice and Care
Salvias are not particularly high maintenance or messy but removing dead blooms and occasional pruning will keep plants dense and encourage reblooming. Spider mites, whiteflies, and aphids can sometimes be a problem but usually they are more of a problem indoors. Fungus can also develop so keep plants deadheaded and pruned.

Companion Planting and Design
Salvias are very effective in mixed borders and in containers. In addition, salvias make great cut flowers, used in both fresh and dried arrangements.

Try These
While there are many varieties of salvia, there are some good, standout varieties that offer great ornamental qualities. Of the scarlet salvia varieties, Saucy™ Red salvia offers big, bold plants to 2 to 3 feet while the Salsa™ series come in a variety of colors and have a dense growth habit from 12 to 24 inches in height. The mealycup salvia also offer good, tried-and-true varieties including 'Victoria' with a deep violet-blue color and 'Strata' with a bicolor silver-and-blue flower color combination.

Spider Flower

Cleome hassleriana

Botanical Pronunciation
klee-OH-mee hass-le-REE-a-nuh

Other Name Cleome

Bloom Period and Seasonal Color
White, pink, purple, and bicolor flowers from
early summer until frost

Mature Height × Spread
3 to 5 feet × 1 to 2 feet

Spider flower is a classic annual with large, rounded, spiderlike flowers with elongated stamens that range from white to pink, purple, or even bicolor combinations. The flowers offer a sweet fragrance all summer long. The flowers are attractive to butterflies and hummingbirds and birds prefer its seed. Their tall, irregular growth habit makes a bold statement in the garden. The lacey, palmate, aromatic leaves have spines at the base so handle with care. While traditional spider plant varieties are large and stately in the garden, new breeding has focused on smaller, more compact forms of this garden favorite. Because of this, a new breed of spider flower is being used virtually everywhere including mixed borders, containers, and in mass plantings as foundation plantings.

When, Where, and How to Plant

Spider flower is remarkably adaptable, growing best in well-drained soil but able to adapt to drier conditions. It prefers full sun but grows well in partial shade. Spider flower can grow quite large so give them room. It's a slender, upright grower; 12- to 24-inch spacing is appropriate. Plants can be purchased in small pots or started from seed indoors six to eight weeks before last frost date or seed can be sown directly after last frost date. You can harvest seedpods in fall for planting the following spring. If seedpods are not promptly removed, plants will self-seed, spreading spider flower throughout your garden.

Growing Tips

Spider flower is not a particularly heavy feeder so fertilizer at planting should be sufficient. It benefits from well-drained soil and will even tolerate dry, sandy soils. Although spider flower performs best with even moisture, once established this hardy plant is drought and heat tolerant.

Regional Advice and Care

Spider flower is basically trouble free although sometimes insects such as aphids, spider mites, and whiteflies can be problematic. Late in the season, powdery mildew and rust may occur, but this adaptable plant seems to endure.

Companion Planting and Design

Spider flowers make their presence known in a mixed flower border and are excellent companions to taller annuals and perennials. Plant them with other similar-sized plants such as dahlias and cosmos or use in the back of a border for height. More compact varieties are excellent in mass plantings or as foundation plantings.

Try These

Sparkler series offers a shorter habit but big, bold flowers that burst with colors ranging from white, blush pink, rose, and lavender. The newest generation of spider flower that are among my favorites display a compact habit and are seedless and disease resistant. Senorita Rosalita® offers a more compact habit to 2 to 4 feet tall, rich lavender flowers, and dark green foliage. Pequeña Rosalita™ is a newer selection offering pink flowers, while Senorita Blanca® displays pale pink flowers. These are real showstoppers and will complement a wide variety of plants.

Sweet Potato Vine

Ipomoea batatas

Botanical Pronunciation
EYE-pome-E-uh bat-at-US

Bloom Period and Seasonal Color
Grown for its colorful maroon, chartreuse, and variegated foliage and trailing habit; offers seasonal color spring, summer, and early fall

Mature Height × Spread
6 to 12 inches × 8 feet plus

Over the years, the horticultural industry has expanded to include what once were exclusively agricultural crops as ornamentals in the landscape. Who would have thought that sweet potatoes could be used for their foliage rather than their edible potato production? The underground tubers of sweet potato vine are not considered edible so just use these plants for their aesthetic value. Because of its fast growth rate, colorful foliage, and adaptability, this vine has become a real force in the gardening world. Foliage can be heart-shaped or deeply lobed and can range in color from deep maroon to chartreuse to variegated leaves featuring green, white, and pink. Sweet potato vine can be used in hanging baskets, mixed containers, or as a mass planting creeping along the ground.

When, Where, and How to Plant
Sweet potato vine is easy to grow, thriving in well-drained, rich soils but adapting to a wide range of soil conditions. For maximum growth, plant sweet potato vine in full sun, although partial shade, especially on variegated types, is acceptable. Keep plants away from soggy, poorly drained soil and deep shade. Plants can be purchased in small pots in the spring and tubers can be dug up in the fall and replanted the following year. Sweet potato vine can also be easily propagated by rooting cuttings. When planting in the garden, be sure to space plants several feet apart to give plants room to grow.

Growing Tips
Sweet potato vine is not a heavy feeder and an all-purpose, slow-release fertilizer at the time of planting should be sufficient to get plants on their way. Incorporating rich, well-aged compost into the planting beds will allow plants to thrive.

Regional Advice and Care
Since sweet potato vine is such a vigorous grower, regular pruning to keep plants from wandering into areas where they are not wanted will be needed. Pest problems are minimal but occasionally sweet potato beetles can chew up the leaves so keep a close eye on your plants.

Companion Planting and Design
Sweet potato vine is a great companion plant to ornamental grasses and other colorful annuals in containers. It is also a very effective groundcover or vine covering on a wall or fence.

Try These
'Blackie' was one of the first of the ornamental sweet potatoes with dark purple to almost black, dissected foliage. 'Ace of Spades' offers heart-shaped leaves with the same striking, dark purple foliage. 'Margarita' is still the most popular and vigorous grower with beautiful chartreuse leaves. 'Pink Frost' is a slower grower but features a combination of green, white, and pink variegation that is quite effective in containers with other plants that offer pink flowers and colored foliage.

Verbena

Verbena spp.

Botanical Pronunciation
vur-BEE-nuh

Other Name Vervain

Bloom Period and Seasonal Color
White, pink, blue, purple, red, cream-colored, and bicolored flowers from May until October

Mature Height × Spread
6 to 14 inches × 1 to 2 feet, depending on species and variety

Verbena is a fairly carefree annual that comes in a variety of vibrant colors and is especially adapted for hot, dry areas of the garden. Verbena can grow as a groundcover or upright flowering plant with rich, green foliage in addition to the rounded, colorful blooms. The three species that are most garden-worthy are garden verbena (*Verbena × hybrida*), moss verbena (*V. tenuisecta*), and clump verbena (*V. canadensis*). Garden verbena offers the most flower colors and is typically trailing to a more upright habit while clump and moss verbenas tend to be more spreading. While garden verbena and clump verbena foliage is thick and lush, moss verbena is much finer and lacey in texture. This diversity of flowers, foliage, and habit make verbena a very versatile and valuable plant. Verbena will attract a variety of butterflies and bees to the garden.

When, Where, and How to Plant
Verbena can be grown from seed or transplants purchased in spring in small pots or cell packs. Annual verbena tends to be slow to germinate, so sow seeds indoors about ten to twelve weeks before the last frost date. Each verbena is different so be sure to follow the instructions on the seed packet. Verbena prefers rich soil but is quite tolerant of poor, dry, or rocky soils as long as it drains. If you have poor soil, incorporate plenty of compost in the spring before planting. Verbena prefers moist, well-drained soil and full sun but will tolerate hot, dry conditions. Spacing depends on the variety but typically plants should be spaced 12 to 24 inches apart.

Growing Tips
A general-purpose, slow-release granular fertilizer will help plants establish and encourage growth during spring and summer. Maintain even moisture but it is drought tolerant.

Regional Advice and Care
Plants may decline and reduce flower production during extended periods of heat and drought. Verbena is a free bloomer but deadheading will result in more consistent reblooming. Pruning is not usually necessary unless plants get too leggy or large for the area. In general verbena is pest and disease free, although powdery mildew and root rot can be a problem in areas where they are overwatered or have poor air circulation.

Companion Planting and Design
Verbena are excellent filler plants for containers, window boxes, and flower beds and trailing types can be used very effectively in hanging baskets and as a groundcover over rock walls and on slopes.

Try These
The EnduraScape™ series are good performers that come in many colors including blush pink, red, lavender, blue, and hot pink. Two of my favorites, which still are relevant today, are 'Homestead Purple' and 'Imagination'. 'Homestead Purple' is a variety of clump verbena that spreads along the ground with dense foliage and bright purple flowers. 'Imagination' is a variety of *V. speciosa* with soft, finely dissected foliage and deep purple flowers. Both are excellent in hanging baskets or as groundcovers.

Wax Begonia

Begonia semperflorens-cultorum

Botanical Pronunciation
beg-own-E-uh semp-PUR-floor-ens colt-OR-um

Other Name Fibrous begonia

Bloom Period and Seasonal Color
White, pink, and red flowers from May until the
first hard frost in fall

Mature Height × Spread
6 to 18 inches × 6 to 12 inches, depending
on variety

Wax begonias are one of those classic annuals that everyone loves, and for good reason. They are adaptable, versatile, and reliable performers in the garden. Wax begonias come in a variety of flower and foliage colors. Flowers range from white to pink and red while the thick, glossy foliage is offered in green or deep bronze. This carefree group of plants creates mounds of color all summer that are rivaled by few annuals. I am absolutely head over heels in love with the newer, large-flowering type wax begonias including the Big® series and the Whopper® series. Both feature unusually large clusters of flowers borne on plants that reach 24 inches in height and width. Wax begonias perform best in flowerbeds, containers, and hanging baskets. They are most effective when used in groupings. Wax begonias are quite low maintenance once established and will perform well in full sun or partial shade.

When, Where, and How to Plant

It is best to plant begonias when the soil is warm and the threat of frost has passed. Wax begonias can be grown in full sun, staying more compact, while in shade they tend to grow taller reaching for sunlight. Wax begonias prefer rich, organic soil. If you have heavy clay or sandy soil, be sure to incorporate a generous amount of compost or well-rotted manure. However, because of their thick leaves, established plantings will tolerate periods of drought. Plants should be spaced 8 to 12 inches apart to allow room to grow and for air circulation to reduce disease. Wax begonias can be purchased in cell packs, small pots, or can also be started from

seed. The seed is very small and should be handled with care. Start seed indoors six to eight weeks prior to planting outdoors.

Growing Tips

A few applications of water-soluble fertilizer will give plants a boost early in the season. If you grow your begonias in pots, lightly fertilizing every few weeks will keep plants at their best. Although plants require well-drained soil they should not be allowed to dry out as they prefer even moisture.

Regional Advice and Care

Wax begonias are relatively pest free but poor soil drainage may result in root rot, which can weaken or kill plants. On larger growing varieties or plants in shade that become leggy and open, lightly cutting them back will help them stay bushy.

Companion Planting and Design

Wax begonias are ideal in mass plantings, foundation plantings, mixed borders, and in containers/hanging baskets.

Try These

The Whopper® and Big® series are both eye-popping hybrids of wax begonia with enormous flowers, dense habits reaching 18 to 24 inches tall, and rich, lustrous foliage. Another series that has gained popularity is the Cocktail® series, which offers a compact habit and a wide variety of flower and foliage colors. The Volumia™ series is also a good performer with bushy plants coming in a variety of colors.

Wishbone Flower

Torenia fournieri

Botanical Pronunciation
tor-EE-nee-uh four-near-EYE

Other Name Torenia

Bloom Period and Seasonal Color
Blue or purple bicolor, tubular flowers that are also available in pink, rose, burgundy, and white depending on the variety; from June until frost

Mature Height × Spread
6 to 12 inches × 6 to 12 inches

Torenia is a very interesting annual that is slowly gaining in popularity in the garden. Its unique tubular to trumpet-shaped flowers are typically blue with a deep purple lower lip and yellow interior. The flower parts within the flower resemble a wishbone of a chicken, hence the common name. This rather low-growing, spreading annual is very striking in a mass planting or container because it is so different from most other flowers. There are many new and exciting varieties of wishbone flower, which offer gardeners a variety of flower colors to choose from. Like begonia and New Guinea impatiens, wishbone flower is another annual being recommended as an alternative to the disease-plagued common impatiens. Wishbone flower is one of those select annuals that thrives in shade and offers a food source for hummingbirds.

When, Where, and How to Plant
Wishbone truly is a shade lover and should not be put in full, exposed sun. It performs rather well in partial shade and will tolerate full shade. Wishbone flower does best in organic, rich, well-drained soil. Seed can be started indoors about six to eight weeks before the last frost or sown directly outdoors after the threat of frost has passed. Of course, wishbone flower can also be purchased as small plants in pots or cell packs. Since wishbone flower does spread, space plants about 8 to 10 inches apart and they will eventually form a dense, low-growing planting.

Growing Tips
Since wishbone flower prefers organic soil, incorporating compost or manure at planting is recommended. In addition, a light layer of mulch is ideal to keep the roots cool and moist during the long, hot days of summer. A general-purpose fertilizer at or soon after planting will help plants establish. For plants in the ground, use a granular fertilizer once a month and for plants in containers, use a well-balanced liquid fertilizer once every other watering. It is important to keep plants well watered in times of drought.

Regional Advice and Care
Wishbone flower will naturally spread and may need to be contained, which can easily be done with pruning. If plants become leggy, especially in excessive shade, they can be pinched back or lightly pruned, which will keep them bushy. Although wishbone flower is generally resistant to disease, root rot and powdery mildew can be an issue. Planting in well-drained soil and areas where there is plenty of air circulation will reduce incidents of disease.

Companion Planting and Design
Wishbone flowers are excellent in a shade garden as an edging plant, in mixed flower borders, woodland gardens, window boxes, hanging baskets, or in containers.

Try These
The Summer Wave® series is an excellent group of plants offering a wide variety of flower colors. This series is heat tolerant and is an especially vigorous performer.

Zinnia

Zinnia spp.

Botanical Pronunciation
zin-EE-uh

Bloom Period and Seasonal Color
White, pink, red, yellow, orange and violet
flowers from spring until frost

Mature Height × Spread
10 to 15 inches × 8 to 12 inches for smaller
varieties; up to 3 feet × 2 feet for larger varieties

Zinnia is an old-fashioned flower that has been used in American gardens for centuries. It originated in Mexico, South America, and the southwestern United States and was brought to Europe from the new world. Traditionally, zinnias were grown for their upright habit and bold flowers and often used as cut flowers but more recently plant breeding has produced lower-growing, more compact varieties that are ideal as bedding plants. Zinnia can now be found in mixed borders, containers, and even hanging baskets. One of the most common diseases of zinnias is powdery mildew, but plant breeders have also developed resistant varieties. These major improvements to this plant has allowed zinnia to be reinvented as a reliable and productive garden annual.

When, Where, and How to Plant
For the most part, zinnia is easy to grow and thrives in moist, well-drained soil and performs best in full sun. Zinnia can be grown from seed or purchased in flats as small plants. Seed can be sown indoors about four to five weeks before the last frost date or directly sown outdoors when frost date has past. Zinnia does not like to be disturbed when it is young so if you're starting your own seed, using peat pots (which are directly planted into the soil) is recommended. Zinnia needs well-drained soil and prefers a rich, organic garden soil. Space plants 6 to 8 inches apart on smaller varieties and 12 to 18 inches apart on larger ones.

Growing Tips
Incorporate compost into soil that is less than ideal and a light application of liquid fertilizer soon after planting and again in the midseason will keep plants vigorous. Maintain even soil moisture.

Regional Advice and Care
The biggest problem for zinnia is powdery mildew, which covers leaves with a white, powdery film in late summer. However, some new varieties are less susceptible to the disease. Avoiding overhead watering, and siting plants in full sun and areas that have good air circulation will reduce incidents of powdery mildew. Also keep a watchful eye out for Japanese beetles, which will chew on the leaves. Pruning to remove dead flowers, especially on taller varieties, is recommended weekly.

Companion Planting and Design
Zinnias are excellent in large masses as cut flowers and smaller varieties can be used as edging plants, in containers and hanging baskets or in mixed borders with other annuals and perennials with similar textures and flower colors.

Try These
So many zinnia varieties and so many ways to use them! Two great performers are the dwarf Star® series, growing to 8 inches tall, which come in a wide variety of colors and are great edging plants. The Profusion series is a bit taller to 12 to 15 inches, but still dense and also a good performer. The Ruffles series is a tall variety with double blooms that make excellent cut flowers.

PERENNIALS
FOR NEW YORK & NEW JERSEY

Like annuals, perennials are herbaceous plants with stems and leaves made of soft tissue that dies back to the ground each fall. The only difference is that unlike annuals, perennials will come back year after year, emerging from the ground in spring when the weather warms up. When used properly, perennials can add great interest to the landscape including a wide range of flower colors, foliage colors and textures, and seedheads and fruit, from spring until early winter.

Selecting Perennials

With so many perennials to choose from, selecting the right ones for your garden can be a daunting task. Listed in this section are a good variety of perennials that will thrive in many different landscape situations. But it is important for you, as a gardener, to follow basic steps to ensure your plants will thrive. The first step is to have a clear understanding of the environmental conditions that your garden has to offer and then match that with the perennials that will grow best in those conditions. It is equally important to know exactly what you want to accomplish in the garden with your perennials, whether creating a perennial border, woodland garden, or foundation planting. This will maximize the effectiveness of your perennials both functionally and aesthetically.

Hostas lining a brick paver path.

Many perennials attract beneficial insects, such as this coneflower (*Echinacea*).

Once you know what growing conditions you have and a clear goal of what you want to accomplish, it is important to select quality plant material from a reputable source. Perennials are typically sold as potted plants from local sources although sometimes root divisions or tubers can be purchased from mail-order nurseries. Starting off with good quality, healthy plants will get your perennials off to a great start.

General Care and Maintenance of Perennials

Although perennials are more resilient than annuals, they still require special care in spring when they are emerging from dormancy and are their most vulnerable. New perennials, especially ones that have been purchased from mail-order sources, also need to be acclimated to their new surroundings. This process includes placing your perennials in a protected place for a few weeks in spring to get them used to the great outdoors (called "hardening off"). This could be a cold frame, cool garage, cool greenhouse, or outdoors in a protected area, such as shade, until it is safe to plant them. Even though your perennials are hardy in the area you live, be sure not to put them out until the last frost date for your area has passed.

One of the most important aspects of growing perennials successfully is proper soil preparation. Proper cultivation and enhancement of the soil is very important when growing perennials because they are going to be there long term. An occasional soil test to evaluate soil pH and fertility is always a good idea. Adding rich, well-aged compost to sandy or heavy clay soils will improve their water-holding capacity and fertility while creating a healthy root zone. One common practice when planting perennials is called "double digging," which involves removing the top layer of soil to the depth of a shovel, setting the soil aside, and then loosening the subsoil another shovel depth. The topsoil is then added back into the planting hole along with soil amendments such as compost, manure, and fertilizer. This provides the plants with a fluffy root zone that roots can easily grow into. This can be done in the spring or fall when plants are not actively growing. New perennials should then be mulched with wood chips, pine straw, or shredded leaves, and watered thoroughly. Watering regularly as needed for the first growing season is important to get plants established.

Perennials are an important part of the cultivated landscape, anchoring the garden with interest during much of the growing season. A well-designed garden must include a good selection of perennials, which help tie the landscape together while offering color and habitat for wildlife such as birds, bees, and butterflies.

Arkansas Blue Star

Amsonia hubrichtii

Botanical Pronunciation
am-SOW-nee-uh HEW-brikt-ee-eye

Other Name Threadleaf star flower

Bloom Period and Seasonal Color
Powder blue, star-shaped flowers in spring;
lacey green foliage all summer turns brilliant
golden yellow in fall

Mature Height × Spread
24 to 36 inches × 24 to 36 inches

Arkansas blue star is a beautiful perennial native to the Southeast. It offers fine, feathery foliage reaching 2 to 3 feet tall that gracefully sways in the summer wind. The upright clumps of soft foliage bear small, star-shaped blue flowers in spring on the tips of each stem. The bright green, needlelike foliage turns an eye-catching bright golden color in fall, setting the landscape ablaze. Blue star is carefree, easy to grow, and adapts to a wide variety of soils and landscape situations. Blue star works best in mixed plantings with perennials, ornamental grasses, and flowering shrubs. Although it complements other plants, Arkansas blue star is very effective in a single mass planting as well. There is no doubt that Arkansas blue star is as beautiful as it is versatile.

When, Where, and How to Plant

Blue star is not finicky and requires very little to succeed in the garden. It is adaptable to a wide variety of soils but performs best in well-drained, rich soil. Incorporate a healthy amount of compost into the soil when planting. Full sun is best but partial shade in the afternoon is acceptable. Blue star should be planted 18 to 24 inches apart to give them room to grow.

Growing Tips

Keep plants well watered during summer droughts. A light layer of mulch (1 to 2 inches) will keep roots cool in the summer. Arkansas blue star is not particular about fertilizer and a general-purpose fertilizer can be applied in spring if needed.

Regional Advice and Care

Blue star is adaptable and not known to be susceptible to pests. Divide plants every few years to keep them vigorous and productive. Divide established plantings in early spring while plants are dormant by gently pulling apart a small section of the root system and transplanting small clumps to other areas of the garden. Wait until late fall when plants are dormant to cut stems back to the ground.

Companion Planting and Design

Blue star works well in mass plantings, in small groupings, as a foundation planting, and in a mixed border with other annuals, perennials, and shrubs. The exceptionally striking yellow fall color makes it very effective when used alongside other plants with similar foliage color and texture, especially those with yellow, orange, and red fall foliage color or fruit. I recommend both species, one of which is mentioned below, because they are quite different in their appearance and equally lovely. Both species are incredibly beautiful in a mass planting, especially in summer and fall because of the striking foliage texture and color.

Try These

This is a standalone species with no cultivated varieties. A closely related species, common blue star (*Amsonia tabernaemontana*), has thicker, dark green leaves and sky blue flowers in spring. 'Blue Ice' is a nice variety that is a bit shorter than the species.

Aster

Aster spp.

Botanical Pronunciation
ASS-tur

Bloom Period and Seasonal Color
Daisylike flowers range from white to pink to blue-purple in summer and fall

Mature Height × Spread
24 to 72 inches × 24 to 48 inches

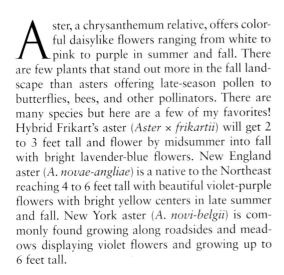

Aster, a chrysanthemum relative, offers colorful daisylike flowers ranging from white to pink to purple in summer and fall. There are few plants that stand out more in the fall landscape than asters offering late-season pollen to butterflies, bees, and other pollinators. There are many species but here are a few of my favorites! Hybrid Frikart's aster (*Aster × frikartii*) will get 2 to 3 feet tall and flower by midsummer into fall with bright lavender-blue flowers. New England aster (*A. novae-angliae*) is a native to the Northeast reaching 4 to 6 feet tall with beautiful violet-purple flowers with bright yellow centers in late summer and fall. New York aster (*A. novi-belgii*) is commonly found growing along roadsides and meadows displaying violet flowers and growing up to 6 feet tall.

When, Where, and How to Plant

Asters in general prefer moist, well-drained soil and full sun, although partial shade is also acceptable. Asters are not particularly fussy so a garden loam will suffice. In poor soils adding compost to the soil will help plants establish. Full sun and good air circulation will reduce the chance for disease. Plants can be purchased in pots in the spring and should be spaced between 12 to 24 inches.

Growing Tips

In a garden setting, a light layer of mulch in spring will keep plants evenly moist and happy. Consistent soil moisture is preferred and a low-nitrogen fertilizer in spring is acceptable.

Regional Advice and Care

Cutting asters back early in the season will help develop dense and productive plants that may not need to be staked. Planting in open, airy locations will reduce issues with rust and powdery mildew. Also, thinning stems to improve air circulation will keep plants healthy and productive. Deadheading will reduce the chance of plants reseeding. Established plants should be divided every few years in spring to keep them vigorous and in bounds. New England and New York asters are hardy to Zone 4 while Frikart's aster is hardy to Zone 5.

Companion Planting and Design

Asters are good in mixed borders with other mid- to late season perennials and can also be used in groupings or mass plantings. Asters are excellent as cut flowers and can brighten up your home in a freshly picked floral arrangement. They work especially well with black-eyed Susan, coneflower, ornamental grasses, and sedum. Some of the taller-growing species and varieties often need staking in the garden to keep them from flopping to the ground.

Try These

There are many good cultivars that range from 12 inches to 3 feet tall including 'Professor Kippenburg', which only grows to 12 inches tall with lavender-blue, semi-double flowers; 'September Ruby' with striking, ruby red flowers; and 'Purple Dome', a semi-dwarf plant reaching 18 inches tall with deep purple flowers. 'Monch' is considered by many as one of the best with lavender-blue flowers and a dense habit reaching 3 feet × 3 feet.

Astilbe

Astilbe spp.

Botanical Pronunciation
uh-STILL-bee

Other Name False spirea

Bloom Period and Seasonal Color
White, pink, and red flower plumes in late spring to summer

Mature Height × Spread
Ranges from less than 12 inches to 4 feet × 2 feet

Astilbe is a delightful, colorful perennial that has gained in popularity over the past few years. It offers spikes of plumelike flowers that range in length from 6 inches to 2 feet depending on the species and variety. The fine-textured, deep green foliage often emerges a copper color especially in red-flowering varieties. *Astilbe × arendsii* is a hybrid that accounts for most of the astilbe on the market today. The compact, spreading species, *A. chinensis* var. *pumila*, can vary in size but tends to creep along the ground and is great as an edging plant or in front of a border. Using a combination of several species and cultivars together can be quite attractive. The key to growing astilbe successfully is to keep them well watered the entire summer.

When, Where, and How to Plant
Astilbe prefers moist, well-drained soil with adequate organic matter. Plants are very sensitive to dry conditions and will burn up if they're left dehydrated. Because astilbe prefers moist, organic soil, be sure to incorporate compost into the soil when planting. Partial shade is best but I have seen plants performing well in full sun as long as they are well watered and mulched. I have also seen plants performing admirably well in dense shade. Propagate by dividing plants in the spring or fall. Plants can be purchased in nursery pots and planted when the weather warms up.

Growing Tips
Astilbe likes moist soil. Mulching new and established plants is *essential* as it will keep plants from drying out so fast. Applying a balanced, granular fertilizer in spring is usually sufficient to keep astilbe happy.

Regional Advice and Care
Plants can be deadheaded after the flowers fade or flowers can be left as seedheads and are interesting the rest of the season and into the winter. Dividing will not only make new plants but will also keep plantings vigorous and productive. Although powdery mildew and spider mites attack astilbe, they typically do not get severe enough to need a treatment with a pesticide, but monitor and treat these problems as needed. In general, astilbe is hardy to Zone 4 with *A. chinensis* var. *pumila* hardy to Zone 3.

Companion Planting and Design
Astilbe is a shade lover that is especially complementary when used with ferns, hosta, daylily, and other woodland plants. They are especially effective in mixed borders and along the edges of paths and can even be used in containers as long as they are kept watered.

Try These
'Bridal Veil' is a beautiful white form to 2½ feet. 'Cattleya' offers large pink blooms and 'Fanal' is an old-fashioned variety with bronze foliage and blood red flowers. *A. chinensis* var. *taquetii* 'Superba' is a big and bold plant growing to 4 feet tall and displaying rosy purple flowers in early summer.

Autumn Joy Stonecrop

Sedum × 'Autumn Joy'

Botanical Pronunciation
SEE-dum

Other Name Autumn Joy sedum

Bloom Period and Seasonal Color
Pink flat-topped flowers from late summer until fall; brown seedheads persist all winter

Mature Height × Spread
12 to 24 inches × 24 inches

In spring, green buds emerge from the ground and elongate to form dense clumps of light green shoots and thick, fleshy leaves. Later in the growing season, Autumn Joy sedum develop clusters of dense, dome-shaped, pink flowers that attracts hordes of bees and butterflies. As the flowers fade, they turn reddish bronze to brown, persisting all winter. New plants can be planted in groupings when the weather warms up and the chance for frost has passed in your region. Like most succulents, Autumn Joy sedum is excellent in hot, dry conditions, even thriving near the seashore. Autumn Joy sedum can even be used in both fresh and dried floral arrangements with the seedheads persisting for quite some time.

When, Where, and How to Plant
Autumn Joy sedum prefers well-drained soil and full sun but will also tolerate partial shade. Plants will thrive in moist soils that are well drained but are also remarkably tolerant of dry, rocky, or sandy soils. Planting in too much shade will cause weak-stemmed plants that will topple over and eventually fade away. New plants can be purchased at a local nursery in spring and planted after frost. Wait until weather has warmed the soil sufficiently before planting your sedum. Cuttings or divisions in spring or fall typically propagate plants. Spacing should be about 18 inches apart.

Growing Tips
Overfertilizing will cause plants to put on a lot of growth, which will eventually fall over. Compost is not typically needed but it's appreciated in poor soils. Mulching at the time of planting will help young plants to establish. Even soil moisture is beneficial but this tough plant tolerates fluctuations.

Regional Advice and Care
Clumps can be divided in spring or fall when plants are dormant; this will keep mature plants from becoming too large and weak. Cutting back plants in early summer to a foot or so results in smaller flowers but a denser, shorter plant that is less likely to fall. Plants can be cut back to the ground in late fall or early winter although many gardeners prefer to leave the dried seedheads until spring.

Companion Planting and Design
Autumn Joy stonecrop is a great companion in a mixed border with other late-season perennials such as aster, chrysanthemum, black-eyed Susan, goldenrod, and ornamental grasses. It is also very effective in one large mass planting. Bumblebees and honeybees are especially enamored by stonecrop, and seem to spend their entire existence attending to the flowers.

Try These
There are several variegated stonecrops including 'Autumn Charm', which features light green leaves with creamy white edges and pink flowers. The variegated stonecrops are very striking in the landscape. Another popular trend in stonecrop breeding are purple leaf varieties. 'Purple Emperor' has rich, dark purple foliage accented by pink flowers, a wonderful combination.

Becky Shasta Daisy

Leucanthemum × superbum 'Becky'

Botanical Pronunciation
loo-KAN-thuh-mum soo-PUR-bum

Bloom Period and Seasonal Color
White daisy flowers with bright yellow centers in early to midsummer, often reblooming later

Mature Height × Spread
36 inches × 24 to 36 inches

Zones Hardy to Zone 5

Shasta daisies have been a favorite in the garden for many years with their bright, pure white flowers in summer. But 'Becky' is a real standout plant with tall, sturdy stems and dark green foliage that form dense clumps of foliage and flowers. Unlike many daisies, 'Becky' does not flop when it reaches maturity or after a heavy rain. The masses of large flowers illuminate the landscape and can also be used effectively as a cut flower. Shasta daisy will attract bees and butterflies to the garden. I have seen 'Becky' used in small groupings or in large, mass plantings and every time I have seen it, it *never* disappoints. For midseason color, it's hard to beat this carefree perennial.

When, Where, and How to Plant

Becky Shasta daisy is a heat, drought, and cold-tolerant plant that adapts to a wide range of soil types and soil pH. Becky Shasta is not particularly fussy and doesn't require highly fertile soils. Adding a generous amount of compost to sandy or clay soils in spring will help plants thrive in their new location. Plants prefer full sun and well-drained soils but will also tolerate light shade. Planting in planters or raised beds will help to improve drainage. New plants should be gently removed from their pots in spring and spaced about 18 inches apart to form a large mass within one growing season.

Growing Tips

A general, balanced granular fertilizer can be incorporated into the soil at planting. A layer of mulch added to the surface of the soil after planting will keep plants from drying out and help them establish. Regular watering is important for the first growing season, especially during times of drought to get plants established.

Regional Advice and Care

Becky Shasta daisy is easy to grow and is not bothered by insects and diseases. Deadheading after the initial flush of blooms has faded often will encourage another round of flowering. Divide established clumps every few years in early spring. The beauty of Becky Shasta daisy is that it does not need staking.

Companion Planting and Design

Becky Shasta daisy is an ideal companion in a mixed border with coneflower, black-eyed Susan, bee balm, and ornamental grasses. It is equally effective as a stand alone planting in one large mass where it is a real focal point in the landscape. It can also work well in a container as long as it is watered regularly or as a cut flower for floral arrangements.

Try These

'Alaska' is a particularly hardy variety growing in Zone 4 with exceptionally large white flowers.

Bee Balm

Monarda didyma

Botanical Pronunciation
muh-NAR-duh DID-ih-muh

Other Name Monarda

Bloom Period and Seasonal Color
Whorled, globular clusters of red, pink, or purple
flowers in midsummer; dark green, scented leaves

Mature Height × Spread
2 to 4 feet × 3 feet

Zones Hardy to Zone 4

This North American native has unique flowers in summer, which attract a wide variety of bees, butterflies, and even hummingbirds. The blooms are whorled, tight rounded clusters of bright red flowers, although there are other colors available by variety. The pointed, aromatic leaves are interesting and deer resistant. This plant has an interesting history in the garden world and is sometimes called Oswego tea because the legendary plant explorer John Bartram discovered it near Oswego, New York, in the 1700s. The leaves were used to make herbal tea and planted in the garden with other edible plants. Because of its unique flower and ability to attract and feed a wide variety of wildlife, bee balm is a real asset to the eco-friendly gardener.

When, Where, and How to Plant
Full sun or partial shade is best for bee balm and air circulation is a *must*. Plants in too much shade or in areas with poor circulation will fail. Moist, organic, well-drained soils are ideal for bee balm and choosing soaker hoses instead of overhead watering may prove beneficial. Bee balm needs rich garden soil so be sure to incorporate copious amounts of compost or manure in the soil when planting. Space plants about 18 to 24 inches apart in spring. Purchasing seeds and sowing in spring or purchasing small plants in pots from a local nursery is recommended.

Growing Tips
A general-purpose, granular fertilizer can be used at time of planting. Mulching plants with about an inch of wood chips, leaves, or other organic material will keep plants from drying out in times of drought. Soils must be evenly moist and plants should not dry out.

Regional Advice and Care
Although powdery mildew can be a problem, siting plants in the right location and proper maintenance is essential for success. Every few years, divide plants as the centers of large plants can die out if left unattended. Deadheading the flowers once they are faded will encourage extended bloom periods.

Companion Planting and Design
Bee balm is often used in a mixed border with other perennials with similar needs such as black-eyed Susan, coneflower, ornamental grasses, asters, and so forth. It is also an excellent cut flower for floral arrangements. Bee balm works well in moist locations near streams and ponds as long as the sites are in full sun.

Try These
'Fireball' has beautiful, ruby-red flowers and a semi-compact habit growing only about half the size as the species. 'Marshall's Delight' has received good reviews for disease resistance and offers purplish pink flowers in summer and an upright habit to 3 to 4 feet tall. 'Cranberry Lace' features pink-lavender flowers with a dark center and a rather compact habit, only reaching 12 to 16 inches in height.

Black-Eyed Susan

Rudbeckia fulgida

Botanical Pronunciation
rud-BECK-ee-uh FULL-jih-duh

Other Name Orange coneflower

Bloom Period and Seasonal Color
Bright golden yellow petals surround dark brown to black centers from summer until fall; dark green leaves

Mature Height × Spread
18 to 30 inches × 24 inches

Perennial black-eyed Susan blooms heavily from midsummer to fall with masses of golden yellow flowers with cone-shaped, dark centers. The upright stems and thick foliage forms large masses or growth within a few years. These colonies will need to be thinned out as they can really take over large areas in the garden. At the same time, this species is quite carefree and easy to grow. It is pest and disease resistant and also tolerates heat and drought. Black-eyed Susan is a favorite of bees and butterflies and birds will also feed on the seed heads. Black-eyed Susan is effective in a mixed border and are also excellent as both fresh and dried flowers for gardeners who want to brighten up their home.

When, Where, and How to Plant
Black-eyed Susan is a vigorous grower and is quite adaptable. It thrives in well-drained, moist soil but will tolerate drier conditions and even heavy soil as long as it is well drained. Adding compost to poor soils will help keep plants happy. Although it's best in sun, black-eyed Susan will perform well in partial shade. Plants can be propagated by seed or divisions. Seed can be sown directly in the ground from spring until a few months before the first hard frost in fall. Plants can also be purchased in pots in spring. Spacing should be 18 to 24 inches apart.

Growing Tips
Black-eyed Susan is relatively easy to grow and does not require regular fertilizer to keep them going strong. A general-purpose, granular fertilizer at planting will suffice. A layer of mulch on the surface of the soil after planting will help plants establish during their first growing season.

Regional Advice and Care
Dividing large clumps every few years in fall will keep plants from spreading too far. Deadheading does not necessarily help plants to rebloom and leaving the seedheads will not only add winter interest, but will also provide a tasty treat for birds. If you must remove the spent flowers, wait until spring to do so and cut the entire plant to the ground.

Companion Planting and Design
Black-eyed Susan is a faithful companion to plants with similar needs such as purple coneflower, daylilies, coreopsis, ornamental grasses, and summer-flowering shrubs.

Try These
'Goldsturm' is by far still the most popular cultivated variety with masses of showy, colorful flowers most of the summer. 'Pot of Gold' is a fine selection, growing slightly shorter than 'Goldsturm' with similar, profuse flowering. *Rudbeckia hirta* 'Herbstsonne' ('Autumn Sun') is a big, bold plant displaying long, drooping sulphur yellow flower petals called rays with green centers. It is a very tall perennial reaching 5 feet in height and is hardy to Zone 4.

Bleeding Heart

Dicentra spectabilis

Botanical Pronunciation
dye-SEN-truh speck-TAB-ih-liss

Bloom Period and Seasonal Color
Deep pink flowers from spring until early summer; heart-shaped flowers have white inner petals giving the appearance of bleeding hearts

Mature Height × Spread
18 to 24 inches × 18 inches

This old-fashioned perennial has been a garden favorite for many years. The soft, fern-like foliage is a perfect backdrop to the long strings of heart-shaped flowers that arch across the plant. The flowers come in both pink and white and can be used together to create quite a show in the garden. Plants will often go dormant upon the arrival of the heat in midsummer. Bleeding heart is a wonderful woodland perennial and is great to mix with other shade-lovers such as ferns, hosta, geranium, and heuchera. Be careful, though, this plant can be poisonous if ingested in large quantities and can be a skin irritant so keep kids and pets away. Bleeding heart is known to be resistant to deer browsing.

When, Where, and How to Plant
Bleeding heart is best grown in a shaded area of the garden but will tolerate full sun if provided even moisture throughout the season. Soil should be well drained, organic, and fertile. Divide the underground stem (called a rhizome) after the plant has flowered and is going dormant to propagate plants. Fresh seed can be harvested and sown in late summer or fall or overwintered in trays that are heeled in the ground for spring germination. Trays should be covered with a light layer of mulch to keep them protected for the cold winter months. Spacing of new plants should be 18 to 24 inches apart to allow groupings of plants room to grow.

Growing Tips
Because bleeding heart likes it cool and moist, mulching plants in spring with a light layer of shredded leaves, pine needles, or wood chips will keep plants happy and protect their roots. Incorporate compost in the soil if needed and stay away from hot, dry, and exposed sites. Use a low-nitrogen, balanced fertilizer in spring if needed.

Regional Advice and Care
Powdery mildew and slugs can be problem with bleeding heart but if plants go dormant in summer, this is not as much of an issue.

Companion Planting and Design
Bleeding heart is a great companion plant to other shade-loving perennials. It works well in a woodland garden and in a mixed flower border. Often it's best to mix this among other plants so that when it goes dormant, there is other foliage to pick up the slack. If you have a cool greenhouse or sunroom that can be kept cool, try forcing plants into flower in winter just in time to give it to your sweetheart on Valentine's Day!

Try These
'Alba' is the white-flowering variety that is also striking in the landscape. 'Gold Heart' has bright golden yellow leaves and adds great contrast to the pink flowers. As the season progresses, its leaves fade to chartreuse and really brighten a shaded area of the garden.

Butterfly Weed

Asclepias tuberosa

Botanical Pronunciation
uh-SKLEE-pee-us too-bur-OH-zuh

Other Name Butterfly milkweed

Bloom Period and Seasonal Color
Bright orange, yellow, and red flowers in late spring, early summer, and early fall

Mature Height × Spread
18 to 36 inches × 24 inches

Zones Hardy to Zone 4

Butterfly weed has vibrant bright orange, yellow, and even red flowers in spring and summer and can sporadically bloom into early fall. Flowers give way to ornamental seedpods and silky seeds that are often dried and used in floral arrangements. Adult butterflies value the nectar and caterpillars will feed on the foliage of several species of *Asclepias* giving this plant group a dual purpose. This versatile plant can be used in a cultivated landscape with other perennials or in a more naturalistic area such as a meadow. As the name would suggest, butterfly weed is a favorite of many species of butterflies and bees including the beloved Monarch butterfly and native bumblebee. Unlike most relatives in the milkweed family, butterfly weed does not have milky sap.

When, Where, and How to Plant
Butterfly weed prefers well-drained soil and even moisture but also tolerates drier conditions and even drought quite well due to its tuberous, thick root system. Butterfly weed performs best in full sun and it can be often found growing in open fields. Plants can be purchased in pots in spring or seeds can be sown in spring. Seed germination is quite variable with a wide range of success rates depending on many factors including age and quality of seed, temperature, moisture, and so forth. Plants should be spaced about 12 inches apart.

Growing Tips
Butterfly weed is an adaptable plant requiring well-drained conditions but highly fertile soil is not necessary. Incorporating compost or manure at planting, especially in poor soils that are rocky or gravelly, will help with moisture retention. Regular fertilizer is not necessary and consistent soil moisture is beneficial.

Regional Advice and Care
Butterfly weed is relatively carefree although aphids and rust may be an issue. Since butterfly weed has ornamental fruit, cutting off spent flowers is not recommended unless it's necessary. It is slow to establish and the extensive root system prefers not to be disturbed so transplanting should be kept to a minimum.

Companion Planting and Design
Butterfly weed is found growing extensively in many parts of the United States. It is an excellent choice for a sunny mixed border, meadow, or prairie with other wildflowers or in groupings with other insect-attracting native plants.

Try These
There are very noble conservation efforts underway to help re-establish butterfly habitat, especially for species such as the Monarch butterfly. Many scientists feel that reduced populations of this species is a direct result of reduced milkweed populations, their main source of food. Another species of *Asclepias*, *A. incarnata*, is a good species for the garden and *A. syriaca*, the common milkweed, can be encouraged in natural areas such as fields and meadows.

Catmint

Nepeta × faassenii

Botanical Pronunciation
NEP-ih-tuh fass-EN-ee-eye

Other Name Nepeta

Bloom Period and Seasonal Color
Lavender-blue flower spikes in summer; gray-green foliage all season

Mature Height × Spread
12 to 18 inches × 24 inches

Catmint is related to catnip, which has been known to drive cats wild with its aromatic leaves! This species, although not as potent as true catnip, still has an effect on cats. It is a vigorous perennial, forming tight, dense mounds of gray-green foliage in spring. As the weather warms, plants will grow fast and produce an initial flush of lavender-blue flowers *en masse*. By late summer, blooming will slow, especially during hot, dry periods. But very often plants will rebloom in early fall as the weather cools. Its dense, mounded habit will reach 18 inches tall rather quickly and spreads to about 24 inches. Although beloved by cats, deer or rabbits do not typically bother the scented leaves. Pollinators such as bees and butterflies will swarm catmint plants all summer.

When, Where, and How to Plant

Catmint is very heat and drought tolerant and actually *thrives* in dry conditions. It prefers well-drained soil and full sun but will also perform well in moist soils and partial shade. Because it prefers well-drained conditions, sometimes it is necessary to incorporate sand or gravel into the soil to ensure good drainage. This particular species of catmint is sterile and cannot be propagated from seeds; however, cuttings or divisions in spring or summer can easily propagate it. Put cuttings in moist sand or perlite, keeping plants moist until rooting occurs. Spacing plants about 18 inches apart will allow clumps to develop and eventually touch.

Growing Tips

Unless there is a soil nutrient deficiency, regular applications of fertilizer are not usually needed. Even soil moisture is preferred.

Regional Advice and Care

Removing spent flowers and cutting plants back about two-thirds after the initial flush of blooms have faded will often encourage reblooming late in the season. Divide large clumps every few years, which will multiply plants and keep them vigorous. Disease and insects are not usually problems with catmint unless the soil drainage is poor and plants are under stress.

Companion Planting and Design

Catmint is an excellent companion in mixed borders with salvia, coneflower, daylilies, and coreopsis and is an excellent edging plant in a rose garden. I have seen this plant used very effectively along walkways, in rock gardens, and herb gardens. It is a great replacement for lavender, which does not like the heat and humidity of the Northeast. Catmint is a great selection for seashore conditions.

Try These

'Walker's Low' is not actually a low-growing plant; it can reach 18 to 24 inches tall with a similar spread. It is undoubtedly one of the best performing catmints and will rebloom late into the season if cut back. 'Six Hills Giant' is a large plant reaching 3 feet tall with showy, dark violet-blue flowers that stand out in the summer landscape. 'Blue Wonder' is 12 to 15 inches tall and wide. It is ideal along the edges of a flowerbed or as a groundcover.

Coral Bells

Heuchera spp.

Botanical Pronunciation HEW-kur-uh

Other Name Heuchera

Bloom Period and Seasonal Color
Pinkish red bell-shaped flowers in late spring and early summer; rich foliage colors all summer and fall

Mature Height × Spread
12 to 18 inches × 12 to 18 inches

Zones Hardy to Zone 4

Like coneflower and hellebore, coral bells have taken the gardening world by storm with myriad new and exciting cultivars offering brilliant colors and bold texture. The two main species that I have grown are *Heuchera sanguinea* and *H. villosa*. *H. sanguinea* forms neat clumps of growth and coral pink flowers while *H. villosa* is a big, bold plant with whitish pink flowers and heart-shaped, hairy leaves. But since the introduction of 'Palace Purple' over two decades ago, gardeners have craved the next best heuchera with leaves of purple, silver, gold, orange, and many other color combinations never before thought possible. While some varieties perform better than others and are often limited by heat and humidity, there is no question that gardeners in the Northeast have a lot to be excited about.

When, Where, and How to Plant
Heuchera needs well-drained soil and prefers even moisture. Coral bells should be given soil with plenty of organic matter. Depending on species and variety, heuchera will grow in sun, partial shade, or full shade. The green leaf or bicolored foliage types can take more sun; those with yellow or brightly colored leaves appreciate some shade. Plants are purchased from nurseries in pots in spring and should be planted about 12 inches apart. Coral bells can be propagated by dividing established plants in spring.

Growing Tips
Topdress the soil surface in spring with a thin layer of mulch to keep plants protected and help replenish organic matter. Apply a well-balanced fertilizer in spring.

Regional Advice and Care
Some gardeners pay no attention to the flowers because the foliage is so intense. For gardeners who want to encourage the floral display, removing spent flowers will extend flowering time. Coral bells are relatively carefree although heavy clay and highly acidic soils will cause plants to perform poorly. Adding sand, gravel, dolomitic lime, compost, and other amendments will help to keep coral bells happy. Coral bells can be divided into halves or quarters in spring every few years to prevent the centers of established plants from dying out.

Companion Planting and Design
Coral bells can be very effective in a shade garden, in groupings, as an edging plant, and even in containers. The foliage and flowers are great complements to astilbe, hosta, geranium, hellebore, and epimedium.

Try These
There are too many coral bells to keep track of but here are a few to consider. 'Citronelle' is a bright golden yellow that lights up the landscape in spring. 'Caramel' offers combinations of apricot to peachy orange leaves with reddish purple undersides. 'Mocha' is a bold plant with rich, blackish purple leaves. 'Rave On' is a special variety with deep greenish purple foliage combined with silver, which is covered with masses of deep pink blooms. 'Autumn Bride' displays bold, light green foliage and large spikes of pure white flowers in fall. It is hardy to Zone 6.

Cranesbill

Geranium × 'Rozanne'

Botanical Pronunciation
jur-AY-nee-um

Other Name Hardy geranium

Bloom Period and Seasonal Color
Blue-violet flowers with a white center
throughout summer

Mature Height × Spread
15 to 18 inches × 18 inches

This group known as hardy geraniums should not be confused with the annual bedding plant known as zonal geraniums (*Pelargonium* spp.) mentioned under the annuals chapter. These perennial geraniums, called cranesbill because of their cranes beak-like fruit, are generally easy to grow and adaptable in the landscape. The hybrid 'Rozanne' is an exceptionally good garden variety with violet-blue flowers with white centers in summer growing between 15 to 18 inches tall with a slightly wider spread. Rozanne cranesbill will flower most of the summer and often into fall and features deeply cut, lacey foliage, which is attractive even when the plant is no longer in flower as it gently weaves its way through the garden. Perennial geraniums are a favorite of pollinators.

When, Where, and How to Plant
Cranesbill thrives in moist, well-drained soils and full sun or partial shade. 'Rozanne' is rather shade and heat tolerant but it is wise to site plants on an eastern exposure giving them protection from the hot afternoon sun. Cranesbill prefers moist, organic, rich soil, so adding well-aged compost or manure will help plants establish. Spring planting of new plants purchased in pots from a local nursery is best in order to get them established. Space new plants about 12 to 15 inches apart and in time they will grow together.

Growing Tips
A light layer of wood chips, leaves, or other types of mulch will help plants in times of drought. Geraniums are not particularly fond of hot, dry conditions and need even moisture in the soil. For plantings that need it, a well-balanced fertilizer can be used in spring.

Regional Advice and Care
Cranesbill in general is quite pest and disease tolerant and 'Rozanne' is no exception. Light pruning of plants during the summer will keep plants more compact and inbounds but severe pruning will reduce reblooming during late summer and fall season. 'Rozanne' is hardy to Zone 5.

Companion Planting and Design
Geraniums as a group are effective in mixed borders and natural areas such as a woodland garden. Because of its spreading habit, 'Rozanne' is also useful as a groundcover, edging plant, in containers, and it's even effective in hanging baskets. Even when not in flower, the fine foliage and interesting growth habit make it desirable in the landscape. This reliable perennial will gently spread its way into the garden among other favorite plants with similar cultural requirements.

Try These
There are several species of cranesbill that are worth trying. Grayleaf Cranesbill (*Geranium cinereum*) is also hardy to Zone 5 and features showy, pale purplish pink flowers highlighted by dark purple veins. Bigroot geranium (*Geranium macrorrhizum*) is a European species with white, pink, or purple flowers growing to 18 inches tall with a similar spread. It has finely dissected leaves that, when crushed, are aromatic.

Ferns

Athyrium, Matteuccia, Osmunda et al

Botanical Pronunciation
uh-THEER-ee-um; muh-TEW-kee-uh; oz-MUN-duh

Bloom Period and Seasonal Color
Interesting, lacey foliage in shades of green, gray, and reddish pink all season

Mature Height × Spread
1 to 5 feet × 2 to 3 feet

Ferns offer unique interest in a shade garden with beautiful textures and colors. Ferns have leaflike structures called fronds which, unlike most plants, in addition to being ornamental, have a reproductive function. Ostrich fern (*Matteuccia struthiopteris*) is a beautiful, bold fern with fronds reaching 5 feet tall and spreading up to 3 feet. Cinnamon fern (*Osmunda cinnamomea*) has 3-foot-tall green leafy fronds with striking, cinnamon-brown fertile fronds emerging from the center of a plant in spring. One of the most garden-friendly and colorful ferns is Japanese painted fern (*Athyrium niponicum* var. *pictum*). This lower-growing fern will grow 12 to 18 inches tall with a slightly larger spread. Its fronds have the most beautiful shades of green and reddish purple on a grayish background that look like an artist painted it. Ferns in general tend to be resistant to deer browsing once fronds have matured.

When, Where, and How to Plant

Ferns can be planted as container plants or bare root in spring after danger of frost has passed. Potted ferns can be planted almost anytime except during hot, dry periods. Most ferns prefer partial shade and moist, organic soil conditions although Japanese painted fern can tolerate more sun. Spacing depends on the species but is typically 12 to 36 inches.

Growing Tips

Ferns really want organic soils and gardeners should try their best to duplicate the conditions ferns would get in a natural woodland. Add a generous amount of compost or other organic matter to the soil at planting. Adding a light layer of leaves or other fine mulch as a topdressing will also help ferns keep cool during summer.

Regional Advice and Care

Some ferns require dividing more than others but generally when the fronds begin to look smaller or the centers of the plants get bare, it's probably time to divide plants. Some ferns develop crowns while other develop matted roots. Clumps or sections of roots can be dug up and replanted in other areas of the garden in spring. Ferns do not typically need regular pruning but let plants die down to the ground and leave the dead fronds for winter. Dead foliage can be cleaned up and removed in early spring. Japanese painted fern and cinnamon fern are hardy to Zone 4.

Companion Planting and Design

The ferns mentioned here are both native and exotic but all are striking from spring to fall. They are great companions to astilbe, lady's mantle, bleeding heart, hosta, heuchera, and other shade lovers. Several fern species can also be used together to make lovely combinations.

Try These

'Burgundy Lace' is a Japanese painted fern with silvery foliage highlighted by heavy burgundy coloration. 'Silver Falls' has pronounced silver foliage with red veins, which offer great contrast. Lady fern (*Athyrium filix-femina*) 'Lady in Red' offers bright green fronds highlighted by brilliant, reddish violet stems.

Foamflower

Tiarella cordifolia

Botanical Pronunciation
tee-uh-RELL-uh kore-dih-FOE-lee-uh

Other Name Tiarella

Bloom Period and Seasonal Color
White flower spikes in spring; heart-shaped, green leaves turn reddish bronze in winter

Mature Height × Spread
6 to 12 inches × 24 inches

Foamflower is a hardy native perennial that is a wonderful addition to a shade garden. The dense clusters of soft green leaves often have reddish burgundy coloration along the veins of the leaf. The long-lasting, white, bottlebrush-like flowers will last for over a month. The matted, spreading growth habit will rapidly develop into thick masses of foliage. Foamflower is ideal in areas of the garden where dappled light shade exists, especially under the shade of conifers such as pines and hemlocks. It is a wonderful companion plant to other shade-lovers such as hostas, geranium, and heuchera, with which it has been hybridized to create an entirely new group of plants called *Heucherella*. Foamflower is relatively resistant to deer and rabbits.

When, Where, and How to Plant
Foamflower is best suited for partial or full shade in moist, rich, organic soils. Because foamflower thrives in rich soils, adding well-aged compost or manure at planting time is highly recommended. Siting plants in full sun or exposed, dry conditions will cause plants to be weak, never fully developing. Poor drainage will kill plants just as easy, so make sure the soil drains. Seeds can be sown in spring just under the surface of the soil and will be ready to transplant in about six to eight weeks after that. Mature plantings can be propagated by dividing large clumps. Spacing should be 12 to 18 inches apart.

Growing Tips
A light layer of leaves or pine straw will keep plants moist and cool during the heat of summer.

Even soil moisture is preferred and a low-nitrogen, well-balanced fertilizer in spring can be applied when needed.

Regional Advice and Care
Foamflower is ideal for colder climates where shade is your only option. Since foamflower spreads quickly, it can easily be divided and replanted in other areas of the garden in late fall.

Companion Planting and Design
There is nothing quite like a mass planting of foamflower in full flower in the spring landscape. It is a wonderful groundcover in a single planting or will work well with other woodland plants such as ferns, hellebores, heuchera, and so forth. It can be used in containers as long as it receives adequate watering.

Try These
'Happy Trails' is a vigorous, trailing grower with a thick black band along the veins of the leaf. 'Neon Lights' offers deeply cut, fuzzy green foliage with distinct black-purple patterns. A hybrid between *Heuchera* and *Tiarella*, × *Heucherella* 'Alabama Sunrise' undergoes several foliage transformations from bright gold with distinctive red veins in spring, to chartreuse leaves accented by red veins in midsummer, finally to shades of orange/pink or coral in fall. Using these showy foliage types in combination with one another can put on quite a show most of the gardening season.

Hosta

Hosta spp.

Botanical Pronunciation HOSS-tuh

Other Name Plantain lily

Bloom Period and Seasonal Color
Lilac, purple, or white flowers; lush green, blue, or variegated foliage in early, mid-, or late summer (depending on species and variety)

Mature Height × Spread
Large types: 2 to 3 feet × 2 to 3 feet; medium types: 18 inches × 18 inches; small types: 8 to 12 inches × 8 to 12 inches (some even smaller)

Hostas are from Asia and have been cultivated in the garden for centuries. They are among the elite for the shady garden. Hostas come in all shapes, colors, and sizes from less than a foot in height to nearly 4 feet. With thousands of named varieties available today, the choices are endless and sometimes exhausting to select. The fleshy, glossy, and sometimes puckered leaves can be green, gold, blue, or variegated in just about any color combination and pattern imaginable. Although not all are ornamental in flower, some species and varieties are quite lovely in bloom with spikes of showy, miniature lily-like flowers. I have seen hostas in every imaginable landscape situation and more often than not, they perform admirably with little fuss.

When, Where, and How to Plant
Hostas perform best in rich, organic, well-drained soil with even moisture and partial shade. When planting, add a generous amount of compost to the soil. Some varieties, especially green foliage types, will perform well in full sun as long as they are watered. Hostas with blue, gold, or variegated foliage should be protected from direct sun. Plants are available in spring at local garden centers in containers and can be planted right after the last frost. Spacing depends on the variety or species with smaller selections spaced at 6 to 12 inches, while larger varieties are spaced 2 to 3 feet apart.

Growing Tips
A layer of wood chips, crushed leaves, or pine needles will also keep plants happy. If needed, use a low-nitrogen, slow-release fertilizer in spring.

Regional Advice and Care
Hostas are wonderfully adaptable garden plants but are not without their share of problems. Slugs and black vine weevil are just two problematic pests. Use slug baits or drown them using a bowl of beer to keep slugs in check. Remove dead leaves from dormant plants in late fall as they may harbor slug eggs. Although hostas do not need to be divided often, a small slice of the roots can be taken in early spring to propagate.

Companion Planting and Design
Hostas are very versatile and can be used in groupings and mass plantings in woodland gardens or in mixed borders with compatible plants such as astilbe, heuchera, hellebore, and ferns. Gardeners should be careful where they use hostas as they can be poisonous to pets.

Try These
'Blue Mouse Ears' is a miniature with thick, blue-green foliage only reaching 6 to 8 inches tall by 12 inches wide. *Hosta sieboldiana* offers big, lush, blue-green leaves and cultivars such as 'Elegans' offers steel blue foliage and light lilac to white flowers. 'Sum and Substance' is a giant, reaching 3 feet tall with a greater spread; its chartreuse leaves in shade turn a striking golden color in sun. 'Great Expectations' is a eye-catching variety with two-tone leaves with blue-green margins and golden yellow centers that change as the season progresses.

Japanese Anemone

Anemone × hybrida

Botanical Pronunciation
an-eh-MOE-nee HIB-rih-duh

Other Name Hybrid anemone

Bloom Period and Seasonal Color
White, pink, and rose-colored flowers from late summer through fall

Mature Height × Spread
2½ to 5 feet × 2 to 3 feet

Zones Hardy to Zone 4

Japanese anemone is an easy-to-grow hybrid perennial that can extend the gardening season well after most of your garden plants have faded. Japanese anemone is in full bloom in fall, a wonderful reminder that the gardening season doesn't end just because summer has. The single, semi-double, and double flowers on long stalks and dense clumps of rich green foliage provide great color and texture in the fall landscape. Japanese anemone has also been touted as a deer-resistant plant. Japanese anemone is effective in large groupings and mixed borders with other fall-blooming perennials. Although some varieties require staking or the flower stalks will fall over, who cares! They are still well worth inclusion in the garden adding rich color at a time when you least expect it.

When, Where, and How to Plant

Japanese anemone grows best in well-drained, rich garden soil and full sun or partial shade. Since Japanese anemone prefers fertile, organic soil, incorporating well-aged compost when planting is recommended. New plants can be purchased in small pots in spring or fall from a local nursery. Plants can be propagated from cuttings although the easiest method of multiplying your plants is through dividing large clumps of anemone. Spacing is generally 18 inches apart or more to give plants room to spread.

Growing Tips

Because Japanese anemone is sensitive to heat and drought, a light layer of mulch in spring will help plants through tough summers. In hot, dry conditions, it tends to suffer and should be well watered during times of drought. A well-balanced fertilizer can be used in spring if needed.

Regional Advice and Care

Japanese anemone can be an aggressive spreader and dividing large clumps every few years will keep plants vigorous and contained. Dividing should be done in the spring to avoid disruption in the fall when it is blooming. Deadheading is not as critical as other plants but flower stalks on some varieties may need to be staked in order to keep them upright. Powdery mildew, Japanese beetles, and flea beetles may be problematic but plants typically perform well in spite of that.

Companion Planting and Design

Japanese anemone works well in mixed borders, cottage gardens or in a mass planting. Using it in combination with other fall bloomers such as sedum, chrysanthemum, asters, and toad lily can make a nice display.

Try These

'Honorine Jobert' is an old-fashioned variety that dates to the Civil War and still dazzles the garden today. It has pure white flowers with a yellow center growing to 3 to 4 feet tall. 'Max Vogel' is an impressive pink-flowering anemone that provides a great show. 'September Charm' offers single, rose pink flowers with flower stalks reaching 2 to 3 feet in height. 'Serenade' offers an extended blooming period with showy pink flowers and dense, spreading habit that covers the ground rather quickly.

Lady's Mantle

Alchemilla mollis

Botanical Pronunciation
al-kuh-MILL-uh MOLL-iss

Bloom Period and Seasonal Color
Chartreuse flowers in June; gray-green leaves
all summer

Mature Height × Spread
12 to 14 inches × 18 to 24 inches

Lady's mantle is one of the most durable, easy-to-grow perennials that will work both in a mixed sunny border and a shaded woodland garden. The mounded, spreading habit and thick, gray-green foliage are an excellent canvas for the delicate, showy greenish yellow flowers in early summer. When the leaves get wet the water beads up, glistening in the summer sun. The flowers can be effective both as fresh and dried flowers in a vase. It grows in a wide variety of soils as long as they are well drained. One very important feature of lady's mantle is its relatively good resistance to deer and rabbits. In addition, lady's mantle, once established, will act as an effective groundcover while suppressing weed growth.

When, Where, and How to Plant

Lady's mantle does best in moist, well-drained soil with organic matter but will also tolerate clay or sandy soils as well. Adding a generous amount of compost, especially to sandy soils, is recommended. It will grow well in full sun or partial shade. Full exposure and hot, dry conditions may cause leaves to scorch. Plants are typically sold in pots from the nursery, although seed can be planted indoors six to eight weeks before the last frost date as well. Seedlings will need to be carefully nursed along until they are large enough to be on their own. Plants should be spaced 15 to 18 inches apart, which also depends on how fast you want plants to grow together, creating a dense mound of foliage.

Growing Tips

Lady's mantle benefits from a light layer of mulch to keep their roots cool during the heat of the summer. Keep plants well watered during periods of heat and drought. A low-nitrogen, granular fertilizer can be used in early spring.

Regional Advice and Care

Lady's mantle can reseed in the garden so removing spent flowers will reduce that possibility and also encourage a sporadic reblooming. One way to multiply your existing plants and keep them vigorous is to divide them every few years. This can be done by gently pulling plants apart in the early spring or fall. Lady's mantle is quite pest resistant and resilient but may need grooming late in the growing season. In early spring, be sure to cut or remove any dead leaves or stems before the growing season.

Companion Planting and Design

Lady's mantle can be grown as a standalone plant in a mass planting, groundcover, edging plant, and even in containers. It is especially effective lining a garden path. The flowers and foliage can also be used in cut floral displays. Lady's mantle is a good companion plant to iris and hardy geranium.

Try These

There are other species of *Alchemilla* but *A. mollis* is still by far the best one for this region. There is an improved form that can be found in mail-order nurseries.

Lilyturf

Liriope muscari

Botanical Pronunciation
lih-RY-oh-pee muss-KAR-ee

Other Name Liriope

Bloom Period and Seasonal Color
Lilac-purple flower spikes in late summer and
early fall; dark green, straplike foliage

Mature Height × Spread
12 to 18 inches × 12 inches

Zones Hardy to Zone 6

Lilyturf is a grasslike perennial that forms dense clumps of foliage and spikes of showy purple flowers in late summer. It is extremely durable and is one of few perennials that are evergreen in many climates. Lilyturf is typically used in mass plantings where it can be used to cover a large area. It is incredibly pest, heat, and drought tolerant and is also resistant to deer, rabbits, and other varmints. What is most attractive about lilyturf is its indestructible nature and its remarkable tolerance of shade, even dense shade. Besides being used as an effective groundcover or edging plant, lilyturf can be used in place of a lawn. In late winter or early spring, mowers set to the highest setting are often used to cut back plantings to remove old foliage.

When, Where, and How to Plant
Lilyturf will adapt to almost any condition but prefers well-drained soil and full sun or partial shade. Lilyturf tolerates dense shade and a range of soils from sandy to heavy clay. Adding compost to sandy or heavy clay soils will certainly help plants develop, though. Avoid poorly drained soils as the plants will not perform well in these conditions. Plants are grown in small containers in the nursery and can be planted in spring. Spacing should be 12 inches apart to ultimately ensure a dense, matted grouping. Dividing in spring will yield many new plants that you can plant around the garden.

Growing Tips
Lilyturf does not require any specific fertilizer or rich garden soil. A light layer of mulch such as woody chips, crushed leaves, or pine straw will help in times of drought for the first growing season. Even soil moisture is best but it will take periods of dry conditions.

Regional Advice and Care
Since lilyturf keeps its foliage most or all of the year, by late winter or early spring the leaves may get beat up during a cold, harsh winter. Plants can simply be cut back with a pruner, hedge trimmer, or even a lawn mower in early spring and new leaves will emerge from the crown. Insects or diseases are not particularly troublesome and usually problems only arise in poorly drained soils.

Companion Planting and Design
Lilyturf is excellent in mass plantings, as a groundcover, and to replace a lawn. It can be used as a edging plant or mixed with ornamental grasses and plants with similar texture. Lilyturf is effective on slopes and for erosion control.

Try These
'Big Blue' offers abundant blue clusters of flowers late in the growing season. 'Variegata' has creamy white leaf margins that are especially effective brightening up a shady area of the garden. *Liriope spicata*, creeping liriope, is a bit finer in texture and is a fast-spreading groundcover that is also effective as a lawn replacement and is hardy to Zone 4.

Peony

Paeonia spp.

Botanical Pronunciation
pee-OH-nee-uh

Bloom Period and Seasonal Color
Late April or early May for tree peonies and mid- to late May for herbaceous peonies. Flowers in white, pink, red, yellow, and bicolors.

Mature Height × Spread
24 to 36 inches × 24 to 36 inches (herbaceous types); 36 to 48 inches × 36 to 48 inches (tree types)

Who doesn't love peonies? Peonies are classic, old-fashioned perennials with a charm that has stood the test of time in gardens all over the world. Although maybe not considered as "hip" as some of the more cultivated perennials today, you can bet that peonies are still highly prized garden treasures. There are two types: herbaceous, which die down to the ground at the end of the season, and tree, which have woody stems. Within the herbaceous peony types available today, most of the garden peonies came from the Chinese peony (*Paeonia lactiflora*) and common peony (*P. officinalis*), while the tree peonies are selections of *P. suffruticosa*. In addition, Itoh peonies are hybrids between herbaceous and tree peonies and are among the most popular peonies available today.

When, Where, and How to Plant

Peonies prefer full sun and moist, rich, organic, well-drained soil so incorporate well-aged compost or manure into the soil at planting. Peonies are typically planted in fall or spring as either bare-root plants or containers. It is important to plant herbaceous peony roots—which have obvious buds, called eyes—about 2 inches *below* the soil. Roots planted too deep will result in poor flowering. Tree peonies are often grafted so plant the graft so that it's covered with 4 to 6 inches of soil, or at least 2 inches above the thick portion of the rootstock if not grafted. Space herbaceous types at 2 to 3 feet; spacing of tree peonies may be up to 4 feet apart.

Growing Tips

Adding a low-nitrogen fertilizer such as 5-10-5 or bone meal will get them off to a good start but do not overfertilize. A light layer of mulch is recommended after planting. Soil should be kept evenly moist.

Regional Advice and Care

Peonies are susceptible to foliage diseases, mostly on herbaceous types. Removing the infected tissue and cutting plants to the ground at the end of the growing season will help reduce future infestations. Fungicides may be another option to reduce disease infestations. Bring a sample of your infected plant to your local agricultural Extension office for recommendations on treatment. Deadheading after flowering allows plants to put energy towards growth and next year's flowers. Peonies do *not* like to be disturbed so dividing or transplanting should be kept to a minimum. Dividing herbaceous peonies should be done in fall.

Companion Planting and Design

Peonies are excellent in mass plantings, mixed borders with sun-loving annuals and perennials, and especially as cut flowers.

Try These

Start slow and choose varieties that work with *your* garden in terms of space and color scheme. 'Scarlet O'Hara' is a wonderfully vibrant red herbaceous peony. Itoh peonies offer the best of both worlds with flowers like a tree peony but foliage that's characteristic of a herbaceous peony. 'Bartzella' is a beautiful variety with large yellow flowers.

Purple Coneflower

Echinacea purpurea

Botanical Pronunciation
eck-ih-NAY-see-uh pur-PUR-ee-uh

Other Name Purple echinacea

Bloom Period and Seasonal Color
Flowers consist of bronze cones surrounded by rosy purple flower petals from mid- to late summer into fall

Mature Height × Spread
24 to 36 inches × 24 inches

Purple coneflower is a very popular perennial with rounded, brown- to bronze-colored, cone-shaped flower heads surrounded by colorful purple petals that range from white to pink or rosy purple, depending on the variety. The upright habit and lush, dark green leaves provide a bold texture in the landscape. Purple coneflower typically has a loose, open habit growing to 2 to 3 feet in height with a slightly less spread. Bees and butterflies gravitate to the flowers all summer and plants are especially favored by native bees including bumblebees. Several species of birds will find a tasty meal in the center of the cone-shaped flower once the seed is ripe. Purple coneflower has many garden uses including colorful perennial, cut flower, deer-resistant plant, and it's used in medicine to boost the immune system.

When, Where, and How to Plant
Purple coneflower prefers moist, rich, well-drained soil and full sun but will tolerate a dry, less fertile soil and partial shade. Established plants can be purchased in spring or seed can be sown that will germinate within two to four weeks. Seed should only be lightly covered with soil, as darkness reduces germination. Space new plantings about 12 to 24 inches apart.

Growing Tips
Although purple coneflower does not typically benefit from additional fertilization, adding compost to the soil at planting will keep plants vigorous and happy. Mulching plants after planting will also help keep soil evenly moist and roots cool during hot periods.

Regional Advice and Care
Although purple coneflower typically does not want to be disturbed, occasionally dividing large plants every few years will allow you to multiply plants and keep them productive. Cutting plants back and deadheading spent flowers will often prolong flowering and reduce reseeding in the garden. Leaving the seedheads attracts birds and also offers ornamental interest in winter. Japanese beetles and powdery mildew as well as other diseases can attack purple coneflower, but it's generally tolerant of pests.

Companion Planting and Design
Purple coneflower is a great companion to tried-and-true perennials such as black-eyed Susan, ornamental grass, coreopsis, daylilies, and other sun-loving plants. It can work well in a cultivated garden or in a natural site such as a meadow.

Try These
Purple coneflower in general can get tall and lanky. 'Kim's Knee High' is a shorter variety to 1 to 2 feet tall but still shorter than the species, displaying rosy pink flowers. 'Magnus' offers larger rosy purple flowers and 'White Swan' is a beautiful white-flowering form with pure white petals that are very striking when combined with the purple varieties. One of my favorites is a PowWow® Wild Berry with vivid rosy purple flowers and a semi-compact habit to 24 inches tall. A real showstopper!

Threadleaf Coreopsis

Coreopsis verticillata

Botanical Pronunciation
kore-ee-OP-siss vur-tiss-ih-LAY-tuh

Other Name Threadleaf tickseed

Bloom Period and Seasonal Color
Bright yellow blooms, early summer to early fall

Mature Height × Spread
18 inches × 36 inches

Threadleaf coreopsis is native to the eastern United States and is one of the easiest perennials to grow and use in the garden. The showy, starlike yellow flowers and soft, lacey foliage all summer give this plant a real presence in the garden. With so many exciting varieties, both old and new, threadleaf coreopsis flowers range from pink to pale yellow and golden yellow. Even when not in flower in early spring and late fall, the fine texture and dark green foliage offer interest in the garden. Bees and butterflies flock to threadleaf coreopsis all summer. It is also considered a deer-resistant plant. Because it is adaptable and trouble-free, threadleaf coreopsis offers versatility in a wide variety of landscape situations.

When, Where, and How to Plant

Threadleaf coreopsis performs best in full sun but light shade is acceptable. Too much shade will cause plants to flower poorly and create more opportunities for disease. Threadleaf coreopsis thrives in moist, well-drained garden loam but tolerates both sandy and clay soils as long as they are well drained. In less than optimum soil conditions, adding well-aged compost to the soil when planting will help plants thrive. Threadleaf coreopsis can be purchased in small containers at a local nursery in spring but are also easy to propagate once established. Simply dig up small root divisions in spring, move them to other areas of the garden, and stand back!

Growing Tips

A light layer of mulch added to the surface of the soil will especially help in times of drought. Even soil moisture is beneficial and, if needed, a well-balanced fertilizer can be added in spring.

Regional Advice and Care

Threadleaf coreopsis will form dense clumps of foliage and flowers reaching 2 to 3 feet in width by the end of summer. These clumps should be divided every few years in early spring or fall, which will keep mature plantings from spreading too aggressively. Once the initial flush of flowers subsides, cut back dead flowers to encourage another flush of blooms in late summer or fall. Although powdery mildew and other diseases can occur, if located in the right conditions, threadleaf coreopsis is rarely high maintenance.

Companion Planting and Design

Threadleaf coreopsis is an excellent companion to other summer-blooming perennials and annuals in a mixed border. It can be used in butterfly gardens and, depending on the variety, can be used as an edging plant, in containers, or in foundation plantings.

Try These

'Moonbeam' is a very popular garden variety with soft yellow flowers and will often spill over and lay on the ground. 'Zagreb' is a more compact variety that tends to stay upright with bright, golden yellow flowers. 'Full Moon' is a hybrid that is part of the Big Bang™ series with large, 2- to 3-inch-diameter, bright yellow flowers that stand out.

Yarrow

Achillea millefolium

Botanical Pronunciation
ack-ih-LEE-uh mill-ih-FOE-lee-um

Bloom Period and Seasonal Color
White, pink, red, cream, and bicolored flowers,
early to late summer

Mature Height × Spread
12 to 36 inches × 24 to 36 inches

The name *Achillea* refers to Achilles from Greek mythology, who used the plant medicinally to stop bleeding and to heal the wounds of his soldiers. Yarrow is an aggressive grower with a matted, spreading habit and flat-topped flowers borne on upright stalks. The soft, green, fernlike foliage has an aromatic scent and the name *millefolium* means "thousand-leaved" referring to the dissected foliage. Yarrow is quite adaptable to a wide variety of soils and drought but requires sun to really thrive in the garden. It is also deer resistant and will attract bees and butterflies. The flowers are excellent both in fresh and dried floral arrangements. Yarrow does need maintenance as it will spread in the garden and may need to be reduced in size or divided every few years to keep it in check.

When, Where, and How to Plant

Yarrow prefers full sun and well-drained, moist soil but is quite tolerant of dry conditions as well. Yarrow is rather carefree and does not require rich soils to survive, but incorporating compost into the soil when planting is beneficial in dry, sandy soils. In partial shade plants often become sparse, may flop to the ground, and can be more susceptible to disease. Yarrow can be purchased in small pots in spring from local garden centers or seed can be sown directly outdoors. It can be easily propagated by dividing established plantings in spring. Yarrow will self-seed so pay close attention to where it spreads in the garden. New plants or divisions can be spaced 1 to 2 feet apart.

Growing Tips

Yarrow is a tough plant and doesn't usually require an abundance of fertilizer. Even soil moisture is preferred but dry periods are acceptable.

Regional Advice and Care

In general, yarrow tends to flop, particularly in hot, humid weather, so plants should be pruned and deadheaded regularly. Cutting back plants in late spring before flowering will help reduce overall plant height. Pruning and deadheading plants after initial flowering will keep plants tidy and encourage additional blooming. Powdery mildew and rust are common diseases of yarrow but overall the plant is not overwhelmed with disease in the right conditions. The main challenge with this plant is to divide it every two to three years to keep it vigorous and under control.

Companion Planting and Design

Yarrow is effective in cottage gardens, mixed perennial borders, and is especially useful in meadows and wildflower plantings. Yarrow will quickly naturalize in areas of the garden that are left wild and less cultivated. Yarrow is an excellent cut flower and is very effective as a dried flower. Often clumps of yarrow are hung upside down to dry, and then are used as needed for long-lasting floral displays.

Try These

Some of the newer varieties are quite attractive including the 'Seduction' series, which offers a compact habit and a variety of colors.

BULBS

FOR NEW YORK & NEW JERSEY

One of the key secrets to a successful garden is to incorporate a wide variety of plants that will grow and look good together. Part of this plan should include bulbs, which provide interest from late winter through spring, summer, and fall. These plants are very different from other ornamentals in the garden, offering unique and beautiful flowers and foliage that diversify your landscape. Bulbs enhance other plants around them and bridge the seasonal and ornamental gap between spring and summer perennials and annuals.

The first signs of life after a long, hard winter are favorites like winter aconite and snowdrops, which tolerate the cold, fluctuating weather typical of late winter and early spring in the Northeast. To simplify this section of the book, the term "bulb" will be used to describe plants growing from bulbs, tubers, tuberous roots, corms, and rhizomes. These are all underground root and storage systems that enable these plants to grow and flower. Most of the plants discussed in this section are winter hardy with the exception of dahlias, which are tender and can be dug up in the fall and replanted the following spring.

Dicentra spectabilis, Tulipa 'Hans Anrud', *Tulipa* 'Peer Gynt', *Pulmonaria longifolia* 'Roy Davidson', *Helleborus niger, Alchemilla mollis,* Hosta

Selecting Bulbs for the Home Landscape

Bulbs can be ordered from mail-order catalogues, online websites, or a local nursery or garden center. It is better to shop early to ensure the best selection. Once you receive your order, check bulbs to make sure they are not soft or damaged. Store them in a cool, dark place until you are ready to plant.

Although most bulbs have relatively short-term bloom periods, often going dormant after flowering, you still have to pay close attention to their cultural needs and function. Bulbs can be selected for

Narcissus in mass planting.

colorful blooms, interesting foliage, and ability to be used in groupings or mass plantings for a showy display. Some bulbs are better than others at being truly perennial. For example, daffodils are one of the most beloved plants because they will multiply and get stronger each year, creating sizeable masses, often referred to as "naturalizing." On the other hand, most large-flowering tulip hybrids and cultivars tend to be treated as annuals, replaced each year because they do not multiply as well and often get weaker each year. Whatever and wherever you choose to plant bulbs in your garden, make sure they'll thrive in the conditions you have provided and plant them in large numbers to make a big impact.

General Care and Maintenance of Bulbs

Most bulbs prefer moist, well-drained soil with a generous amount of organic matter. If you have heavy clay or sandy soils, add compost or manure and turn over the top 12 inches of the soil before planting. If you are adding fertilizer in spring to garden beds, bulbs will absorb those nutrients. A soil sample should be taken for large plantings to be sure the pH and nutrients are right for the bulbs you have chosen. Add a light application of bone meal or blood meal if phosphorus and nitrogen are lacking in the soil. Animals will sometimes dig up bulbs to get to these organic fertilizers so a low-nitrogen, well-balanced fertilizer can be used as a substitute.

Most winter-hardy bulbs can be planted in fall for the following season. Bulbs can be planted as long as the ground is not frozen but should be planted in early to mid-autumn. Planting depth is *very* important and varies by the species and size of the bulb. Read the directions on the bulb package. Or as a general rule, plant bulbs at a depth two to three times greater than the height of the bulb. Once your bulbs are planted, add a 1- to 2-inch layer of wood chips or pine straw to the soil's surface, and water thoroughly. After flowering, hardy bulb foliage should not be cut back until the foliage starts to die back and turn yellow. Cutting plants back prematurely will impact the plants' ability to store energy for next year.

Allium

Allium spp.

Botanical Pronunciation AL-ee-um

Other Name Flowering onion

Bloom Period and Seasonal Color
Early, mid-, and late summer flowers in white, pink, purple, or yellow

Mature Height × Spread
6 to 60 inches × 12 to 24 inches

Zones In general, the alliums listed are hardy to Zone 4

The *Allium* family is familiar to gardeners because we are usually growing them in the vegetable garden as garlic, chives, leeks, and onions. But members of the *Allium* family are not only edible, they can be ornamental as well. These flowering bulbs have colorful, globular flowers that attract bees, butterflies, and other pollinators while resisting pests such as voles, rabbits, chipmunks, squirrels, and deer. It's hard to imagine a summer border without these colorful flowering bulbs that require little care. Even when the flowers fade, the seedheads remain and offer interesting texture in the garden. Dried or fresh, the flowers can be cut for a floral display. They are a bit pricier than the average flowering bulb but are well worth the investment.

When, Where, and How to Plant
Alliums will tolerate most soils as long as they are well drained but they thrive in moist, organic soil. They prefer basking in full sun where they will flower most reliably. Bulbs should be planted in fall, and spacing should be at least three or four times the width of the bulb.

Growing Tips
Alliums benefit from adding some well-aged compost to the soil, especially in dry, sandy soils or heavy, clay soils. Once established, plants do not need much water and in fact bulbs will rot if given too much water. A light mulch layer will protect flowering onion during cold winters and reduce the potential for premature sprouting, which can cause frost damage to foliage and flowers.

Regional Advice and Care
Alliums are carefree, pest-resistant plants that pay great dividends year after year with little maintenance. Once flowers have faded, they can be left or cut back but do not remove foliage or flowers before they have faded unless you are harvesting them for their flowers.

Companion Planting and Design
Alliums are ideal for a summer border with other sun-loving perennials and annuals. They should be used in groupings to create a colorful display. Some of the smaller alliums work well in rock gardens and with other dwarf plants. Alliums are very effective when mixed with fine-textured plants such as coreopsis, ornamental grasses, and *Amsonia* but are equally striking against bold-textured plants such as hosta.

Try These
A classic allium that has been popular for many years is giant onion (*A. giganteum*) with 4-inch-diameter, lilac flowers that stand atop 4-foot-tall stalks. 'Purple Sensation' offers 2- to 4-inch-wide purple flowers that reach 2 to 2 ½ feet high. 'Globemaster' has large, deep purple flowers reaching 3 to 4 feet tall. Drumstick allium (*A. sphaerocephalon*) is an early summer bloomer growing 2 to 3 feet tall with small, two-toned, burgundy-green flower heads. German garlic (*A. senescens* subsp. *glaucum*) is a delicate plant reaching 6 to 12 inches tall and displaying silvery gray-green foliage and lilac to lavender flowers in late summer.

Autumn Crocus

Colchicum autumnale

Botanical Pronunciation
KOLL-chi-kum aw-tum-NAY-lee

Other Name Colchicum

Bloom Period and Seasonal Color
Lavender-pink flowers in early fall with the absence of foliage

Mature Height × Spread
6 to 8 inches × 6 to 8 inches

Zones Hardy to Zone 4

Autumn crocus looks similar to, but is not related to, nor should be confused with, Dutch crocus, which blooms in spring. This fall bloomer has spring foliage, which yellows and goes dormant by summer and is followed by bright lavender-pink flowers in fall. In contrast, the spring-flowering crocus has foliage and flowers in early spring in a wide variety of color combinations. Autumn crocus is very colorful and noticeable in fall since it displays all flowers and no leaves. New varieties are available in double flowering forms and white blooms. They work very well in mass plantings, naturalized areas, or in small groupings around other dwarf plants. Autumn crocus is toxic if eaten and animals will keep their distance.

When, Where, and How to Plant
Autumn crocus should be grown in well-drained, moist soil with plenty of organic matter. It will also flower best in full sun or partial shade. Add well-aged compost or manure to sandy loam soils and heavy clay soils to keep the soil friable (loose). Bulbs should be purchased in late summer and planted 3 inches deep and 6 inches apart.

Growing Tips
Mulching new plantings will keep them cool in the summer and protected from fluctuating temperatures in winter. Crocus like even moisture and a general-purpose fertilizer at planting is beneficial.

Regional Advice and Care
Autumn crocus need good drainage; poor drainage will result in the bulbs rotting. Slugs may be a problem on summer foliage so keep a close eye on the foliage and use nontoxic slug bait. Reduce watering in summer when leaves begin to fade so the foliage does not get wet regularly. Autumn crocus often has flowers that will flop over, especially if watered from overhead irrigation. Plants can be divided right after foliage has gone dormant in summer.

Companion Planting and Design
Autumn crocus are perfect in small, open areas of the garden between existing plants to fill those voids. They work well in woodlands, rock gardens, and in combination with dark green groundcovers where they will pop up through—and stand out against—the foliage. Unfortunately, you have to live with the foliage for a while but the fall display is worth it. Planting autumn crocus among creeping plants such as perennial geranium will help to conceal the foliage.

Try These
'Alboplenum' is a double white form with frilly, white flowers. 'Album' is a single white flowering variety that will brighten up the garden. 'Pleniflorum' is a double flowering variety with rosy pink flowers. There are other species of *Colchicum* that are worth trying, all bringing something unique to the garden. *C. speciosum* has dark, reddish violet flowers that look similar to tulips.

Crocosmia

Crocosmia spp.

Botanical Pronunciation
kroe-KOZ-mee-uh

Other Name Montbretia

Bloom Period and Seasonal Color
Red, yellow, and orange tubular, nodding
flowers borne along arching stalks in summer

Mature Height × Spread
2 to 3 feet × 1 to 2 feet

Zones Hardy to Zone 5

Crocosmia is a colorful flowering bulb that paints the landscape with brightly colored flowers in summer. The tubular, one-sided flowers are grouped along arching flower stalks that grow up from dark green, pleated, swordlike leaves that look similar to gladiolus leaves. The flowers are magnets for hummingbirds and pollinating insects. Crocosmia is also an excellent cut flower and can make a gorgeous bouquet. There are quite a few cultivated varieties ranging in flower color from golden yellow to orange and scarlet red. Crocosmia is a wonderful addition to a mixed summer border and close attention should be paid to using these bright, warm colors with complementary colors and textures from plants such as ornamental grasses, black-eyed Susan, and coreopsis.

When, Where, and How to Plant
Crocosmia prefer moist, well-drained soil and full sun or partial shade. In full sun, be sure to keep plants well watered during times of heat and drought. Bulbs should be planted 2 to 3 inches deep and 6 to 8 inches apart.

Growing Tips
Crocosmia does *not* like dry, rocky soil and requires even moisture in the soil. Add compost or manure to sandy loam soils and mulch plants so they have a source of organic matter and protection from freezing temperatures. Use a general-purpose fertilizer in spring as plants emerge from the soil.

Regional Advice and Care
Crocosmia is susceptible to spider mites and if left untreated, significant infestations will impede growth and flowering. Check with your local nurseries for recommendations on low toxicity pesticides such as horticultural oil or soap. If it is a light infestation, hose plants down with cold water, once a day. In colder Zones of 5 and 6 where temperatures could get below 0 degrees Fahrenheit, remove the bulbs in fall, keep them indoors but do not let them completely dry out, and replant in spring.

Companion Planting and Design
Crocosmia are ideal in a summer flower border with other brightly colored perennials and annuals. They can be a real focal point in the summer landscape. Plant in groups of 12 bulbs or more. Crocosmia can also be grown in containers and moved into a cool, dry place in winter.

Try These
'Lucifer' is a hybrid with rich, scarlet-red flowers reaching 2 to 3 feet in height. 'Walberton Yellow' offers bright yellow flowers reaching about 18 inches tall. 'Bright Eyes' offers a profusion of yellow-orange flowers with red centers that arch outward along each stem. 'Solfatare' is a hybrid bred in the late 1800s featuring apricot-yellow flowers and dark green leaves.

Daffodil

Narcissus spp.

Botanical Pronunciation nar-SISS-us

Other Name Jonquil

Bloom Period and Seasonal Color
Colorful white, pink, orange, bicolors, and several shades of yellow in early spring

Mature Height × Spread
6 to 18 inches × 6 to 12 inches

Zones Generally hardy to Zone 4; some hardy to Zone 3

Daffodils are among the most diverse and useful flowering bulbs in the garden. There are sixty species of daffodils and ongoing breeding has yielded many new and exciting cultivated varieties for gardeners to enjoy. Quite frankly, whether using some of the old standbys or some of the new hybrids, you can't go wrong with daffodils for spring color. They work in just about every landscape situation imaginable, are resistant to deer and rabbits and continue to multiply each year. There are different classes of daffodils, from miniatures to large, bold varieties, some with small-cupped flowers, others with larger cups, bicolor and double flowers, and some having a sweet fragrance. Many of these varieties can be planted together to create a stunning spring display.

When, Where, and How to Plant
Daffodils tolerate sandy and clay soils but prefer well-drained, organic garden loam. During planting incorporate a generous amount of compost into the top 12 inches of soil. Bone meal or a low-nitrogen balanced fertilizer can also be used. Daffodils prefer full sun or part shade and too much shade will reduce flowering. Plant new bulbs in early to mid-fall at a depth of two to three times deeper that the height of the bulb. Most daffodil bulbs should have at least 3 inches of soil over them. Spacing depends on the size of the plant and flower but as a general rule, it should be 6 to 12 inches apart.

Growing Tips
Adding a 1- to 2-inch layer of mulch on the soil surface will help protect bulbs from weather fluctuations and freezing and thawing soil. Soil should be kept evenly moist and apply fertilizer in spring.

Regional Advice and Care
Daffodils have few pest problems but bulbs will rot in poorly drained soil. After flowering has finished, do not cut back foliage to the ground until it starts to yellow and go dormant. Cutting back foliage prematurely will often affect flowering the next year. Daffodils do not need dividing very often but if plants are too large or unproductive, divide with a garden fork in early fall. Daffodil hardiness is greatly dependent on the species, hybrid, and variety, so check for the hardiness before buying them.

Companion Planting and Design
Daffodils are effective in large masses or small groups, mixed borders, rock gardens (dwarf varieties), window boxes, containers, and as cut flowers. They are great companions to crocus and snowdrops.

Try These
'King Alfred' is a well-known, large growing daffodil with golden yellow flowers and it's great for naturalizing. 'Mount Hood' emerges a creamy yellow but changes to ivory white. 'Tête-à-Tête' is a wonderful dwarf variety with delicate, golden yellow flowers. There are so many outstanding varieties available, do some research and pick the best ones for you.

Dahlia

Dahlia hybrids

Botanical Pronunciation
DAL-yuh

Bloom Period and Seasonal Color
Various types of flowers in a wide range of colors from white, yellow, pink, purple, orange, red, bicolors, and more

Mature Height × Spread
1 to 5 feet × 1 to 2 feet

Zones Not hardy; dahlia is an annual

Dahlias are native to Mexico and Central America and today's garden varieties are primarily hybrids. This highly cultivated plant continues to be bred for improved flower colors and sizes and for foliage color and quality. A new trend with dahlias today is to develop dwarf and semi-dwarf varieties that do not need staking. Dahlias are classified by their flower type, including single, anemone, collarette, waterlily, decorative, ball, pompon, cactus, orchid, peony, and stellar forms. All of these choices in size, foliage type, flower type, and color are enough to make a gardener dizzy but excited at the same time. Dahlias are very useful because they can be incorporated into almost any sunny summer border with a wide range of perennials, annuals, and flowering shrubs.

When, Where, and How to Plant
Dahlias prefer moist, organic, well-drained soil and full sun to produce the most quality flowers. Dahlias like organic soils so add a generous amount of compost or manure to the planting hole. A general-purpose, slow-release, low-nitrogen fertilizer applied at planting will give plants a boost in spring. Light afternoon shade and protection from strong winds is recommended. Dahlias grow from tubers, which can be purchased in spring. Plant tubers of larger varieties up to 6 inches deep and shorter varieties, 2 to 3 inches deep. Spacing should be 1 (shorter varieties) to 3 (taller varieties) feet apart.

Growing Tips
Add a 1-inch layer of mulch to keep roots cool in summer. Using a liquid application of hydrolyzed fish emulsion will give plants a quick-release, low dose of nitrogen in the heat of summer. Soil should be kept evenly moist and should not be allowed to dry out completely.

Regional Advice and Care
Root rot, powdery mildew, aphids, and mites can be an issue. Monitor your plants and check with your local nursery or agricultural Extension office for treatment recommendations. On taller varieties, stake and tie up plants as they grow. Deadhead spent flowers a few times a week to remove faded blooms and to encourage new ones. Pinching back plants early in the growing season will encourage bushier plants. In fall, tubers will have to be dug up, cleaned, and stored in newspaper in a cool, dry place until the following spring.

Companion Planting and Design
Dahlias are effective in containers, mixed borders, and as a cut flower. Plant heights can range from low-growing border dahlias to large show dahlias.

Try These
The Melody® series is a good border dahlia coming in a variety of colors and only reaching 24 inches tall. I love the dwarf Dark Angel® series with its dark purple foliage and a variety of colors including yellow, orange, red, pink, and dark purple. For the larger dahlias, check out the American Dahlia Society website (www.dahlia.org) or the Mid Island Dahlia Society website (www.midislanddahlia.com) for more information.

Daylily

Hemerocallis spp.

Botanical Pronunciation
hem-ur-oh-KAL-iss

Bloom Period and Seasonal Color
Large, funnel-shaped flowers come in every color but blue in summer along with clumps of long, fleshy, dark green leaves

Mature Height × Spread
1 to 3 feet × 1½ to 2 feet

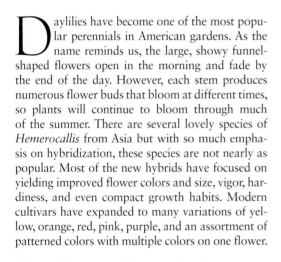

Daylilies have become one of the most popular perennials in American gardens. As the name reminds us, the large, showy funnel-shaped flowers open in the morning and fade by the end of the day. However, each stem produces numerous flower buds that bloom at different times, so plants will continue to bloom through much of the summer. There are several lovely species of *Hemerocallis* from Asia but with so much emphasis on hybridization, these species are not nearly as popular. Most of the new hybrids have focused on yielding improved flower colors and size, vigor, hardiness, and even compact growth habits. Modern cultivars have expanded to many variations of yellow, orange, red, pink, purple, and an assortment of patterned colors with multiple colors on one flower.

When, Where, and How to Plant
Daylilies prefer full sun or partial shade and moist, well-drained soil. They are not picky about soil and will grow in average soil conditions but thrive in rich, organic soils so add well-aged compost to sandy or clay-based soils. New plants can be purchased and planted in spring and should be spaced 18 to 24 inches apart. New bulbs should be planted deep enough to accommodate their roots but the crown, where the leaves and roots meet, should be only 1 to 2 inches below the soil surface.

Growing Tips
A 1- to 2-inch layer of mulch once a year in spring will keep plants thriving and productive. Daylilies are drought tolerant once established but should be watered in times of drought to reduce stress. In severe droughts with no watering, plants will often go dormant. A general-purpose fertilizer can be applied in spring.

Regional Advice and Care
Thrips and spider mites may infest daylilies but using cold water to wash them off the foliage or using insecticidal soaps can help. Divide plants in fall to reduce large, oversized plantings and to maintain vigor of the plants. Deadhead spent flowers to keep plant tidy and productive.

Companion Planting and Design
Daylilies are great companions to ornamental grasses, black-eyed Susan, purple coneflower, and other summer-blooming perennials. They do well in mixed flower borders, mass plantings, and they can be used effectively on slopes and woodland gardens.

Try These
'Stella de Oro' is a dwarf selection with golden yellow flowers and a growth habit of only reaching 12 to 18 inches tall. 'Happy Returns' is a repeat-bloomer, which features 3 ½-inch-diameter ruffled, lemon-yellow flowers reaching 18 inches tall above the arching, linear foliage. Like dahlias, there are too many great cultivated varieties and species of daylilies to mention and to do this plant group justice, you should check out the American Daylily Society website (www.daylilies.org) or check with your local daylily society chapter. The Long Island Daylily Society is a very active group on Long Island (www.lidaylily.org).

Dutch Crocus

Crocus vernus

Botanical Pronunciation
KROE-kuss VUR-nuss

Other Name Spring crocus

Bloom Period and Seasonal Color
Early spring flowers in white, yellow, purple, and striped forms

Mature Height × Spread
4 to 6 inches × 4 to 6 inches

Most cultivated varieties of crocus today are from species and hybrids, which are listed under *Crocus vernus*. These early spring-flowering bulbs are native to Europe and are actually in the *Iris* family. Flowers come in quite an assortment of colors from white to yellow and purple as well as striped, bicolor selections. Flowers open during the day but close at night and often remain closed during rainy or cloudy days. The thin, grasslike foliage will go dormant in late spring after flowers have finished. Dutch crocus will multiply and form large drifts of flowers, which can be divided if desired. Dutch crocus can be used in many ways including mass plantings, along path edges, in containers, and in rock gardens with other dwarf plants.

When, Where, and How to Plant

Dutch crocus do well in well-drained soil with even moisture. They prefer sandy loam or even rocky soils that drain well. Full sun or partial shade is best for flowering. Avoid heavy clay soils and poor drainage as plants will perform poorly and bulbs will rot. Plant small bulbs 2 to 3 inches deep and 3 to 4 inches apart in fall.

Growing Tips

Although Dutch crocus thrive in moist soils that are very well drained, adding well-aged compost to the soil at planting will benefit plants as long as you do not overdo it. Add a 1-inch layer of wood chips, shredded leaves, or pine straw to keep plants protected from freezing temperatures.

Regional Advice and Care

Dutch crocus is an easy bulb with few problems. However, rabbits, squirrels, chipmunks, and other animals will dig them up, eat them, and move them around the garden. Try using a barrier such as mesh screen or repellents to keep animals away from your crocus plants. If you grow Dutch crocus in a lawn area, do not mow down their leaves for at least six weeks after blooming so the plants have a chance to go dormant and put resources back into the bulb for next year. Mowing too early will affect flowering and plant health. Plants can be divided in fall while they're dormant.

Companion Planting and Design

Dutch crocus are excellent in woodland gardens, mixed borders, rock gardens, and along pathways where they can be easily seen. They work well as companions to other dwarf flowering bulbs such as dwarf varieties of daffodil, snowdrops, and grape hyacinth.

Try These

Try the new mixtures offered by bulb companies. Species crocuses generally bloom earlier than the hybrids, so using them together will often result in extended spring bloom. Saffron crocus (*C. sativus*) is a showy fall-bloomer with clusters of lilac purple flowers. *C. tommasinianus* is squirrel-resistant with colors varying from pale lavender to deep reddish purple with a white throat. *C. speciosus* is a fall bloomer with goblet-shaped, lilac-blue flowers with deeper blue veins.

Iris

Iris spp.

Botanical Pronunciation
EYE-riss

Bloom Period and Seasonal Color
Flowers range from white, pink, blue, purple, yellow, and many other color combinations.

Mature Height × Spread
6 inches to 3 feet × 6 inches to 2 feet

Zones Japanese iris is hardy to Zone 4; other types are hardy to all Zones

Iris has been a beloved plant for centuries in many cultures and can be found in gardens all over the world. Iris bloom in spring and have a complex flower with several distinct flower parts including an upright shield called a "standard" and a drooping lower part called a "fall." Iris is adored for its diverse flower colors and is interesting when not in bloom because of its green, swordlike leaves. Iris species vary greatly and can found from miniatures only growing 6 inches tall and wide to 3-foot-plus-tall plants with half the spread. There are many different types including bearded, beardless, and crested types, which describe the flowers. Some iris spread by rhizomes (underground stems) and others are bulbous. Iris is also deer resistant.

When, Where, and How to Plant
Each iris species is slightly different but in general they prefer moist, well-drained, organic soils and full sun but will also grow in light afternoon shade. Add rich, well-aged compost to heavy clay soils or sandy soils. New plants can be purchased bare-root or in pots in spring. If you purchase a bulbous type iris, such as Japanese and Siberian species, plant bulbs 3 to 5 inches deep and the same spacing. If you are planting iris with rhizomes, such as bearded iris, cover with ½ inch of soil and space 12 to 24 inches apart.

Growing Tips
A well-balanced, low-nitrogen granular fertilizer application in spring is recommended. Bearded iris prefers neutral or slightly acidic soil and lime can be used to raise soil pH. The beardless types such as Japanese and Siberian iris prefer moist and acidic soils.

Regional Advice and Care
Borers, root rot, and leaf spot can be problematic. Remove infected leaves or stems as soon as you find them. Cut back faded flowers, removing the entire stalk once blooming is finished. Bearded types can be cut back as foliage turns yellow and divided in late summer. The fleshy rhizomes can be cut in pieces with a spade or pulled apart with a garden fork and replanted. Dividing every few years will keep plants vigorous. Beardless types, such as Siberian, Japanese, and Dutch iris, do not like to be disturbed but when plants become too large and unproductive, divide them in early spring or fall.

Companion Planting and Design
Iris work well in a mixed border, as cut flowers, and some can even be used in containers.

Try These
Bearded iris bloom in spring and come in a wide variety of colors. Siberian iris (*Iris sibirica*) grow in wet soils but will also grow in well-drained, moist soils. Siberian iris offers blue-purple flowers, occasionally lavender or white. Japanese iris (*I. kaempferi*) prefers moist soil and display large, showy flowers ranging from blue, pink, purple, and white.

Lily

Lilium spp.

Botanical Pronunciation
LIL-ee-um

Bloom Period and Seasonal Color
Summer blooms in white, pink, purple, red, yellow, and orange, sometimes having spots or striping

Mature Height × Spread
1 to 7 feet × 1 to 2 feet

Zones Most are generally hardy to Zone 4 but that varies among specific cultivars and types

Lilies are another classic flowering bulb that still dominate gardening catalogues and are sought after by gardeners who crave their striking colors and fragrance all summer. There are three main groups of lilies: European species, Asiatic species, and North American species. All three have been hybridized to create beautiful garden selections. These hybrids are highly prized in the horticultural industry and there is a lot of interest with breeding of lilies, producing improved cultivated varieties for gardeners who want a reliable cut flower and versatile perennial. There are many types of lilies available but among the most popular are the Asiatic hybrids, Oriental hybrids, and trumpet lilies. Some species and hybrids are more fragrant than others—and some not at all—but the Oriental types are a good choice if you want that sweet perfume. Pollinators frequently visit the trumpet-shaped flowers.

When, Where, and How to Plant

Lilies will grow in average, well-drained soil and full sun or partial shade. They thrive in rich, organic soil so add a generous amount of compost or manure at planting time; soil should not be allowed to dry out. New bulbs can be planted in fall and, although depth is dependent on species or type, a good rule of thumb is to plant the bulb two to three times deeper than the diameter of the bulb. Spacing also varies but planting lilies 8 to 12 inches apart is acceptable.

Growing Tips

Lilies also benefit from a cool root environment so add 1 to 2 inches of mulch to the soil surface to moderate soil temperature and moisture. Soil should be evenly moist; add a low-nitrogen fertilizer in spring.

Regional Advice and Care

Lilies are fairly pest free although aphids, virus, and bulb rot can occur. Often taller plants will need staking to prevent them from falling over, especially in windy locations. Plants should be deadheaded right after flowering and the entire plant cannot be cut back until the leaves start fading and turning yellow.

Companion Planting and Design

Lilies can be grown as single clumps or in groupings in mixed borders and can be used as cut flowers or in containers.

Try These

There are many good mixtures or individual cultivated varieties available and you should shop in local nurseries or mail-order catalogues to choose the best colors and types for your needs. 'Star Gazer' is an established variety with deep crimson flowers edged with white and spotted and a delightful fragrance. 'Casa Blanca' offers huge, pure white, fragrant flowers that illuminate the landscape. 'White Elegance' is a hardy version of an Easter lily with long, white, trumpet-shaped blooms. Speciosum lily (*L. speciosum* var. *rubrum*) is a lovely species with ruby-red, 6-inch-wide, fragrant flowers with reflexed petals.

Snowdrop

Galanthus spp.

Botanical Pronunciation
guh-LAN-thus

Bloom Period and Seasonal Color
Pure white nodding flowers with a touch of green at the inner base emerge in late winter and early spring

Mature Height × Spread
6 to 12 inches × 6 to 12 inches

Zones See "Try These"

Like winter aconite, snowdrops are the early risers of the garden. The common name refers to the resemblance the flowers have to drops of snow. It is exciting to see the flowers of snowdrop poking through the snow, reminding us that spring is just around the corner. Snowdrop comes in different sizes, depending on the species, and are related to the popular indoor flowering bulb *Amaryllis*. Snowdrops are native to Europe and Asia and prefer the cooler environment of the Northeast. If given the right growing conditions, this vigorous flowering bulb will spread and naturalize in the landscape. It is deer resistant and will even grow in heavy clay soils. Snowdrop is an excellent groundcover in mass under large deciduous trees where grass won't grow.

When, Where, and How to Plant

Snowdrops prefer moist, well-drained, organic soil but will tolerate clay soils as well. Snowdrop is not fussy but if soil is sandy or heavy clay, add a generous amount of compost and apply a light layer of mulch on the surface of the soil. Full sun or partial shade is best for flowering and it grows well under deciduous trees where it will be in full sun in early spring but under partial shade after it finishes flowering. Plant bulbs in fall at a depth of 2 to 3 inches and about 2 to 4 inches apart.

Growing Tips

Snowdrops prefer even soil moisture and adding a balanced fertilizer at planting is beneficial.

Regional Advice and Care

Snowdrops are easy to grow and require little care. After flowering, do not cut back foliage until it turns yellow as the plants go dormant in late spring. In ideal growing conditions, snowdrops will self-seed and send off bulb offsets. Snowdrops can be divided in fall.

Companion Planting and Design

Snowdrops are effective in large masses or smaller groupings. They can be used in rock gardens, foundation plantings, woodland gardens, containers, planted under deciduous trees, and even in a lawn. Snowdrops are a great companion plant to winter aconite and glory of the snow (*Chionodoxa*).

Try These

Giant snowdrop (*Galanthus elwesii*) grows to 12 inches tall and has noticeably large white flowers to 2 inches long. They are hardy to Zone 4. Common snowdrop (*G. nivalis*) is a more petite plant only growing 6 to 9 inches tall with smaller, more delicate white flowers. Summer snowflake (*Leucojum aestivum*), a close relative, actually blooms in the spring with large, white, bell-shaped flowers reaching 12 to 18 inches tall. It is hardy to Zone 4. Spring snowflake (*L. vernum*) is about half the size and blooms a few weeks earlier than summer snowflake. Both are excellent additions to the spring garden.

Tulip

Tulipa spp. and hybrids

Botanical Pronunciation
TEW-lih-puh

Bloom Period and Seasonal Color
Early, mid-, and late spring species and varieties
with flowers in a rainbow of colors and types

Mature Height × Spread
6 inches to 3 feet × 6 to 8 inches

Zones Not hardy; used as an annual or short-
term perennial

Tulips are a pleasant reminder that spring has arrived. They have a rich garden history dating to the sixteenth century during the Ottoman Empire in Turkey when they were imported to Europe. In Holland, "Tulipmania" dominated society, where they were so valuable that people traded their family possessions or used tulip bulbs as currency. Tulips are versatile, growing in containers, flowerbeds, or as a cut flower. There are many classes of tulips from large Darwin types to parrot tulips with ruffled flowers to dwarf species reaching only 6 to 9 inches. Although beautiful, tulips are not persistent, long-lasting perennials. The majority of the showy cultivars and hybrids are treated as short-lived perennials, lasting only a few years and growing weaker with diminishing flowers as time goes by. However, there are some species that are longer lived.

When, Where, and How to Plant
Tulips should be planted in full sun and well-drained soil. Tulips thrive in organic soils so add compost to sandy or clay soils. Bulbs should be planted in mid- to late fall when the weather is consistently cool but not freezing. Plant at an average depth of three times the diameter of the bulb. Space no more than 6 inches apart.

Growing Tips
Add a light layer of mulch on the surface of the soil to protect bulbs from freezing and thawing and dry spring weather. If needed, use a low-nitrogen,

well-balanced fertilizer at planting or when leaves emerge in spring. Keep soil evenly moist.

Regional Advice and Care
Tulips are not usually around long enough to worry about pests, although deer and squirrels cause major headaches. Use repellents or barriers to protect your prized tulips. In poorly drained soil, bulbs will rot, so be sure to plant in well-drained conditions. Tulips are generally shorter lived, although some of the species are longer lived. Otherwise, plant away and just know your tulips will have to be replaced every few years.

Companion Planting and Design
Tulips should be planted in bunches to make a real showy display. Smaller varieties and species can be used in a rock garden or with other smaller bulbs such as crocus or pansies. Plant extra bulbs so they can be used as a cut flower in spring.

Try These
'Apeldoorn' is a big and bold variety reaching 2 feet tall with bright colors including red, golden yellow, and others. Parrot tulips are always unique and fun with featherlike flower petals in a wide range of solid colors and color combinations. Two species that work well in a rock garden with other dwarf flowering shrubs is *Tulipa tarda*, with small star-shaped white flowers with a yellow center growing 6 to 9 inches tall, and *T. turkestanica*, with white flowers with yellow-orange centers growing 8 to 10 inches tall.

Winter Aconite

Eranthis hyemalis

Botanical Pronunciation
air-AN-thiss hye-em-AY-liss

Bloom Period and Seasonal Color
Bright yellow flowers surrounded by lobed leaves in late winter and early spring

Mature Height × Spread
4 to 6 inches × 4 to 6 inches

Winter aconite is surely a sight for sore eyes after a long, hard winter as they pop their bright yellow, cup-shaped, buttercuplike flowers through the snow in late winter. Delicate, deeply lobed leaves surround the flowers as they emerge. The flowers will warm the bare landscape and should be used along a garden path near the house where they can be enjoyed. This European native thrives in the cold climates of New York and New Jersey with average care and growing conditions. The plant will spread and act as a groundcover as it naturalizes in the landscape. Winter aconite is not susceptible to pests and in fact is deer resistant. After flowering, leaves turn yellow and go dormant by late spring as the temperatures get warmer.

When, Where, and How to Plant

Winter aconite prefers moist, rich, organic soil that is well drained but is adaptable. Incorporate several inches of compost to sandy loam or clay soils. Full sun or partial shade is best for flowering. As trees leaf out in spring, winter aconite may be in more shade but typically that is not a problem since they are soon dormant by that time. Tubers can be planted in late summer or early fall at a depth of 2 to 3 inches and spaced at least 3 inches apart.

Growing Tips

Winter aconite tolerates average soil as long as even moisture is maintained. Watering is not as important in late summer and fall when plants are dormant. A light layer of fine wood chips, shredded leaves, or pine straw after planting will keep plants happy.

Regional Advice and Care

Winter aconite is carefree and easy to grow. It may self-seed or will naturalize into larger clumps over time with good growing conditions. Plants can be divided in late spring or early summer but once planted, should be disturbed as little as possible. Soak tubers in water overnight before planting.

Companion Planting and Design

Winter aconite is an excellent plant for a woodland garden, along garden paths, rock gardens, in containers, and around trees and shrubs. It should be sited someplace close to the house where it can be appreciated in winter. Winter aconite is a great companion plant to snowdrops and when used together, they can offer a wonderful display before most plants have emerged.

Try These

There are several other early spring bloomers that will also enhance the late winter and early spring landscape. Glory-of-the-snow (*Chionodoxa luciliae*) is a carpet of lilac blue, star-shaped flowers, which have a white center. Siberian squill (*Scilla siberica*) has deep blue flowers that look like tiny drooping bells.

ORNAMENTAL GRASSES

FOR NEW YORK & NEW JERSEY

When you think about grass, you naturally have thoughts of a well-manicured "lawn" or "turf." But not all grass species are strictly used for mowed grass areas. Ornamental grasses have dominated the American landscape since the 1980s when German-born landscape architect Wolfgang Oehme and American James Van Sweden used these free-flowing, natural forms in their landscape designs. These well-known designers and plantsmen brought ornamental grasses to the forefront with their mass plantings and unique use of color and texture. While this popular trend continues today, what has changed is the types of grasses that are preferred. Now the trend is to use more native grasses rather than their exotic counterparts because of the threat of invasive species, and to support habitat for native animal species. In a garden setting, ornamental grasses can offer a low-maintenance alternative to lawns and other high-maintenance plantings while offering beautiful texture and color to the garden in all four seasons.

Selecting Ornamental Grasses for the Home Landscape

Many species of both native and exotic ornamental grasses are noninvasive and aesthetically pleasing. While in the past, landscapes were dominated by maiden grass

Grasses provide soothing, soft texture all growing season.

(*Miscanthus* spp.), fountain grass (*Pennisetum* spp.), and blue fescue (*Festuca* spp.), these popular grasses have now taken a back seat to more preferred natives such as switch grass (*Panicum virgatum*), little bluestem (*Schizachyrium scoparium*), and Hakone grass (*Hakonechloa macra*). With so many new species and cultivated varieties available to gardeners, it's mind-boggling and somewhat overwhelming.

However, this chapter offers some clear and distinct choices that stand out above the rest because of their ornamental qualities, landscape function, and adaptability.

Ornamental grasses should be selected with several key attributes in mind. We are most attracted to ornamental grasses for their showy, colorful foliage, interesting flower heads, and unique growth habits. Select the grass that fits your landscape based on how large they will grow. Will they fit into the area of the garden you have for them, and will they look their best there? For example, grasses with golden or variegated foliage are best in partially shady areas of

Wait for ornamental grasses to go dormant before cutting them back.

the garden with lots of green foliage around them so they stand out. These wonderful accent plants, such as variegated Hakone grass, can really brighten a drab area. Ornamental grasses look best when they're used in groupings or mass plantings in a foundation planting or mixed border. They also work very well with sun-loving perennials and annuals.

Even more important than how good these ornamental grasses will *look* in the garden is will they perform well in the conditions you have to offer them? Before purchasing a large quantity of ornamental grasses from the local nursery, find out if they are hardy and able to perform well in the soil and light you have in the garden. Ornamental grasses are rather adaptable, carefree plants that adapt well to most situations, but even they have limitations.

General Care and Maintenance of Ornamental Grasses

While most ornamental grasses in this section prefer full sun, a few select grasses also thrive in partial shade. Ornamental grasses adapt to a wide variety of soil but well-drained, moist soil with some organic matter is ideal for most. In general, ornamental grasses should be planted in spring after the threat of frost has passed. Water these grasses for the first growing season until they become established. After that, most species will need only occasional watering and aftercare. There is a lot of debate when ornamental grasses should be cut back. I believe that you should leave your ornamental grasses alone until early spring so the birds and other animals can use them for cover. They will also give you great texture and color in the winter months. Then the brown stems and seed heads can be cut low to the ground so the next season's growth can emerge. This cutting back process should always be done once a year when plants are dormant.

Feather Reed Grass

Calamagrostis × acutiflora

Botanical Pronunciation
kal-uh-muh-GRAHSS-tiss uh-kew-tih-FLORE-uh

Bloom Period and Seasonal Color
Green foliage turns golden yellow in fall, pink flowers in early summer turning golden brown later in the season

Mature Height × Spread
3 to 5 feet × 1½ to 2½ feet

Zones Hardy to Zone 5

Feather reed grass is a lovely, clump-forming ornamental grass that can be used in groupings or as a standalone plant. It has distinctly upright stems with lush, green foliage and plumelike flower heads from summer through fall and winter. The flower heads are quite showy and will gently wave in a summer breeze. Birds will be attracted to the seedheads. Feather reed grass prefers moist soils and will even tolerate occasional flooding in a low area of the garden such as a rain garden. This is one of those grasses that is a good replacement for the potentially invasive maiden grass (*Miscanthus sinensis*) because of its size and inability to set seed (because it is sterile). It is outstanding in a mass planting.

When, Where, and How to Plant
Feather reed grass prefers moist, well-drained soil and full sun or partial shade. It will tolerate heavy, clay soils as well. Feather reed grass thrives in rich, organic soil so add compost to the soil at planting time. In hot, exposed sites it will perform best if given light shade in the afternoon. Plants can be purchased in containers in spring and should be spaced 18 to 24 inches apart.

Growing Tips
A 1- to 2-inch layer of wood chips on the surface of the soil after planting will help in times of drought. The best time to mulch plants is in early spring after they have been cut to the ground. This plant does not require much other than even moisture in the soil and adequate sunlight.

Regional Advice and Care
Feather reed grass is pest free and, like most ornamental grasses, is quite deer resistant. Seedheads and foliage should be left all winter but pruned to the ground in early spring. This will encourage new growth and a dense plant to develop.

Companion Planting and Design
Because of its upright habit and extraordinary flower display, feather reed grass can be used as a single specimen in a mixed border or in a mass planting. It is a good companion to other sun lovers such as coreopsis, purple coneflower, black-eyed Susan, and other ornamental grasses. Feather reed grass can also be used in a rain garden with other moisture-loving plants. It is also a wonderful cut flower.

Try These
'Karl Foerster' is a popular variety named after an extraordinary German nurseryman. It was awarded the perennial Plant of the Year in 2001. Its dense growth habit will reach 2 to 3 feet tall but with the feathery flower heads it can extend to 5 feet. Korean feather reed grass (*Calamagrostis brachytricha*) offers bright green leaves reaching about 2 feet and large, feathery plumes of pinkish flowers in late summer, extending a foot or two more. The flowers fade to creamy beige in fall and finish to a straw brown color in winter. It's hardy to Zone 4.

Hakone Grass

Hakonechloa macra

Botanical Pronunciation
ha-koe-neh-KLOE-uh MAY-kruh

Other Name Japanese forest grass

Bloom Period and Seasonal Color
Bright to medium green leaves form mounds of
cascading foliage; yellow-green flowers in midsummer

Mature Height × Spread
12 to 18 inches × 18 to 24 inches

Zones Hardy to Zone 5

This is one of my favorite grasses and after planting it in your garden, it will be yours too! This Asian species has wide, pointed leaves and a graceful, cascading habit that form mounds of dense foliage. There are several gold and variegated cultivated varieties, which are actually more popular than the green-leaved species. In partial shade these brightly colored leaves are stunning but plants should be used selectively or they may be overpowering. This grass is ideal for a moist shade garden and can easily be mixed with broadleaved evergreens and shade-loving perennials and ferns. Unlike some of the grasses offered in this section, Hakone grass is not evergreen and the leaves will turn golden yellow to bronze in winter but will persist, offering winter interest.

When, Where, and How to Plant

Hakone grass prefers rich, organic, acidic soil and partial sun. Hakone grass grows best in organic soils so add well-aged compost to soils that are clay based or sandy loam. Do not plant this grass is very dry, rocky soils. The green leaves of the species are tolerant of full sun but the variegated varieties should be protected from the afternoon sun. Plants can be purchased in spring in containers and should be spaced 12 to 18 inches apart.

Growing Tips

A 1- to 2-inch layer of wood chips or shredded leaves is ideal to keep the roots cool in summer. Even moisture should be provided in hot, dry periods of summer or the leaves may get scorched. An application of low-nitrogen granular fertilizer can be applied in spring.

Regional Advice and Care

Hakone grass is a carefree plant that will do its best work in shade. It is not bothered by pests and diseases and is considered deer resistant. Plants can be cut back in late winter or early spring. Hakone grass is not an aggressive spreader and dividing to keep plants in bounds is not needed regulary. Divide establish plantings every few years in early spring.

Companion Planting and Design

Hakone grass is ideal for a woodland garden and in a mixed border with other shade-loving perennials and shrubs. The variegated forms are effective accent plants and are quite striking in a grouping or mass planting. Hakone grass can also be used in container plantings.

Try These

'Aureola' is a variegated form with primarily golden leaves with green striping. It is best in partial shade as full sun will often burn these plants and dense shade turns plants chartreuse green. 'All Gold' has brightly colored golden-yellow leaves with no green stripes. I have seen this plant with reddish hues in fall, which stopped me in my tracks. 'Fubuki' displays green leaves striped with creamy white. Whichever one you pick, you are not likely to be disappointed with any of them.

Little Bluestem

Schizachyrium scoparium

Botanical Pronunciation
skizz-uh-KEER-ee-um skoe-PAIR-ee-um

Bloom Period and Seasonal Color
Blue-green foliage in summer; reddish bronze to orange in fall; purplish bronze flower heads with silvery white seedheads in winter

Mature Height × Spread
2 to 3 feet × 1 ½ to 2 feet

Little bluestem is another meadow grass found on roadsides and in large fields that is stunningly beautiful most of the year. There is no question it is most effective in large numbers but smaller, individual plantings or groupings in a garden setting can be quite attractive as well. The growth habit is loose and upright as it matures, forming upright clumps of blue-green foliage in summer. If the foliage weren't enough, the purplish bronze flower heads display silvery white seedheads in fall, many of which will hang on. Birds eat the seeds. The foliage display in fall is breathtaking as it turns brilliant shades of reddish bronze to bronzy orange in winter. Individual clumps have a broomlike effect but large masses will sway in the wind and look like amber waves of grain!

When, Where, and How to Plant
Little bluestem grows in moist, well-drained, organic soil but will also tolerate drier conditions. It also tolerates poor, infertile soils and heavy, clay soils. Little blue stem benefits from organic soil so add compost in the soil and as a topdressing when planting. Full sun is best for maximum growth and keeps plants upright, as shade will cause plants to flop over more. Plants are slow to grow from seed so in spring purchase plants in small pots. Space 6 to 12 inches apart.

Growing Tips
Little bluestem thrives in soils with even moisture but can take periods of dry conditions. Regular

fertilizer is not needed but if it's used, apply a low-nitrogen fertilizer in spring.

Regional Advice and Care
One potential drawback of this plant is that it will also flop in late summer, especially in rich, fertile soils or after a heavy rain. Planting in tight groupings rather than single plants may help keep plants erect. Some of the new varieties tend to be less prone to this issue. In early spring cut plants down to encourage new growth and flowers for the growing season.

Companion Planting and Design
Little bluestem is most effective in groupings and mass plantings in natural, open areas if you have the room. It can be used in smaller numbers in mixed borders with other grasses and sun-loving perennials.

Try These
'The Blues' emerges in spring with clumps of striking blue-green foliage changing to reddish bronze in fall. 'Blaze' is a unique variety transforming from gray-green with purplish tints in late summer, to pinkish orange to reddish purple to vivid red in fall. 'Standing Ovation' is an upright form that has been developed to stay vertical and is less likely to flop like the species. Big bluestem (*Andropogon gerardii*) is an entirely different species that is quite larger than little bluestem. It displays silvery gray to blue-green foliage and turns reddish bronze to coppery yellow in fall. Big bluestem can reach 4 to 6 feet tall with about half the spread. Hardy to Zone 4.

Mexican Feather Grass

Nassella tenuissima

Botanical Pronunciation
nuh-SELL-uh ten-you-ISS-ih-muh

Bloom Period and Seasonal Color
Tufts of fine green foliage bear silvery to light golden blond flowers in early summer changing to deep golden yellow to amber in fall and winter

Mature Height × Spread
18 to 24 inches × 18 to 24 inches

This Southwestern native grass (also found under *Stipa tenuissima*) is as tough as it is beautiful. The soft, fine texture of the foliage and feathery flowers are an impressive combination. Green tufts of soft, fine foliage emerge in spring and give rise to long, silky flowers that range in color from blond to creamy yellow changing to striking golden yellow to amber in the cooler temperatures of fall and winter. This soft texture is especially breathtaking when the grass is blowing in a soft summer breeze. As a native to a hot, arid climate, Mexican feather grass prefers hot, dry conditions and is drought and heat tolerant. It is pest resistant and has been reported as deer resistant. Mexican feather grass is a summer delight that can be used in groupings or as individual plants in a mixed border with other sun-loving grasses and perennials.

When, Where, and How to Plant

Mexican feather grass prefers very well-drained soils that are on the dry side. Sandy loam and even rocky soils will do just fine. They do not like heavy soils that hold too much moisture. Full sun is preferred although a bit of light shade is acceptable as well. Plants should be purchased in small pots in spring and planted well after the danger of frost has passed in mid- to late spring. Spacing should be 12 to 18 inches apart but can be closer if you want them to fill in quicker.

Growing Tips

Mexican feather grass does not need many soil amendments to survive. A light layer of mulch for new plantings will help plants get established. Regular mulch will also protect the roots of these plants in winter. Keep plants watered until they are established and then leave them alone.

Regional Advice and Care

Mexican feather grass is a pest-free, easy-to-grow plant that thrives in the warmest areas of the garden. Plants can be propagated by seed or larger, established plants may be divided in spring but be careful with these delicate plants. It's hardy to Zone 7 but may grow in Zone 6 with protection and mulch.

Companion Planting and Design

Mexican feather grass is ideal in a sunny border with other grasses and summer-blooming perennials such as purple coneflower, coreopsis, black-eyed Susan, catmint, asters, and other ornamental grasses. There is nothing like a mass planting of Mexican feather grass along a pathway as you brush by its soft texture.

Try These

Another species with soft, fluffy flowers that makes a real textural statement in the landscape is pink muhly grass (*Muhlenbergia capillaris*). It displays big clouds of puffy pink flowers that develop in fall and dominate the landscape. Pink muhly grass has very much the same cultural requirements as Mexican feather grass, growing in hot, dry locations into Zone 6.

Prairie Dropseed

Sporobolus heterolepis

Botanical Pronunciation
spore-OB-uh-lus het-ur-oh-LEEP-iss

Bloom Period and Seasonal Color
Open, airy flower clusters are pink with brown hues in late summer and early fall along with dense clumps of fine foliage that transform from medium green in summer to golden yellow, orange, and light bronze

Mature Height × Spread
2 to 3 feet × 2 to 3 feet

Prairie dropseed is yet another underutilized native grass that is worth inclusion into the garden. This prairie grass gets its name from the seed that drops to the ground in the fall. This clumping, dense grower has very fine foliage reaching about 15 inches tall and 18 inches wide but with the addition to the loose, open clusters of flowers, it can reach 2 to 3 feet tall with a similar spread. The flowers offer interesting tints of pink and brown and offer a fragrance similar to coriander. The medium green summer foliage changes to very attractive shades of golden yellow to orange and often fades to light bronze in the winter. This eco-friendly plant provides a valuable food source for birds and is also deer resistant.

When, Where, and How to Plant
Prairie dropseed is very tolerant of a wide range of soils including heavy clay. It thrives in soils that are well drained and have a dry to medium moisture retention. Prairie dropseed will perform best in full sun. It is exceptionally tolerant of drought and will tolerate the root competition of surrounding trees as long as it is not in too much shade. In general, prairie dropseed is slow growing and also slow to establish. Although seed can be sown in spring, I recommend purchasing plants grown in small containers. Spacing should be 15 to 18 inches apart.

Growing Tips
Prairie dropseed prefers drier soils so adding compost or manure is not usually necessary. Regular watering until plants are established and a light layer of mulch is beneficial to new plantings. Regular fertilizer applications are not typically needed.

Regional Advice and Care
Prairie dropseed is a pest-free, drought- and pollution-tolerant native and is also deer resistant. Plants can be cut back in late winter or early spring for the upcoming growing season. Plants *can* be propagated by seed, although self-seeding is not typical. Divide large clumps in early spring, which is somewhat difficult because of their extensive root systems.

Companion Planting and Design
Prairie dropseed is a good companion plant to other native grasses such as sedge and little bluestem. It will also look good in a mixed sunny border with flowering perennials, in rock gardens, and it's effective in a mass planting. Its one of few ornamental grasses mentioned here that can tolerate hot, dry areas near the seashore, dry slopes, and deer.

Try These
'Windbreaker' is a variety of *Sporobolus wrightii* with a large growth habit to 7 to 8 feet tall and a similar spread. This sturdy, upright grower offers very showy flower heads in summer.

Sedge

Carex spp.

Botanical Pronunciation
KAIR-ecks

Bloom Period and Seasonal Color
Thin, grasslike foliage forming low, mounded clumps and short flower stalks

Mature Height × Spread
12 inches × 12 inches

Zones Hardy to Zone 5

M any plant professionals feel that ornamental sedge is like the Rodney Dangerfield of the plant world: They get no respect! It is true that sedges are relatively unpopular compared to many ornamental grasses. But these grasslike plants are gaining in popularity thanks to the hard work of many good growers, designers, and plant professionals. Sedges are low-growing, tough, and easy-to-grow plants with durable foliage that come in a wide variety of colors. Sedge leaves can also be very fine, similar to fescue, or wide, looking very much like liriope. The advantage of planting sedges in the landscape is that they are not only easy to grow, but very diverse, adding unique ornamental characteristics to the landscape. In addition, they are typically drought, shade, and pest tolerant.

When, Where, and How to Plant
Sedges in general prefer moist, well-drained soil but also tolerate wet soils as well as dry, rocky soils. Adding compost to heavy clay or sandy soils will help. They thrive in areas with some form of shade, from light to medium, but some will tolerate dense shade. Morning sun and afternoon shade is good for most sedges. Purchase plants in spring and space 10 to 12 inches apart.

Growing Tips
Sedges are not heavy feeders and don't need regular fertilizer applications. Mulch new plantings lightly to benefit in times of drought. Even soil moisture is preferred but sedges can take periods of drought.

Regional Advice and Care
Sedges are fairy indestructible and I admire them for their resilience and unique beauty. They resist pests and diseases and also are *not* a favorite of deer and rabbits. Sedges have durable foliage and don't necessarily need to be pruned back each spring but if needed, dead or damaged leaves can be pruned out or the entire plant can be cut back hard. Plants are usually propagated by seed or divisions in spring.

Companion Planting and Design
There are not many groundcovers that will tolerate dry shade but sedge fills this role nicely. Sedges can be used as groundcovers, as edging plants in a mixed border or foundation planting, and look especially good with other grasses and fine-textured perennials. Sedges look their best in a mass planting in a woodland garden. They can also be used in containers mixed with other plants.

Try These
Appalachian sedge (*Carex appalachica*) has a very fine texture forming a tidy, clumping growth habit. A similar species, oak sedge (*C. pensylvanica*), is a soft, delicate groundcover that can be a substitute for a lawn for shady spots. It is very happy under the shade of an oak tree; it's hardy to Zone 4. A variety of Japanese sedge grass (*C. morrowii* 'Ice Dance') is a Japanese native offering bright, variegated leaves similar to liriope. 'Ice Dance' sedge prefers some moisture and should be cut back in early spring.

Switch Grass

Panicum virgatum

Botanical Pronunciation
PAN-ih-kum vur-GAY-tum

Other Name Panic grass

Bloom Period and Seasonal Color
Medium green leaves turn shades of yellow and tan in fall, pinkish flowers fade to beige

Mature Height × Spread
3 to 6 feet × 2 to 3 feet

Zones Hardy to Zone 4

Switch grass is quickly becoming "the" native grass to plant in large, commercial sites as well as backyard gardens. It features dense, upright growth that starts off olive green and matures to medium green to blue-green in summer. The combination of lush foliage and profusion of loose, airy flower heads make this grass very desirable. The foliage and flowers offer habitat and food for birds. In fall, plants turn golden yellow, sometimes with tints of orange, and eventually tan for winter. Switch grass is quite genetically diverse with varieties offering a range of sizes and ornamental qualities. Switch grass can grow large, reaching 3 to 6 feet tall with about half the width. Its size and showy flower display in summer, fall, and winter make it another appropriate replacement for maiden grass (*Miscanthus sinensis*).

When, Where, and How to Plant

Switch grass performs well in a variety of soils from sandy to heavy clay. However, giving them rich garden soil with organic matter is desirable. In poor soils, add a generous amount of compost and mulch the surface of the soil after planting. It prefers moist, well-drained soil and full sun but will also tolerate partial shade. Plants should be purchased and planted in spring as container-grown plants. Spacing should be 2 to 3 feet apart but may change by variety.

Growing Tips

Keep soil evenly moist and use a low-nitrogen, general-purpose fertilizer if needed, in spring.

Regional Advice and Care

Switch grass is a rugged, tough plant that is easy to care for once established. It can be propagated by seed and will often self-seed. Because of its spreading root system, it can be multiplied by root divisions in spring. Prune plants back to the ground in spring to remove old growth and encourage new. Switch grass is very pest and disease resistant, drought tolerant, cold hardy, and deer resistant.

Companion Planting and Design

Switch grass is a meadow grass that has expanded its range to the world of the cultivated garden. It enjoys moist soil and can be used in groupings or mass plantings by itself or in a mixed border with other grasses, sun-loving perennials such as black-eyed Susan and purple coneflower. Switch grass works well near ponds and can also be used in rain gardens.

Try These

'Dallas Blues' is a bold variety with wide, striking blue foliage and unusually large flower heads tinged with purple. This plant needs room but it's very effective in a mass planting. The foliage of 'Heavy Metal' emerges metallic blue in spring, then changes to a golden yellow in fall. 'Shenandoah' is a unique variety with reddish pink flower clusters and green foliage with red tips in spring and summer that turn rich burgundy red in fall. The foliage eventually turns beige for winter. This variety is compact and slower growing, generally to 4 feet.

Turf Grass

Various genera

Botanical Pronunciation
Varies

Bloom Period and Seasonal Color
Dark green leaves and a fine texture; most enjoyed from early spring to late fall

Mature Height × Spread
2 ½ to 4 inches × varying spread

Lawn or "turf grass" is a popular part of gardening and this is especially true in the northeast. But while I am not a big fan of lawns, using them selectively to accent other landscape plants such as bulbs, perennials, groundcovers, shrubs, and trees can be attractive and functional. The three main species of cool-season grass used regularly are perennial rye grass (*Lolium perenne*) Kentucky bluegrass (*Poa pratensis*), and fescue (*Festuca* spp.), which mainly consists of tall fescue and fine fescues. Although lawns are typically high maintenance, they don't have to be. This section offers some tips that allow you to maintain a beautiful lawn while being eco-friendly. These non-traditional practices include raising mowing heights, mulching grass clippings in place, using organic fertilizers, and changing watering practices to reduce waste.

When, Where, and How to Plant
Most turf grass prefers moist, well-drained soil with plenty of organic matter. Fescues are known for their durability and shade tolerance. Rye is prized for fast germination and tolerance to moist soil conditions. Kentucky bluegrass is prized for its beautiful color, dense growth habit, and ability to thrive in full sun or partial shade. Turf grass is usually planted in spring or fall as seed or sod. Seed rates vary by species but in general 3 to 6 pounds of seed per 1,000 square feet is acceptable.

Growing Tips
Incorporate a generous amount of well-aged compost before planting. Be sure that the ground is level and smooth before planting. As a general rule,

apply no more than 1 pound of nitrogen per 1,000 square feet for fast-release fertilizers and up to 2 pounds per 1,000 square feet on slow-release fertilizers. Read the fertilizer bag for specific instructions. Depending on soil conditions and sun exposure, water turf deeply during each watering, but infrequently (once or twice a week). This helps plants develop deep, well-established root systems.

Regional Advice and Care
Turf grass can have many pest and disease problems so monitor your grass regularly for issues and treat as needed. Aerate soil annually and remove heavy thatch layers. Overseed once a year in spring or fall and do not mow grass too short. To reduce stress on the grass, raise mower blades 3 to 4 inches above the ground, especially in drought. This creates a dense lawn that will be thick and lush.

Companion Planting and Design
Try a balanced mixture of turf grass or tailor the selection of a mixture to your specific growing conditions. Tall fescue is an excellent drought- and wear-tolerant grass but it is coarser than all of the other species.

Try These
There are many turf grasses that are disease and pest tolerant with improved ornamental qualities. Zoysiagrass (*Zoysia* spp.) is a warm-season grass that is virtually indestructible. Coarse, blue-green foliage turns yellow in winter but will green up again with warm weather in spring. It is the lowest-maintenance, toughest grass you will find.

FLOWERING TREES AND SHRUBS

FOR NEW YORK & NEW JERSEY

Trees and shrubs provide structure, privacy, and offer year-round interest with color and texture in the garden. They are the "bones" of the landscape, filling the voids between annuals, perennials, bulbs, and grasses and offering shelter and shade. There are so many good species of trees and shrubs for the home landscape and endless new cultivated varieties that make gardening even more exciting than ever. Today, trees and shrubs are being developed with improved vigor, pest resistance, and tolerance to heat, humidity, drought, and cold while also offering improved aesthetic value—all of which give gardeners more options than ever.

Selecting Flowering Trees and Shrubs

These days, shopping in a local nursery is like a smorgasbord of plant material that is typically dominated by flowering trees and shrubs of many shapes, colors, and sizes. Many tried-and-true favorites that we grew up with have been reinvented and are once again the shining stars of the garden. These include dogwood, forsythia, hydrangea, magnolia, lilac, and viburnum, just to name a few. These garden favorites, more so than any other plant group, offer multiple seasons of interest with flowers, fruit, foliage, bark texture, and a presence that is undeniable.

When selecting flowering trees and shrubs it is important to consider several factors including the growing conditions you have to offer, the landscape function you require, and how large the tree or shrub you select will ultimately grow. Like any other garden plant, the soil, light conditions, exposure, and many other factors will limit what you can grow. Knowing what you are trying to accomplish and the functions your trees and shrubs are expected to provide, whether it's as a specimen, grouping, or screen, is just as important. But probably the most overlooked factor when choosing trees and shrubs is how large they will grow. The notion of, "I'll just prune it" never works out and often leaves your woody plants misshapen and unproductive. For this reason, it is critical that you understand how tall and wide a new tree or shrub will get before it is purchased and sited in the garden. It all goes back to the notion of "right plant for the right place," which is a much more successful goal.

Flowering trees, such as this red buckeye, can be effective as single specimens in a lawn.

General Care and Maintenance

Flowering trees and shrubs do not have the same requirements as herbaceous plants. Their needs are far different, and gardeners must understand and keep up with maintenance practices such as pruning, watering, mulching, fertilizing, and identification of pests and diseases. Regularly monitoring your garden will help to keep on top of all of these requirements. With global climate change more of a factor, paying close attention to the health and maintenance of your flowering trees and shrubs is more important than ever.

While the discussion of proper planting, pruning, and other general care is discussed in more detail under "plant maintenance" on page 173, it is important to reiterate basic growing tips needed to maintain your trees and shrubs. For example, when planting new trees and shrubs, be sure to dig the planting hole three times wider than the width of the rootball or container but not necessarily as deep. In fact, the bottom of the planting hole should be firm and not fluffy to reduce the chance of the plant settling. In addition, the tree or shrub should be planted slightly above the grade of the soil. Last, backfilling the soil once the plant height is satisfactory is the time to add compost, manure, or other soil amendments to the planting hole.

After planting is complete, a light layer of mulch and a regular watering schedule is imperative. Typically, trees and shrubs require supplemental watering for the first two growing seasons in order for their root systems to become established. Once that happens, your new trees and shrubs should be on their own. However, there are exceptions to the rule. For example, shallow-rooted plants such as rhododendrons or hydrangea often require watering during dry periods even when they have established in the landscape.

Buckeye

Aesculus spp.

Botanical Pronunciation
ESS-kew-lus

Bloom Period and Seasonal Color
Mid-spring or early summer depending on the species, long flower spikes and dark green leaves

Mature Height × Spread
6 to 20 feet × 8 to 15 feet

Zones Bottlebrush and red buckeyes are hardy to Zone 4

Several species of buckeye are worthy of inclusion in the home garden, for several reasons. Buckeyes offer multiple seasons of interest, adaptability, and function in the landscape. While they need room to grow, they can be grown both as large shrubs and small trees. Bottlebrush buckeye (*Aesculus parviflora*) is a four-season plant displaying dark green, palmlike foliage and long, white bottlebrush-like flowers in July. In addition, the leaves turn a beautiful golden yellow in fall and the smooth, gray bark glistens in winter. Red buckeye (*A. pavia*) has glossy green leaves and spikes of deep red flowers in mid-spring. Although it starts off shrubby, it will eventually become a small tree. Both are deer resistant and are also pest and disease resistant.

When, Where, and How to Plant
Buckeyes prefer moist, well-drained soil and full sun or partial shade. Since both of these species grow as woodland plants in their native habitat in the Southeast, they are especially adapted for shade. Although once established they are relatively drought tolerant, watering in times of severe drought will reduce heat and drought stress on these wonderful native plants. Buckeyes do have a brown, chestnut-like seed, which is *not* edible by humans. Seeds ripen in the late summer/early fall and can be planted then, provided the squirrels don't find them first. Bottlebrush buckeye generally is sold in large containers and will spread rather quickly. Red buckeye is generally sold as a balled-and-burlapped plant. Since both or these species need space, plant 10 to 12 feet apart or plant as single specimens.

Growing Tips
Buckeyes are generally easy to grow but prefer organic soils. Adding well-aged compost at time of planting and mulching the surface of the soil with leaves, wood chips, or pine straw will benefit new plantings. Keep soil moist.

Regional Advice and Care
Buckeyes are related to the horse chestnut, but unlike their big cousin, are quite pest and disease resistant. While common horse chestnut leaves are typically "scorched" by late summer from leaf diseases, these two buckeyes species usually remain untouched. Red buckeye doesn't generally need pruning except when it is young to train it into single stem trees. However, bottlebrush buckeye requires selective pruning every few years to keep it inbounds in the landscape. This can be done in early spring by removing older, mature stems and leaving younger, more vigorous stems.

Companion Planting and Design
Buckeyes are excellent as single specimens in a lawn, in groupings, and even as a screening plant. Bottlebrush buckeye specifically spreads quite a bit and will provide a dense screen even when there are no leaves in winter.

Try These
There is a cultivated variety of bottlebrush buckeye 'Rogers', which blooms a bit later and displays noticeably larger blooms 18 to 30 inches long.

Beautyberry

Callicarpa spp.

Botanical Pronunciation
kal-ih-KAR-puh

Bloom Period and Seasonal Color
Pinkish purple flowers develop into striking purple fruit in late summer and early fall, persisting into late fall

Mature Height × Spread
3 to 6 feet × 3 to 6 feet

Zones Common beautyberry: hardy to Zone 5; American beautyberry: hardy to Zone 6

Beautyberry is a carefree, upright, multi-stemmed shrub that has a nondescript appearance most of the growing season, but by fall it's a showy plant that we can't live without. Bunches of rich purple fruit are accented by yellow fall foliage. It is a favorite food of birds that often pluck the fruit off the plant before the onset of cold weather in early winter. The fruit display, especially when the leaves have fallen off, is nothing short of spectacular. Two excellent species are common beautyberry (*Callicarpa dichotoma*), which only grows 3 to 5 feet tall, and the lesser-known American beautyberry (*C. americana*), which grows 4 to 6 feet tall with an equal width. Common beautyberry is a delicate, fine-textured plant while American beautyberry is coarser, with large leaves to 6 inches long.

When, Where, and How to Plant

Beautyberry is easy to grow and does best in well-drained, moist soil in full sun or partial shade. Beautyberry is not particularly fussy, but adding compost to the soil at planting will help plants thrive in their new location. Purchase plants in spring and they'll flower and fruit the same year. Plants can be propagated by seed and usually show up in the garden as birds will spread them around. Spacing is typically 3 to 5 feet apart with plants eventually growing together to form a thick layer of vegetation.

Growing Tips

In poor, sandy soils, regular watering may be needed to keep plants happy. A light layer of wood chips in spring will help keep plants from drying out during times of drought. Apply a well-balanced, granular fertilizer in spring, as needed.

Regional Advice and Care

Beautyberry is not a high-maintenance plant but some pruning is required to keep plants looking their best. With common beautyberry I recommend cutting plants back to 12 inches in early spring once every few years to keep them compact and productive since they bloom on new, vigorous growth. American beautyberry can be pruned this way or it can be selectively pruned if you do not want to lose the height of the plant all at once.

Companion Planting and Design

Beautyberry is a great fall plant, illuminating landscapes with bright, showy fruit and fall color. It is effective in mixed borders, woodland plantings, as foundation plants, and as an informal hedge. It is a *great* plant to attract a variety of birds into the garden.

Try These

American beautyberry only recently became available in northern gardens thanks to progressive thinking growers. Besides the species with its deep, purple-magenta fruit, 'Welch's Pink' is an interesting pink variety forming big bunches of fruit. Common beautyberry varieties are very popular; 'Early Amethyst' features a profusion of amethyst-purple fruit developing earlier than many beautyberries. 'Duet' is a lovely variegated form with distinct yellow-and-green leaves and white fruit. As an accent plant, it's outstanding.

Butterfly Bush

Buddleja davidii

Botanical Pronunciation
BUD-lee-uh duh-VID-ee-eye

Other Name Summer lilac

Bloom Period and Seasonal Color
Spikes of white, blue, pink, purple, reddish purple, and yellow flowers all summer

Mature Height × Spread
5 to 10 feet × 3 to 8 feet

Zones Hardy to Zone 5

Butterfly bush is an Asian native that has long been considered a garden favorite for its long, arching flowers that come in a wide range of colors lasting all summer. The sweetly fragrant flowers attract butterflies as well as bees, hummingbirds, orioles, and other bird species, which will also feed on the seed in winter. This fast-growing shrub will thrive in the heat of the summer and never miss a beat. Many varieties reach up to 10 feet tall with a slightly smaller spread but many new dwarf varieties stay much smaller, which is ideal for the residential landscape. While butterfly bush has no real fall color, its long, slender dark green leaves with silver undersides shimmer in the summer wind.

When, Where, and How to Plant

Butterfly bush is ideal in full sun and should not be put in shade if you want it to perform well. Soil must be well drained but does not have to be rich garden soil. Sandy, gravelly, and even clay soils are just fine; in fact, just about any soil works as long as it drains and is not soggy. Adding compost to poor soils at planting in spring will help plants grow a healthy root system. Butterfly bush propagates by seed and is often considered invasive in some gardens, so pay close attention to wandering seedlings. Depending on variety, space 4 to 8 feet apart.

Growing Tips

A general-purpose, granular fertilizer in spring will help give plants a boost as they go into summer.

Regional Advice and Care

Butterfly bush is susceptible to several pests including Japanese beetles, aphids, and spider mites. An application of a low-toxicity insecticide such as horticultural oil or soap may be necessary but consult with your local garden center or Extension office. Prune in early spring while plants are dormant, down to 12 inches from the ground. This form of rejuvenation pruning each spring (or at least every other spring) will keep plants dense and productive. Removing dead flowers reduces the chance of seedlings in the garden and it also encourages more flowering.

Companion Planting and Design

Many environmentalists feel butterfly bush can be invasive and it does not benefit native butterflies so I recommend planting it along with natives so you have diversity. Use discretion with this plant and try it in a mixed border, foundation planting, grouping, and use smaller varieties in containers. Butterfly bush has shown it's rather good where deer are prevalent and it's excellent in seashore conditions.

Try These

My favorites include 'Honeycomb', which offers golden-yellow flowers, and 'Nanho Blue', offering blue flowers and a compact growth habit growing 3 to 5 feet tall and wide. 'Pink Delight' is a standard grower with huge 12-inch-long pink flowers. Lo & Behold® are available in several colors and only reach heights of 2 to 3 feet.

Crabapple

Malus spp.

Botanical Pronunciation
MAL-us

Bloom Period and Seasonal Color
Clusters of white, pink, or reddish pink flowers in mid-spring followed by glossy red or yellow fruit

Mature Height × Spread
15 to 25 feet × 15 to 25 feet

Zones Most are hardy to Zone 4

Crabapples are undoubtedly among the most durable, versatile, and diverse flowering trees available today. Although crabapples had diminished in popularity over the years, recently they have enjoyed a resurgence in the American garden. Approximately thirty-five species and over 800 garden varieties of crabapples can be found in landscapes all across the world. Crabapples offer showy, single white, pink, or reddish purple flowers in spring, and small fruit that look similar to miniature apples. The fruit typically develop in late summer and fall. The flowers are a very important food source for a wide variety of pollinators and the fruit, while tart, are eaten by birds and other small animals. Crabapples are incredibly adaptable to a wide range of environmental conditions and offer great functions in the landscape.

When, Where, and How to Plant

Crabapples are incredibly tolerant, adapting to heat, cold, drought, pollution, less than ideal soils and pH, and light exposures. Though crabapples tolerate a wide variety of soils, adding well-aged compost at planting is helpful, regardless of how tough they are. Although they thrive in full sun, I have seen crabapples perform admirably in shade. For best results, plant in full sun with plenty of air circulation and moist, well-drained soil. Crabapples establish best if purchased and planted in spring. Space at least 12 to 15 feet away from other trees and garden structures.

Growing Tips

Crabapples prefer even soil moisture.

Regional Advice and Care

Crabapples are prone to several serious leaf and branch diseases, including leaf spot, apple scab, and fireblight. Many new selections have been developed that offer superior resistance to these diseases. Crabapples are fairly high maintenance in regards to pruning. Crabapples will develop water sprouts and suckers (vegetative shoots that grow from the branches and roots). This growth produces leaves but no flowers, reducing floral display and often causing trees to become overgrown. An ongoing pruning program is needed to keep plants aesthetically pleasing and productive. Remove suckers and water sprouts in summer after flowering; if you have established plantings, this should be done gradually over three years.

Companion Planting and Design

Use crabapples as single specimens, in groupings, lawns, or even in large planters. Young trees can be trained as an espalier, which is the art of pruning plants flat against a building or garden structure.

Try These

New varieties offer improved disease resistance and ornamental value and hold onto their fruit well into winter. 'Callaway' features pink buds and showy white flowers that develop into larger-than-normal fruit, which is edible. 'Red Jewel' has beautiful white flowers and glossy, bright red fruit. 'Snowdrift' is small with a dense habit and a profusion of white flowers and orange-red fruit. Sugar Tyme™, my favorite, offers pink flower buds opening to pure white flowers, eventually developing large, glossy, deep red fruit, often persisting into late winter.

Crape Myrtle

Lagerstroemia indica

Botanical Pronunciation
lag-ur-STREE-mee-uh IN-dih-kuh

Bloom Period and Seasonal Color
Blooms mid- to late summer from white to pink, lavender, and red. Dark green foliage in summer turns brilliant shades of orange and red

Mature Height × Spread
From 2 × 3 feet to 25 × 30 feet

Zones Hardy to Zone 6 but benefits from shelter on exposed sites

Once only considered a plant for warmer climates, crape myrtle has emerged as an exceptionally good performer in northern climates. Clusters of long, crinkled flowers in late summer paint the landscape with bright colors. After the flowers have finished, bunches of green, round capsule-like fruit form. In spring, newly emerging leaves often unfold bronzy red before maturing to a glossy medium to dark green. In autumn, the leaves change to brilliant shades of yellow, orange, and red and the smooth, multicolored bark provides exceptional interest all year, especially in winter. Crape myrtle is very heat and drought tolerant and is ideal in hot, exposed sites even thriving near the seashore. Crape myrtle comes in many forms from low-growing shrubs to tall, vase-shaped trees.

When, Where, and How to Plant

Crape myrtle does particularly well in hot, dry conditions and full sun. Partial shade is acceptable but too much shade will result in leggy, poorly performing plants. Crape myrtle thrives in moist, well-drained soil but tolerates sandy and clay loam soils. New plants in containers or balled-and-burlapped should be planted when the soil has had a chance to warm up in spring. Spacing depends on the variety and should be 2 to 3 feet for smaller varieties and 10 to 12 feet for large varieties.

Growing Tips

A low-nitrogen granular fertilizer applied in early spring will help stimulate growth and promote flower production. A light layer of mulch or pine straw will help protect roots from fluctuating soil temperatures and varying soil moisture while adding organic matter to the soil.

Regional Advice and Care

Crape myrtle blooms on current season's growth and pruning right after blooms fade may extend the blooming season. Crape myrtles grow fast, so if significant pruning is needed, selective pruning while the plant is dormant in late winter is recommended. On larger plants the canopy can be thinned and top growth cut back to branches no thicker than your pinky finger. Remove young, thin branches from the lower part of the plant leaving several mature, main stems to develop.

Companion Planting and Design

Crape myrtle can be used as a small specimen tree or large shrub, mass planting, informal hedge, tall screen, and in combination with summer-blooming shrubs or perennials. It tends to break dormancy later than most plants, so be patient.

Try These

Dynamite® ('Whit II') is one of the most spectacular varieties of crape myrtle with deep red flowers and a tall habit that can exceed 15 feet in height. 'Natchez' is a tree form with pure white flowers and cinnamon-brown bark that is beautiful all four seasons. 'Pocomoke' is a low growing form to 24 inches tall with deep pink flowers making it ideal for the home landscape. Razzle Dazzle® series grow 2 to 4 feet tall and are excellent for gardens with limited space.

New Jersey Tea

Ceanothus americanus

Botanical Pronunciation
see-uh-NOE-thus uh-mair-ih-KAY-nus

Other Name Mountain sweet

Bloom Period and Seasonal Color
Clusters of white flowers in late summer and textured, dark green foliage

Mature Height × Spread
2 to 3 feet × 2 to 3 feet

Zones Hardy to Zone 6

This beautiful, eco-friendly, but underutilized shrub has a lot to offer the home gardener. It's a compact, dense shrub with late-season blooms that attract many species of pollinators including butterflies, bees, wasps, flies, and hummingbirds and is also known to be deer resistant. The colonists used New Jersey tea during the Revolutionary War as a substitute for the tea plant, which is where it got its name. Ceanothus is a little-known group of plants but several species and cultivars have emerged to illustrate what this group of plants has to offer. New Jersey tea and its relatives are very effective with other shrubs and perennials in the late-summer landscape. The time has come for this wonderful, easy-to-grow shrub to get the attention it deserves.

When, Where, and How to Plant
New Jersey tea prefers moist, well-drained soil and full sun or partial shade but it's adaptable to drier conditions in rocky or sandy soils. It can "fix" nitrogen, allowing it to survive in infertile soils. The addition of compost or manure is not necessary but in dry, sandy soils that will help plants, especially during droughts, but it tolerates heat and drought quite well. Small plants can be purchased and planted in spring and are most effective when used in groupings. Cuttings in midsummer can also propagate plants. It can also be propagated by seed, collected in fall, which are soaked for twelve hours and sown in soil and given cold, moist treatment for three months. Spacing should be 18 to 24 inches apart to give plants the space they need.

Growing Tips
A layer of mulch on new plantings will also help to keep plants cool in summer and add organic matter to the soil as it decomposes. This plant does not have a high fertilizer requirement and typically just takes what it is given and it thrives. Keep soil evenly moist but it can tolerate periods of drier conditions.

Regional Advice and Care
New Jersey tea is very pest resistant and as long as it has a good amount of sunlight and well-drained soils, it will perform very well. Lightly pruning New Jersey tea in late winter or early spring is best to shape plants. No severe pruning should be done late in the growing season.

Companion Planting and Design
New Jersey tea can work well in a naturalistic garden, among wildflowers and meadow plantings, or it can also work in a cultivated garden with other flowering shrubs. It works best in small groupings and can be used in foundation plantings, mixed borders, and butterfly gardens.

Try These
Several hybrids and cultivated varieties are worth including in your landscape. *Ceanothus × pallidus* 'Marie Simon' offers large, billowy, pink flowers and interesting foliage while Marie Bleu™ offers soft blue flowers.

Dwarf Fothergilla

Fothergilla gardenii

Botanical Pronunciation
fah-thur-GILL-uh GAR-den-ee-eye

Other Name Dwarf witch-alder

Bloom Period and Seasonal Color
White blooms in mid-spring, dark green leaves turn yellow, orange, red, and maroon in fall

Mature Height × Spread
2 to 3 feet × 2 to 3 feet

Zones Hardy to Zone 5; tolerates Zone 4 with protection

Dwarf fothergilla is a lovely native flowering shrub related to witch hazel. If offers three seasons of interest with frilly, white bottlebrush-like flowers in April/May, dark green leaves, and a dense, upright growth habit. The real show is in fall when the foliage changes to brilliant colors that rarely disappoint. The more sun the plant is given, the more vibrant the colors tend to become. The only real enemies of this plant are poor drainage and dry, hot conditions. Dwarf fothergilla is very useful as a foundation planting or in a small grouping in a woodland garden. There are several beautiful cultivated varieties, a few of which offer striking blue foliage in summer. Next time you are looking to landscape your house, put down the azaleas, roses, and lilacs, and reach for a fothergilla!

When, Where, and How to Plant

Fothergilla is sensitive to drought and should be grown in moist, acidic, well-drained soil. Heavy, clay soils with poor drainage will also spell doom for these plants. In addition to good garden soil, fothergilla benefits from organic matter added to the soil at planting time. Full sun is best for flowering but partial shade is acceptable. New plants are typically grown in containers and can be planted in early to mid-spring. Spacing should be about 3 to 4 feet apart as it will spread and sometimes form colonies.

Growing Tips

Well-aged compost is preferred as well a light layer of wood chips or pine straw to keep roots cool in summer. Keep soil moist and use a well-balanced, granular fertilizer in spring.

Regional Advice and Care

Dwarf fothergilla is relatively pest free and easy to care for provided adequate moisture is given during drought. Pruning is generally not needed unless plantings get too large for the area they are growing in. Modest summer pruning right after flowering can reduce the size of your shrubs but this must be less than one-third of the overall size of the plant.

Companion Planting and Design

Dwarf fothergilla works really well as a foundation planting, in borders, groupings, and in a woodland garden. It is a good companion plant to other spring-blooming plants such as dogwood, magnolia, rhododendron, and mountain laurel.

Try These

Although a variety of a different species, large fothergilla (*F. major*) 'Mt. Airy' is the most popular and reliable performer of cultivars available today. It offers abundant flowers; rich, blue-green foliage that turns brilliant shades of yellow, orange, and red in fall; and a dense upright habit to 6 feet. 'Blue Shadow' is a striking selection that has bright blue foliage in summer, making it a *great* accent plant. 'Red Licorice' displays brilliant red fall color even in shade.

Eastern Redbud

Cercis canadensis

Botanical Pronunciation
SUR-siss kan-uh-DEN-siss

Other Name Judas tree

Bloom Period and Seasonal Color
Purplish flower buds open to rosy pink, pealike flowers in early to mid-spring

Mature Height × Spread
20 to 30 feet × 25 to 35 feet

Zones Hardy to Zone 4

Eastern redbud is a native that can be found in woodlands, along highways, and in gardens across the eastern United States. The bright, rosy pink flowers in early to mid-spring brighten up the landscape. Eastern redbud is what I call a "drive by" plant because it can be seen in flower even from a far distance. Clusters of flowerbuds form along thick stems and the main trunk. It is in the legume family and forms long seedpods after flowering, which attract a variety of birds. The bold, dark green leaves are heart shaped and do not offer any significant fall color, although sometimes display a pale to medium yellow. Young trees are compact, upright, and rounded while older specimens are irregular and spreading.

When, Where, and How to Plant
Some members of the legume family "fix" nitrogen from the atmosphere, making them tolerant of infertile soils. Redbud does *not*, but it doesn't seem to matter, as this tree is still plenty tough. Soil must be well drained because poorly drained, soggy soils can cause root rot and weak, stressed trees. Add compost to sandy or heavy clay soils. Full sun or partial shade is preferred, ideally an eastern exposure offering morning sunlight and afternoon shade. Spring planting is best and spacing should be about 15 feet apart.

Growing Tips
A light layer of wood chips or pine straw will help during droughts. Soil should be kept evenly moist but can be allowed to dry out a bit. A light application of a general-purpose fertilizer in spring gives plants a boost going into summer.

Regional Advice and Care
A few insects and diseases bother redbud, such as stem cankers, leaf diseases, and wood decays, but it's still a worthwhile plant. Corrective pruning when plants are young to remove co-dominant stems, crossing branches, or to thin heavy canopies can be done in late winter. Prune to shape in midsummer.

Companion Planting and Design
Use Eastern redbud as a single specimen lawn tree, in small groupings, or in partially shaded woodlands. It is often found growing along highways and roadsides where it creates a haze of color in spring. Butterflies, bees, and other pollinators are attracted to the small, pealike flowers.

Try These
'Appalachian Red' is not quite true red but hot pink and is almost fluorescent in the landscape. 'Forest Pansy' has rich, glossy, deep reddish purple leaves that fade to greenish purple; however, 'Merlot' is said to hold its color better. Lavender Twist® is a beautiful weeping form with pink flowers and lush, dark green leaves that weep to the ground like a waterfall. 'Royal White' is a bit of an oxymoron because it is a "white redbud," but its magnificent white flowers are very attractive. The Rising Sun™ displays striking golden-yellow to orange-salmon foliage before fading to chartreuse and finally light green.

Flowering Dogwood

Cornus florida

Botanical Pronunciation
KORE-nus FLORE-ih-duh

Bloom Period and Seasonal Color
Spring, white or pink blooms; green summer
foliage turns reddish maroon; glossy red fruit

Mature Height × Spread
20 to 30 feet × 20 to 30 feet

Zones Hardy to Zone 5

Like apple pie and the Fourth of July, flowering dogwood is an American classic! This iconic native tree has a rather complex flower structure with the colorful part of the inflorescences known as a bract, which is actually a modified leaf. Dogwood has four white or pink bracts that surround a less conspicuous and not particularly ornamental cluster of small flowers. The pollinated flowers transform into red, glossy fruit in fall and are one of the most prized sources of protein for birds, which strip the fruit clean by winter. Flowering dogwood displays brilliant shades of orange, red, and maroon fall foliage. As plants mature they develop rough, gray, alligator skinlike bark. Needless to say this popular tree is a four-season treasure that will brighten any garden.

When, Where, and How to Plant
Flowering dogwood has very specific needs. Well-drained, acidic garden loam with plenty of organic matter is ideal. Plant flowering dogwoods in spring with generous amounts of compost added to the planting hole. Sun exposure is very important; dogwoods should be planted on an eastern exposure so they have morning sun and afternoon shade. This will reduce disease and keep plants protected from the heat of the afternoon summer sun. They tolerate full sun as long as they're well irrigated and mulched. Space 12 to 15 feet apart.

Growing Tips
A 1- to 2-inch layer of wood chips will help keep roots cool in summer and replenish organic matter. Avoid watering in the afternoon or evening to minimize foliage staying damp. Use a low-nitrogen, granular fertilizer in spring if needed.

Regional Advice and Care
Serious problems include powdery mildew, anthracnose, and leaf spots but gardeners should not be discouraged. Much has been learned about how to grow dogwood, which includes good air circulation, adequate sunlight, and proper watering. Prune after flowering to reduce size or train young trees

Companion Planting and Design
Flowering dogwood works well in partially shaded woodlands with holly, rhododendron, and other acid-loving plants. It can be used as a single specimen or in small groupings, sprinkled across the landscape. In the residential garden, dogwood is often the focal point, adding structure and height.

Try These
'Appalachian Spring' is a white-flowering variety tolerant to heat and humidity as well as disease. 'Cherokee Brave' is one of the best pink varieties with deep pink flower bracts and excellent red fall color. Researchers and growers such as Dr. Elwin Orton of Rutgers University and nurseryman Don Shadow of Winchester, TN, have championed the cause of reintroducing dogwood and its virtues to the American gardener. These include superior varieties of *Cornus florida* as well as hybrids offering large, showy flowers, disease resistance, and adaptability in the landscape. Celestial™ and Venus™ are two from the Stellar® series from Rutgers.

Glossy Abelia

Abelia × grandiflora

Botanical Pronunciation
uh-BEEL-yuh gran-dih-FLORE-uh

Bloom Period and Seasonal Color
Pinkish white flowers early summer until late fall, leaves turn maroon in fall and winter

Mature Height × Spread
6 feet × 6 feet (new varieties often smaller)

Zones Hardy to Zone 6

Glossy abelia is one of very few shrubs that blooms all summer and often continues well into fall. Masses of small, tubular, pale pink to white flowers cover the plant from June to as late as Thanksgiving, sometimes. Glossy abelia can be evergreen or semi-evergreen depending on the severity of the winter. Its dark green, glossy leaves persist most of the year and turn rich shades of reddish maroon in late fall and early winter accented by rosy pink flower stalks that turn brown and persist well after the flowers have fallen off. Arching branches cascade downward giving this shrub a very graceful appearance. Glossy abelia is frequently visited by bees and butterflies all summer and is a very versatile shrub for a wide variety of landscape situations.

When, Where, and How to Plant
Glossy abelia prefers moist, well-drained soil but is adaptable to a wide variety of soils including sandy and clay soils as long as it is not in a soggy situation. Adding compost or manure will help plants develop a healthy root system. Glossy abelia thrives in full sun or partial shade and performs remarkably well in heat and drought. Plants can be purchased from a local nursery in spring in containers, but don't expect plants to do much early in the season. Abelia needs warm temperatures to really get going, and the hotter it gets in summer, the better it seems to perform. Spacing should be 2 to 3 feet apart depending on variety.

Growing Tips
A general, balanced granular fertilizer in spring will give plants a boost. Mulching plants with wood chips will help during hot, dry periods in summer. Abelia thrives in soil that is kept evenly moist.

Regional Advice and Care
Abelia is very pest and disease resistant with no real issues. Pruning is not often needed but plants can be sheared as a hedge during the growing season. It can be selectively pruned by removing older stems or rejuvenated by pruning all stems down to the ground in early spring. Since abelia blooms on new growth, it will flower the same year that it is pruned.

Companion Planting and Design
Abelia is a wonderful companion plant to perennials and other flowering shrubs such as butterfly bush, roses, and spirea. Glossy abelia can be used as a formal or informal hedge, foundation planting, and in a mixed border.

Try These
'Rose Creek' is an outstanding semi-dwarf variety growing to 3 feet tall and wide. It requires very little maintenance and will bloom longer than most abelia varieties. Fragrant abelia (*Abelia mosanensis*) is a relatively unknown species with lustrous, dark green leaves that turn reddish maroon in fall; it has a graceful, upright habit. A profusion of pinkish white flowers in spring will perfume the landscape. Fragrant abelia is a favorite of butterflies and bees and is deer resistant. Hardy from Zones 5 to 9.

Greenstem Forsythia

Forsythia viridissima 'Bronxensis'

Botanical Pronunciation
for-SITH-i-a vir-i-DIS-si-ma

Bloom Period and Seasonal Color
Delicate yellow flowers in early spring followed by dark green leaves

Mature Height × Spread
1 to 2 feet × 2 to 3 feet

Forsythia has been a household name in American gardens for about a century. Its golden-yellow blossoms seem to be the unofficial sign that spring is here. But this popular plant is quite possibly the most tortured one in the typical home garden. I have often seen forsythia sheared into gumdrops, round pom poms, and tight hedges mainly because most species just get too big for the average residential landscape. But Greenstem forsythia is a low-growing, dwarf version that will not overtake the garden. It allows gardeners to experience that early spring flush of color without the large, spreading, full-scale forsythia that can quickly outgrow the garden. 'Bronxensis' was grown from seed in 1939 at the New York Botanical Garden in the Bronx.

When, Where, and How to Plant

Greenstem forsythia is rather adaptable but is best in full sun or partial shade and moist, well-drained soil. It will tolerate poor soils as well and is quite drought tolerant once established. Though greenstem forsythia does not need organic soils, in sandy or heavy clay soils, adding compost or manure is a good idea. New plants can be purchased in spring and should be planted about 18 inches to 2 feet apart. Greenstem forsythia can tolerate cool nights so planting early in the season when a chance of frost is still possible is not typically a problem.

Growing Tips

Mulching new plantings with 1 to 2 inches of wood chips will help in times of drought. A general-purpose, granular fertilizer in spring will get plants off to a good start. Keep soil evenly moist even though this plant can take drier conditions.

Regional Advice and Care

Greenstem forsythia, unlike most of the full-sized species and varieties, does not need a lot of pruning. Pruning older plants back to the ground every few years in late winter will rejuvenate them and keep them productive. Because forsythia blooms on old wood, a hard pruning will cost you one year of bloom but it will keep plants vigorous and productive over time. Greenstem forsythia is resistant to pests and diseases and is also drought and heat tolerant.

Companion Planting and Design

Greenstem forsythia is ideal as a foundation planting, groundcover, edging plant along slopes for erosion control, in woodland gardens with adequate sunlight, and it can even be used in containers.

Try These

'Kumson' is a very interesting cultivated variety offering dark green leaves highlighted by silver venation. The combination is simply stunning and it is great as a foliage plant to accent the landscape. Although a different species, 'Fiesta' is a variegated form with a striking combination of yellow and green leaves.

Hydrangea

Hydrangea spp.

Botanical Pronunciation hy-DRAIN-juh

Bloom Period and Seasonal Color
Early summer to mid-fall with rounded, lacecap, or cone-shaped flowers of white, pink, or blue

Mature Height × Spread
2 to 4 feet × 3 to 6 feet on smaller types;
4 to 12 feet × 8 to 10 feet for larger species

Hydrangeas are the most cultivated and widely popular plants in the world. Hydrangeas are loved because of their versatility, diversity, and unmatched landscape value. They offer distinct, identifiable flowers ranging from white to pink to deep blue. Flower types include rounded flowers called mopheads, flat lacecap types, and elongated, pyramidal flower heads called panicles. For the East Coast, six species are widely used: smooth hydrangea (*H. arborescens*), climbing hydrangea (*H. anomala* subsp. *petiolaris*), panicle hydrangea (*H. paniculata*), oakleaf hydrangea (*H. quercifolia*), mountain hydrangea (*H. serrata*), and the star of the show—big leaf hydrangea (*H. macrophylla*). Smooth hydrangea blooms on new growth with large, round, white flowers in early to midsummer. It is a large shrub with thin stems reaching 3 to 5 feet in height and spread. Climbing hydrangea is a vine and will sometimes appear shrubby when it can't find anything to climb onto. It has white, lacecap-like flowers in early summer and lustrous, dark green leaves. Panicle hydrangea is the largest of hydrangea growing as a large shrub or small tree 6 to 12 feet tall. White, pyramidal flowers peak in late summer and continue through fall, changing to purplish pink. Oakleaf hydrangea is a spreading, rounded shrub blooming in early summer with elongated, cone-shaped, white flowers that eventually fade to pink and then brown. The oak leaf-shaped, dark green leaves have a leathery texture and turn brilliant shades of reddish maroon in fall. In winter, the older stems are attractive, often peeling and displaying a beautiful cinnamon-brown color. Mountain hydrangea is a mini version of big leaf hydrangea with many of the same attributes; its rounded white, pink, or blue flowers peak in midsummer. But the real king is big leaf hydrangea. It is sometimes referred to as the florist hydrangea since it is found in florist shops. It is the most adored and cultivated of flowering shrubs with over 1,000 varieties and more on the way. It is typically a rounded 4×4-foot shrub with large, lustrous leaves but its size can vary depending on growing conditions and variety. It is truly a rock star of the garden! Recent hydrangea breeding has focused on developing hydrangeas that are more compact and offer a wider variety of flower colors, as well as improved adaptability and vigor. Big leaf hydrangea typically blooms on old (second year) growth, setting flower buds the previous year. One of the biggest frustrations among gardeners is the lack of quality blooming from big leaf hydrangeas. This is often due to pruning at the wrong time or a cold winter that damages or kills flowers buds, seriously reducing flowering the following year. Today's breeding and evaluation programs focus on developing and introducing varieties that bloom on *new* growth, often called rebloomers or recurrent bloomers. These selections tend to bloom more reliably regardless of when they are pruned or whether they die back from a cold, hard winter.

When, Where, and How to Plant

Keep them well hydrated in summer. Failure will result in poorly developed, stressed plants with wilted or crinkled leaves and inconsistent flowering. Panicle and oakleaf hydrangeas are rather drought tolerant when established, but most need supplemental watering during summer. In general, hydrangeas prefer moist, well-drained soil and partial shade.

Hydrangeas benefit from rich, organic soils, which helps retain soil moisture. Adding well-aged compost or manure to the soil at planting will ensure the success of new plants. Plants can be grown in full sun but require regular watering and mulch to keep roots cool. Even well-watered hydrangeas may wilt in full sun. The flower color on certain species such as big leaf and mountain hydrangea is influenced by soil pH. Acidic soils yield blue flowers while alkaline soils result in pink flowers. For smaller types, space 2 to 4 feet apart. For larger types, space 8 to 10 feet.

Growing Tips

Maintain soil moisture; a 1- to 2-inch layer of wood chips, crushed leaves, or pine straw helps in drought. A well-balanced, granular fertilizer in spring gives plants a boost. Take a soil sample to establish how acidic or alkaline the soil is. To encourage blue flowers, add aluminum sulfate and to encourage pink flowers, add pelletized or granular lime.

Regional Advice and Care

Proper pruning is essential for hydrangeas to look good and flower reliably. Smooth hydrangea (*H. arborescens*) blooms on new growth and each spring, cutting plants down to 6 inches from the ground like a perennial encourages new, vigorous growth and loads of flowers. Panicle hydrangea, which are not typically pruned this drastically, also bloom on new growth and cutting back plants significantly in spring is not a problem. This applies to the new, reblooming varieties of big leaf hydrangea as well, but not the older varieties. However, all other species mentioned bloom on previous seasons' growth so pruning

anytime before flowering will significantly impact flower production. Instead, modest pruning right *after* flowering is acceptable and will keep plants dense and productive. Deadheading keeps plants tidy and clean. Hydrangeas are relatively trouble-free provided they are given good soil and adequate moisture. Smooth hydrangea is hardy to Zone 4 and possibly 3 with some protection. Panicle hydrangea is hardy to Zone 3 while oakleaf hydrangea is hardy to Zone 5. Mountain hydrangea and the new, reblooming big leaf hydrangea varieties are hardy to Zone 5, but the older varieties of big leaf hydrangea do not do well in Zone 5 without protection.

Companion Planting and Design

Use in groupings, mass plantings, foundation plantings, informal hedges, as specimens, and even in containers. Smaller varieties are excellent companions to perennials and other flowering shrubs such as butterfly bush, roses, and viburnum. Flowers can be harvested and dried for arrangements, but do not cut the tip off the stem as that will often cut the next year's flowers off.

Try These

'Annabelle' is a large, white-flowering smooth hydrangea with 12-inch flowers. Invincibelle® Spirit offers rosy-pink flowers fading to a soft pink. Panicle hydrangea cultivar Baby Lace® is a wonderful compact variety reaching only 4 feet tall with a profusion of pure white flowers. 'Limelight' is stunning with lime-green flowers maturing to pure white. It is truly one of the best performers in the garden. Vanilla Strawberry™ displays large white flowers that mature to a rich strawberry pink color. Oakleaf hydrangea has several dwarf varieties including 'Sikes Dwarf', growing to 2 to 4 feet tall and wide. 'Snowflake' offers huge, double flowers that are excellent in dried flower arrangements. 'Ruby Slippers' has white flowers that quickly change to deep pink. As for big leaf hydrangeas, some of the reblooming types such as Endless Summer® series, which offers rounded, mophead flowers while Twist-n-Shout® is a beautiful lacecap type. Bloomstruck® is the latest in this series with genes from both of these varieties. It has wonderful, thick, dark green foliage and showy, round blooms that keep on coming all summer. 'Dooley', named after the great college football coach at the University of Georgia, Vince Dooley, is hard to find but it's stunning in full bloom with enormous blue flowers.

Japanese Kerria

Kerria japonica

Botanical Pronunciation
KAIR-ee-uh juh-PON-ih-kuh

Bloom Period and Seasonal Color
Bright golden yellow flowers in mid-spring with dark green, pleated leaves and green stems

Mature Height × Spread
3 to 6 feet × 6 to 8 feet

Zones Hardy to Zone 5 but will grow in Zone 4 with protection

Although it may be difficult to see the family resemblance, Japanese kerria, also called Japanese rose, *is* a member of the rose family. It is a spring-flowering shrub with rounded, bright yellow flowers that cover each stem. Flowers can be single or double depending on variety. After the main flush of flowers in spring, kerria can also sporadically rebloom into summer. Its upright growth habit; thin, olive green twigs; and sharply serrated leaves provide ornamental value throughout the gardening season. Japanese kerria is especially effective in partial shade where it will brighten a dark, dull corner of the garden with its stunning floral display. In addition to dark green leaves, kerria may also have variegated leaves, which are especially attractive in shade.

When, Where, and How to Plant
Japanese kerria prefers moist, well-drained acidic soils and full sun or partial shade. Poorly drained soils may result in root rot; incorporating compost or other types of organic matter will benefit this plant. Kerria is remarkably shade tolerant and will perform fairly well in full shade. Plants can be purchased from a local nursery in spring in containers and should be planted slightly above the soil grade or on berms to ensure good drainage. Spacing should be 3 to 4 feet apart and plants will eventually form large clusters of stems.

Growing Tips
In spring, well-balanced granular fertilizer can be used but do not overdo it as it may result in more foliage and reduced flower production. Mulching with wood chips or pine straw in spring will keep soil moist and help plants in times of drought.

Regional Advice and Care
Kerria flowers on the previous year's growth so pruning should be done soon after flowering in early summer. Shrubs that are performing poorly can be selectively pruned or rejuvenated by cutting them down to the ground in late winter or early spring. Dead wood pruning is often needed on this plant and that too can be done in late winter. Keep plants in areas with good air circulation and drainage to avoid leaf spots, twig blights, and root rot. Kerria performs best in a sheltered location in extremely cold climates.

Companion Planting and Design
Kerria can be used in mass plantings, small groupings, and in shade gardens as an accent plant. It can also work well as an informal hedge or screen. Kerria is a great companion plant to shade loving plants such as hosta, astilbe, and hydrangea.

Try These
'Golden Guinea' offers unusually large golden single flowers that are a nice contrast to the rich, green leaves. 'Picta' has creamy white variegated leaves that provide a beautiful accent to a shade garden. 'Pleniflora' is an unusual double-flowering form with ruffled yellow flowers. 'Shannon' is a striking variety with large, single bright yellow flowers that arrive earlier than most kerria.

Japanese Snowbell

Styrax japonicus

Botanical Pronunciation
STYE-racks juh-PON-ih-kuhs

Other Name Japanese styrax

Bloom Period and Seasonal Color
Small white flowers in late spring and dark green leaves all summer

Mature Height × Spread
20 to 30 feet × 20 to 30 feet

Zones Hardy to Zone 5

Japanese snowbell is a small- to medium-sized flowering tree with several seasons of interest. In late spring, white, slightly scented, bell-shaped flowers form and cover the entire tree. The flowering will continue for several weeks. During summer, dark green, lustrous leaves turn yellow or red-tinged, but fall color is not usually overwhelming. The smooth, sinuous, fissured, gray brown bark is especially interesting during the winter months. Japanese snowbell is a nice tree for a home landscape and can be used as a single specimen in a lawn or in a mixed border with flowering shrubs. I have seen specimens look especially striking in a partially shaded woodland. There are quite a few interesting cultivated varieties, which are listed in this description.

When, Where, and How to Plant
Japanese snowbell prefers moist, well-drained soil with plenty of organic matter. It thrives in full sun or partial shade (it benefits from some shade in warmer climates). In cold climates and during harsh winters it will experience some die back. Be careful not to damage the rootball when planting this tree as it may affect its overall health and ability to establish in the garden. Japanese snowbell is best if planted in spring and should be spaced 12 to 15 feet apart from other trees and garden structures.

Growing Tips
Japanese snowbell thrives in rich, organic soil so add compost to the planting hole with new plantings. A 1- to 2-inch layer of wood chips will

keep plants thriving. Soil should be kept evenly moist for best results. Use a low-nitrogen fertilizer in spring if needed.

Regional Advice and Care
Japanese snowbell requires regular pruning since it is notorious for suckering at the base and may need cleaning up every few years when it's older. Remove suckers in midsummer. Although it's not seriously affected by diseases and insects, bark diseases can be an issue, possibly enhanced by mechanical injury by mowers and weed trimmers so keep your distance and do not injure the bark of the tree. Seedlings may pop up in the garden so monitoring and removal may be needed to keep this plant from spreading.

Companion Planting and Design
It's excellent as a patio tree, in a lawn area, or in a woodland garden. Japanese snowbell also works well with other flowering shrubs and small trees such as rhododendron, dogwood, and viburnum.

Try These
'Emerald Pagoda' is a lovely selection with larger, darker, and more leathery leaves as well as larger white flowers than the species. 'Pink Chimes' offers beautiful pink flowers in spring while 'Carillon' displays an unusual weeping habit. Fragrant snowbell (*Styrax obassia*) is another species with larger, medium to dark green leaves, and large, fragrant white flower clusters. It's a bold-textured tree ideal as a specimen or in a shaded woodland garden.

Japanese Stewartia

Stewartia pseudocamellia

Botanical Pronunciation
stoo-AR-tee-uh soo-doe-kuh-MEEL-ee-uh

Bloom Period and Seasonal Color
White flowers with bright yellow centers in early summer; foliage turns yellow, orange, and red in fall

Mature Height × Spread
20 to 35 feet × 15 to 20 feet but can get larger

Zones Hardy to Zone 5; possibly to Zone 4 with protection

Japanese stewartia is a non-invasive exotic species offering four seasons of interest with interesting leaves, showy flowers, and beautiful, exfoliating bark. This magnificent tree is proof that not all exotics are bad. Bees pollinate the flowers, becoming frequent visitors to the garden. This midsummer bloomer will have a flush of blooms in late June and early July and sporadically bloom through part of midsummer. The brilliant shades of orange, red, or maroon leaves are stunning in the fall landscape. Stewartia has the most beautiful bark, which typically flakes off in fall revealing a smooth, multicolored brown, beige, and gray. The landscape value of stewartia is unrivaled because in addition to its aesthetic value, it is easy to grow and will adapt to a wide variety of landscape situations.

When, Where, and How to Plant
Stewartia is carefree; prefers moist, well-drained soil; and will grow in either full sun or partial shade. It will also grow in full shade but will not usually flower heavily in those locations. Avoid planting stewartia in hot, dry, or windy sites. Stewartia should be planted in spring and it's usually sold as a balled-and-burlapped plant. Patience is a virtue, as new plantings will take several years to establish, but once they do they grow at a moderate rate. Spacing should be 10 to 15 feet apart, or just plant one as a single specimen.

Growing Tips
Stewartia prefers rich soil so adding compost when planting and mulching new plantings will benefit both new and established plantings. Soil should be kept evenly moist and a general, well-balanced fertilizer can be used in spring if needed.

Regional Advice and Care
Stewartia is pest free and rather adaptable to soil and light conditions. Pruning is not usually necessary unless there is dead wood or crossing branches. If pruning is needed, it can be done while plants are dormant or right after flowering.

Companion Planting and Design
Japanese stewartia is a beautiful specimen tree perfect for a lawn, woodland, or when it's mixed with other small flowering shrubs or trees such as dogwood, rhododendron, and viburnum.

Try These
Mountain stewartia (*Stewartia ovata*) displays large white flowers with yellow to purple centers. This native tree is a bit harder to find in commerce but is well worth the effort. Tall stewartia (*S. monadelpha*) is an Asian native with smaller, delicate leaves, white flowers, and a distinctly upright habit with cinnamon brown bark. It is quite heat tolerant compared to other species of stewartia. Both species are hardy to Zone 5. Other good varieties, which are results of hybrids, are 'Milk and Honey', which has a profusion of large, white flowers, graceful growth habit, and reddish tan bark. 'Ballet' also has large flowers, a broad, spreading habit, and fall color ranging from red to orange-brown.

Landscape Rose

Rosa spp.

Botanical Pronunciation
ROE-zuh

Bloom Period and Seasonal Color
White, yellow, pink, and red flowers from late spring until frost; glossy green leaves

Mature Height × Spread
18 inches × 4 feet to 24 inches to 4 feet

Zones Hardy to Zone 5; some hardy to Zone 4 with some protection

We love roses for their colorful, fragrant flowers and undeniable presence in the landscape. While there are many traditional tea roses and climbers that have been used in the garden, the roses presented here are a bit different. These are more recently developed landscape roses, offering a shrubby habit and excellent pest resistance. While maybe not as flashy as their old-fashioned counterparts, landscape roses offer extended flowering; spreading, upright, dense habits; and remarkable durability. The best attribute they have is their resistance to well-known diseases such as blackspot, mildew, rust, and more. A wide range of flowers, from single to semi-double to double, display bright colors including white, yellow, salmon, pink, and red. Landscape roses require much less care than traditional roses—even less pruning!

When, Where, and How to Plant
Like all roses, landscape roses require full sun and prefer moist, well-drained soil. However, they adapt to partial shade and hot, dry conditions once established. Adding well-aged compost or manure when planting is recommended. Landscape roses do not usually require pesticides to keep them disease free. New plants can be purchased in containers and planted when the soil warms up in spring. Space about 3 to 4 feet apart.

Growing Tips
Landscape roses do not require regular fertilizer applications but a general-purpose granular fertilizer, especially in sandy soils, will keep plants flourishing. Keep well watered. Mulching new plantings will keep their roots cool in summer and protect them in winter.

Regional Advice and Care
Landscape roses do not usually need the regimented pruning required of hybrid tea roses but do need occasional trimming to keep them dense and productive. More severe pruning in early spring can be done to reduce the size of plants that are too overgrown. While disease and insects are still possible in landscape roses, infestations are much less likely. Landscape roses do not require deadheading to continue to bloom although it always helps keep plants tidy.

Companion Planting and Design
Landscape roses make excellent informal hedges, screens, mass plantings, and foundation plantings. They are excellent companion plants to other flowering shrubs and herbaceous plants such as butterfly bush, spirea, coneflower, black-eyed Susan, and ornamental grasses. Some smaller varieties are used in containers and raised planters.

Try These
Knock Out® roses are excellent performers with several selections including Blushing Knock Out®, Double Knock Out®, Pink Knock Out®, Sunny Knock Out®, and the original Knock Out® growing 3 to 4 feet tall and wide. Flower Carpet® roses are a wonderful series with a low-growing habit to 2½ feet × 3 to 4 feet. They come in many colors and are known for their pest resistance and heat and drought tolerance. The Drift® series are groundcover type roses staying a bit shorter than Flower Carpet® roses but they're just as beautiful, offering a wide range of vibrant colors.

Lilac

Syringa spp.

Botanical Pronunciation
sur-ING-guh

Bloom Period and Seasonal Color
Sweetly fragrant pink, rose, and purple flowers
in spring

Mature Height × Spread
4 to 6 feet × 6 to 12 feet

Zones Most are hardy to Zone 3

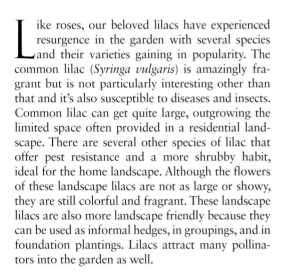

L ike roses, our beloved lilacs have experienced resurgence in the garden with several species and their varieties gaining in popularity. The common lilac (*Syringa vulgaris*) is amazingly fragrant but is not particularly interesting other than that and it's also susceptible to diseases and insects. Common lilac can get quite large, outgrowing the limited space often provided in a residential landscape. There are several other species of lilac that offer pest resistance and a more shrubby habit, ideal for the home landscape. Although the flowers of these landscape lilacs are not as large or showy, they are still colorful and fragrant. These landscape lilacs are also more landscape friendly because they can be used as informal hedges, in groupings, and in foundation plantings. Lilacs attract many pollinators into the garden as well.

When, Where, and How to Plant

Lilacs prefer moist, rich, well-drained soil and full sun or partial shade. They will tolerate a wide variety of soil pH and are particularly adapted for higher pH soils. Soil can be amended with well-aged compost or manure when planting in spring. They are tolerant of heat and humidity and quite cold tolerant. It is important that the soil drains, otherwise root diseases can occur. Lilacs are typically sold in containers. Spacing should be 3 to 4 feet apart or more.

Growing Tips

An application of general-purpose fertilizer can be applied in spring. Lightly mulching plants will keep soil evenly moist and cool in summer.

Regional Advice and Care

Pruning landscape lilacs is usually minimal. If needed, selective pruning can be done in late winter or early spring to remove older, less productive stems, which will encourage a compact habit and vigorous growth. The landscape lilacs listed here are quite resistant to disease and insect problems such as powdery mildew and borers.

Companion Planting and Design

Landscape lilacs are effective as informal hedges, foundation plantings, in groupings, or in mixed borders with other flowering shrubs or perennials.

Try These

Meyer lilac (*S. meyeri* 'Palibin') offers violet purple flowers, delicate, lustrous leaves, and a compact growth habit to 4 feet tall and 6 feet wide. The Fairytale® series are dwarf lilacs that offer various shades of pink flowers, dark green foliage, and dense growth habits. Fairy Dust®, Prince Charming®, Sugar Plum Fairy®, Thumbelina®, and Tinkerbelle® all offer something unique. Bloomerang® is a dwarf with pinkish purple flowers in spring, often reblooming in summer. Littleleaf lilac (*S. microphylla* 'Superba') is one of my favorites with glorious pink flowers and small, heart-shaped leaves. It can reach 6 feet tall with a wider spread to 8 to 10 feet but only with very old specimens; it's hardy to Zone 4.

The Little Girl Hybrid Magnolias

Magnolia 'Ann', 'Betty', 'Jane', 'Judy', 'Pinkie', 'Randy', 'Ricki', 'Susan'

Botanical Pronunciation mag-NOLE-yuh

Bloom Period and Seasonal Color
Reddish purple flowers in early spring (April, early May)

Mature Height × Spread
10 to 15 feet × 10 to 15 feet

Zones Hardy to Zone 4

In the mid-1950s these hybrids were developed at the US National Arboretum. They were results of crosses between *Magnolia liliiflora* 'Nigra' with *M. stellata* 'Rosea', two species with somewhat compact growth habit (compared to many other magnolias). The intent of this breeding program was to retain the showy flowering characteristics of the parent plants but to develop later flowering magnolias to reduce the risk of frost damage, which is often a problem with magnolias. The resulting Little Girl series, also known as "The Girls," includes 'Ann', 'Betty', 'Jane', 'Judy', 'Pinkie', 'Randy', 'Ricki', and 'Susan', which are dwarf and ideal for the residential landscape. Flower colors range from pink to deep reddish purple and trees will sometimes sporadically flower in summer.

When, Where, and How to Plant
Magnolias in general prefer moist, well-drained soil and full sun or partial shade. Full sun is best for the most flower production and dense growth habit. They are remarkably tolerant of a wide range of soils and pH but are most happy in rich garden soil. Although magnolias are adaptable, adding well-aged manure or compost will help trees establish and thrive. Plant magnolias in spring. They are usually grown as single specimens but if planted in groupings or along with other shrubs or trees, they should be spaced 10 to 12 feet apart.

Growing Tips
A general-purpose, granular fertilizer in spring is recommended, especially in very well-drained soils.

Add a 1- to 2-inch layer of mulch to new plantings. Keep soil moist during times of drought.

Regional Advice and Care
Some diseases and insects attack magnolias, but none are usually too serious and can be tolerated. Prune after flowering in early summer, although with the Little Girl series this is not typically a requirement since they do not grow very large. Removing water sprouts or crossing branches is sometimes needed.

Companion Planting and Design
The Little Girl series are best as single specimens in a lawn area or in large borders or in small groupings. It is an excellent companion plant to other early-blooming trees and shrubs such as forsythia, flowering cherry, or some of the early-blooming rhododendrons.

Try These
Besides the Little Girl series, *M. × loebneri* 'Leonard Messel' offers pinkish purple, star-shaped flowers that sparkle in early spring landscapes. 'Galaxy' displays reddish purple flowers and an upright, pyramidal habit. Some of the most coveted magnolia varieties today are the hybrids with yellow flowers. It all started with 'Elizabeth', from the great Brooklyn Botanic Garden with creamy, butter yellow flowers that have a lemony fragrance. 'Judy Zuk', named after the former director of the garden, offers golden-yellow flowers with a purple base and a fruity fragrance. 'Butterflies' and 'Goldfinch' offer rich golden-yellow flowers that warm the bare spring landscape.

Old-Fashioned Weigela

Weigela spp.

Botanical Pronunciation
wye-JEE-luh

Bloom Period and Seasonal Color
Rosy pink flowers in spring

Mature Height × Spread
6 to 8 feet × 8 to 10 feet

Zones Hardy to Zone 5

Although the name suggests that weigela is an "old-fashioned" shrub, it has seen a renaissance over the past decade. Several new and exciting cultivated varieties have emerged including ones with dark purple foliage, variegated foliage, and various flower colors. This easy-to-grow shrub produces masses of pink, trumpet-shaped flowers in spring, which often sporadically continue through late summer. The dark green leaves and graceful, spreading habit offer interest all season as well as landscape function as an informal hedge and screen. Weigela is very versatile and can be effective as a standalone plant or it can be mixed with other flowering shrubs, trees, or perennials. With few pests and great adaptability, it's not difficult to understand why it continues to be a garden favorite.

When, Where, and How to Plant

Weigela is not particularly picky and adapts to a variety of soils and light exposure. For best results, weigela should be planted in full sun and moist, well-drained soil. In poor soils, add well-aged compost. However, it will tolerate sandy and clay soils, a wide variety of soil pH, and partial shade. Spring planting is ideal; space 3 to 4 feet apart.

Growing Tips

Mulch new plantings to help plants establish and to protect them during drought. Keep soil evenly moist and apply a well-balanced fertilizer in spring.

Regional Advice and Care

Weigela is relatively carefree and not bothered by diseases and insects. Prune to keep weigela healthy and productive. Every few years selectively remove older, mature stems, leaving younger, more vigorous ones. Weigela blooms on previous season's growth so flowering will be sacrificed for one season if severe pruning is needed. If you're pruning to shape or maintain a dense growth habit, prune after flowering.

Companion Planting and Design

Use weigela like forsythia, viburnum, and spirea. It is effective in mass plantings, groupings, informal hedges, and foundation plantings. Dwarf varieties are excellent companions to herbaceous plants and can be used as foliage plants in containers.

Try These

Midnight Wine® ('Elvera') is an excellent dwarf growing 18 to 24 inches tall and wide. The combination of deep maroon leaves and bright pink flowers is striking. 'Minuet' is compact, to 2 to 3 feet tall, with dark green leaves and ruby red flowers. My Monet® is a groundcover with reddish pink flowers and variegated leaves highlighted by white and pink leaf edges. 'Red Prince' is an upright, large shrub with bright red flowers and rich, dark green foliage. Flowers often sporadically continue into summer and fall. 'Rubidor' offers bright yellow foliage and red flowers. It is an excellent cut-back shrub used just for its foliage. 'Variegata' grows 4 to 6 feet tall with cream-colored leaf edges and deep rose flowers. Wine and Roses® is a striking variety with deep burgundy leaves and rosy-pink flowers similar to Midnight Wine® but larger.

Ornamental Flowering Cherry

Prunus spp.

Botanical Pronunciation PROO-nus

Bloom Period and Seasonal Color
White, pink, or rose-colored flowers in early to mid-spring, foliage turns yellow, orange, and red in fall

Mature Height × Spread
15 to 20 feet × 10 to 20 feet, depending on species and variety

Ornamental flowering cherries are specifically grown for showy flowers, foliage, and bark interest and not for edible fruit. These ornamental trees offer a wide range of flower colors, from white to deep rosy pink as well as rich green foliage that changes to beautiful shades of yellow, orange, and reddish maroon. Some cherries (or their plum relatives) also have reddish maroon foliage in summer. Cherries can offer quite a diverse selection of bark colors and textures, which are most noticeable in winter. Cherry tree bark has small glands called *lenticels*, which are arranged in an irregular pattern along stems and the main trunk. While many cherries grow too large for the average residential landscape, the species and varieties mentioned here are quite suitable for the home environment.

When, Where, and How to Plant
In general, flowering cherries perform best in moist, well-drained, acidic soil and full sun or partial shade. Flowering cherries should be planted in spring and are typically sold as balled-and-burlapped plants. Spacing varies widely among species but 10 to 15 feet apart is a good rule of thumb.

Growing Tips
Fertilize flowering cherries in spring with a balanced granular fertilizer. A 1- to 2-inch layer of wood chips will help plants establish and keeps the soil moist in times of drought.

Regional Advice and Care
While they're tough, flowering cherries are susceptible to a variety of insects and diseases such as stem and bark diseases and scale, so monitoring them is essential to detect these issues early. Cherries typically do not require regular pruning but if needed, modest pruning can be done after flowering.

Companion Planting and Design
Flowering cherries are useful as single specimens in a lawn, in groupings, or in combination with other spring bloomers such as magnolias, serviceberry, dogwood, and viburnum.

Try These
Okame cherry (*Prunus × incam* 'Okame') is an upright grower with delicate, single, rosy pink flowers in early spring, blooming around the same time as magnolias. 'Okame' cherry grows 20 to 30 feet tall with a slightly smaller spread and is hardy to Zone 6. My favorite is Hally Jolivette cherry (*P. × 'Hally Jolivette'*), which is an old-fashioned variety ideal for small landscapes. The light pink to nearly white flowers are breathtaking in spring. Hally Jolivette cherry will reach 15 feet tall, with a similar spread, and is hardy to Zone 5. There are purple-leaved plums and cherries with pink flowers and rich, reddish maroon leaves all summer. Blireana plum (*P. × blireana*) has double pink flowers and reddish purple foliage in early spring, fading to green in summer. It grows to 20 feet tall and is hardy to Zone 5. *P. cerasifera* 'Atropurpurea' can grow to 25 feet tall offering small pink flowers followed by deep reddish purple leaves. 'Thundercloud' has deep purple foliage and delicate pink flowers that are fragrant; it's hardy to Zone 5.

Rhododendron

Rhododendron spp.

Botanical Pronunciation roe-doe-DEN-drun

Bloom Period and Seasonal Color
Flowers from white, pink, purple, and red with lustrous, evergreen foliage

Mature Height × Spread
6 to 8 feet × 6 to 10 feet

Zones Small leaf types: hardy to Zone 5; large leaf types: hardy to Zone 6

Rhododendrons are a diverse group of shrubs that offer masses of colorful blooms in spring and lush, evergreen leaves. There is incredible variety within this group of plants with hundreds of varieties available to the home gardener. There are two main groups of evergreen rhododendron: small leaf types, known as lepidotes and large leaf types, known as elepidotes. The small leaf types tend to be smaller in stature and will tolerate a bit more sun than the larger leaf types. The clusters of bell-shaped flowers range from white to pink, rose, and lavender. Rhododendrons are most effective in groupings and are especially effective in a woodland. In winter, rhododendrons provide structure and bold texture with their lustrous evergreen foliage and dense, rounded growth habit.

When, Where, and How to Plant

Rhododendrons require rich, moist, acidic (pH about 5.5), well-drained soil with plenty of organic matter. Avoid planting in heavy, clay soils that are poorly drained. Rhododendron prefers partial shade though small leaf types tolerate more sun. An ideal site is under the dappled shade of pine trees with a light layer of mulch such as pine straw or shredded leaves. Plant in spring or fall but don't plant after October. Spacing is very dependent on the species, but generally 4 to 6 feet is ideal.

Growing Tips

Rhododendron has a very fine, fibrous root system that must be protected from drought by mulching and regular watering during summer. Apply a slow-release fertilizer in spring if needed, which can be determined by a soil test.

Regional Advice and Care

Rhododendrons require regular care to survive and thrive. They are susceptible to many pests and diseases but most importantly, their soil, light, and moisture levels *must* be right. Prune to maintain a dense, vigorous habit after flowering. More severe pruning to reduce overall size or to rejuvenate plants should be done in late winter or early spring. Deadheading is especially important on younger plants to encourage growth and future flowers, not seed.

Companion Planting and Design

Rhododendrons provide landscape functions as mass plantings, specimens, screens, informal hedges, foundation plantings, and in shaded woodlands.

Try These

Weston Nurseries, Hopkinton, MA, developed many small leaf rhododendrons that are ideal for the home landscape. 'PJM' is the original with lavender-pink flowers, dark green leaves turning maroon in winter, and an upright growth habit. 'Landmark' offers bright, reddish pink flowers that light up the landscape. 'April Snow' offers masses of double, pure white flowers as early as late April. Of the large leaf types, my favorites are 'Scintillation' offering gorgeous pink flowers with a yellow center and lush, deep green foliage, and 'Taurus' with spectacular dark red flowers that will stop you dead in your tracks. The ever-popular 'Roseum Elegans' is an old-fashioned variety with rosy purple flowers and a reputation to be very tough. It's sometimes criticized as common and overused but it's colorful and it performs, so what's not to like?

Shadblow Serviceberry

Amelanchier spp.

Botanical Pronunciation am-ul-LANK-ee-ur

Other Name Shadbush

Bloom Period and Seasonal Color
White flowers in spring; leaves turn yellow, orange, and reddish maroon in fall

Mature Height × Spread
6 to 20 feet × 8 to 15 feet

Serviceberry is a tall, upright native shrub or small tree that can grow as a single stem specimen or a multi-stem planting. There are several species that are garden worthy including *Amelanchier canadensis* and *A. × grandiflora*. They offer small bouquets of white flowers in spring, followed by new foliage that is often bronze colored before it matures to medium to dark green. The leaves turn brilliant shades of yellow, orange, and red in fall depending on the amount of light they are growing in. One of the best features of this plant is the blueberrylike fruit that ripen by early summer. You will have to beat the birds to them as they are favorites of wildlife but it will be worth it as the fruit are sweet and succulent.

When, Where, and How to Plant
I have seen serviceberry growing in cool, moist, woodland conditions and on exposed sites near the seashore. Serviceberry is tolerant of salt, pollution, drought, and heat. It typically thrives in well-drained, moist soil with adequate organic matter but it will tolerate sandy soils as well. If planted in poor soils, adding a generous amount of compost or manure to the soil will be beneficial. It will even tolerate moist conditions and occasional flooding. Full sun or partial shade is best, but full shade is not recommended as it will weaken plants too much. Plants can be purchased in large containers or balled and burlapped and should be spaced 10 to 15 feet apart.

Growing Tips
Mulching your serviceberry with 1 to 2 inches of wood chips will help in times of drought. Soil should be kept evenly moist.

Regional Advice and Care
Serviceberry is susceptible to rusts, leaf spots, and other diseases that can affect leaves and fruit. Planting serviceberry in open areas with plenty of air circulation will help. A partly shaded area with dappled light and morning sunlight and afternoon shade is ideal. On multi-stemmed plants, selective pruning to remove older, less vigorous stems will keep plants dense and productive. This can be done every few years in late winter or early spring by pruning stems as close to the ground as possible. *A. × grandiflora* is hardy to Zone 4.

Companion Planting and Design
Serviceberry is effective in small groupings or as a single specimen in a woodland garden, in a lawn area, or even as a tall screen or informal hedge. Serviceberry works well in a naturalistic setting. The smooth, silvery gray bark offers winter interest.

Try These
Wonderful varieties of *A. × grandiflora* that offer good fruit and striking fall color include 'Autumn Brilliance', 'Autumn Sunset', and 'Ballerina'. 'Prince William' is a vigorous but somewhat compact variety of *A. canadensis* reaching 10 feet × 8 feet at maturity.

Slender Deutzia

Deutzia gracilis

Botanical Pronunciation
DEWTZ-ee-uh grah-sill-iss

Bloom Period and Seasonal Color
Clusters of pure white flowers in mid-spring

Mature Height × Spread
2 to 4 feet × 3 to 4 feet

Zones Hardy to Zone 4

Slender deutzia is a low-maintenance flowering shrub, which performs well year after year with little or no maintenance. This old-fashioned shrub has become more popular over the years because new varieties have emerged as garden-friendly additions to the landscape. In addition to the pure white flowers in spring, the leaves are petite and slender and the branches are arching and graceful, as the name suggests. Fall color can be shades of red and maroon but is not usually overwhelming. Slender deutzia is incredibly adaptable, growing in most soils and becoming quite drought tolerant once established. Because of its grace and elegance, slender deutzia is ideal as an informal hedge, foundation planting, and with other dwarf shrubs and perennials.

When, Where, and How to Plant
Slender deutzia is a carefree, happy-go-lucky plant that performs well and asks for very little in return. With the exception of wet soils, it is very adaptable to soil type and pH. Slender deutzia is adaptable but adding compost to the planting hole will help plants establish in sandy and clay soils. Full sun or partial shade is best for maximum flowering. Plants can be propagated by sowing seed in fall but semi-hardwood cuttings taken in midsummer after flowering is the most preferred. Because of its spreading, mounded habit, plants can be spaced 2 to 3 feet apart.

Growing Tips
Mulching new plantings is desirable to reduce the effects of drought in summer. Keep soil evenly moist and use a well-balanced, granular fertilizer in spring.

Regional Advice and Care
Slender deutzia is pest, drought, and heat tolerant and also quite cold hardy. Pruning should be kept to a minimum so that the naturally graceful habit is allowed to flow in the landscape. While regular pruning is not typically necessary, occasional rejuvenation pruning to cut plants back to 12 inches in spring will allow unproductive, leggy plants to develop into low, mounded plants. If drastic pruning is needed, older stems can simply be thinned out every few years.

Companion Planting and Design
Slender deutzia is ideal in gardens where room is limited. They work very well as unpruned, informal hedges, low screens, in foundations, or in mixed borders with other summer-flowering trees, shrubs, and perennials.

Try These
There are several varieties including the ever-so-popular 'Nikko', which is a very low, mounded shrub that hugs the ground and roots in as it creeps. Fall color tends to be a bit better on this variety. Chardonnay Pearls® offers golden-yellow new foliage that fades to chartreuse. It is ideal in partial shade. 'Variegata' offers leaves that are splashed with creamy white variegation. Some variegated forms offer yellow and green variations in the leaf.

Spirea

Spiraea spp.

Botanical Pronunciation
spy-REE-uh

Other Name Bridal wreath

Bloom Period and Seasonal Color
White flowers in spring or white and pink flowers in summer

Mature Height × Spread
2 to 5 feet × 2 to 5 feet

Spirea is an old-fashioned flowering shrub that has been used in home gardens since the late 1800s. Like hydrangeas, roses, and lilacs, spirea as a group is hardy, colorful, and versatile. Spireas offer small bouquets of white or pink flowers with the spring bloomers often referred to as bridal wreaths. There are two very distinct types of spirea: spring-blooming types and summer-blooming types. The spring-bloomers flower on the previous season's growth and have one flush of flowers. The summer-blooming types flower on new growth and tend to have an extended period of bloom. These two groups are quite different but can easily be incorporated into a mixed border, foundation planting, or used as an informal hedge.

When, Where, and How to Plant
Spirea prefers full sun or partial shade and well-drained, loamy garden soil. However, they are quite tough and tolerate all types of soils except those that are soggy. Spring is an ideal time to plant spirea from containers, although early fall is acceptable. Space plants 2 to 4 feet apart.

Growing Tips
Spirea will benefit from adding compost to the soil and mulching lightly once planting is completed. Add balanced fertilizer in spring to give plants a boost going into summer. Keep soil evenly moist.

Regional Advice and Care
Spirea is susceptible to insects such as aphids and scale and should be monitored closely. Generally,

spring-blooming spirea should be modestly pruned with a hand shear after flowering and summer-blooming types should be pruned while dormant in early spring. Cutting dormant summer-blooming types down to the ground will result in dense, compact, and floriferous plants.

Companion Planting and Design
Spirea can be used in mass plantings, foundation plantings, mixed borders, and are excellent as low edging plants or informal hedges.

Try These
Bumald spirea (*Spiraea × bumalda*) is a dwarf shrub forming a dense, mounded habit reaching 2 to 4 feet tall with a similar spread. The new reddish pink leaves unfold in spring and change to blue-green when they're mature. The small, flat-topped flower clusters are borne on new growth in summer ranging from white to deep pink. Japanese spirea (*S. japonica*) 'Little Princess' is a true dwarf reaching 2½ feet tall. The lush, dark green leaves, pink flowers, and dwarf habit make this an excellent choice for a rock garden or foundation planting; it's hardy to Zone 4. Snowmound spirea (*S. nipponica* 'Snowmound') displays pure white flower clusters on previous season's growth in late spring and early summer. This species is hardy to Zone 4 but can be grown in Zone 3 with protection. Thunberg spirea (*S. thunbergii*) has a graceful, fine texture with masses of delicate white flowers in spring and small leaves in summer. 'Ogon' offers soft, yellow leaves changing to pale green; it's hardy to Zone 4.

Summersweet Clethra

Clethra alnifolia

Botanical Pronunciation
KLETH-ruh al-nih-FOE-lee-uh

Other Name Sweet pepperbush

Bloom Period and Seasonal Color
Summer, white or pink flowers; fall, golden yellow foliage

Mature Height × Spread
6 to 8 feet × 4 to 6 feet

Summersweet clethra is known for its durability, adaptability, and multiple seasons of interest in the landscape. This rounded, spreading shrub is a real attraction in summer with spikey flowers that have a sweet fragrance in late summer and early fall. The flowers attract bees, butterflies, and even hummingbirds to your garden. The seedpods are not only interesting in fall and winter, but they will provide a food source for birds as well. Summersweet are incredibly adaptable, growing in almost every landscape situation imaginable from a typical garden setting to full sun near the seashore to wet soils near a stream or pond in a shaded woodland. In the garden it works very well with other summer-blooming shrubs and perennials.

When, Where, and How to Plant
Summersweet clethra will tolerate poorly drained, heavy soils or sandy, dry soils as well as heat, drought, salt, and pollution. It performs best in rich, well-drained garden soil. It thrives in full sun or partial shade and will even perform admirably in dense shade. Although seed can be harvested and sown in fall, cuttings or root divisions are the best ways to propagate this shrub. Spacing should be 4 to 5 feet, although some of the smaller growing varieties can be closer.

Growing Tips
Summersweet clethra doesn't require much fertilizer, but if needed, a general-purpose granular fertilizer application in spring gives plants a boost. Adding compost to the soil and a light layer of mulch will help plants establish quickly. Keep soil evenly moist for best performance.

Regional Advice and Care
Pests such a spider mites can be a problem in dry sites but overall it's a rock-solid plant with very few needs. Clethra has a spreading root system and will send up suckers as it grows so regular pruning will keep plants in check. Selective pruning can be done in spring to maintain established plants. If you're pruning in summer, prune plants lightly while spring pruning can be more aggressive.

Companion Planting and Design
Summersweet clethra is a native shrub that can be used in a mixed border, foundation planting, informal hedge, and companion plant to perennials. It is ideal in a woodland garden or in areas where poor drainage is an issue. It is a good plant to attract pollinators and birds and can be used in small groupings, mass plantings, or as a single specimen.

Try These
'Compacta' is an old-time variety and my favorite from New Jersey with a dense habit and extremely dark green foliage and 6-inch-long white flowers. 'Hummingbird' is one of the most popular varieties, with a low, spreading habit growing 2 to 3 feet tall. 'Sixteen Candles' is also dwarf with large, white flowers that look like candles on a cake! 'Ruby Spice' offers deep pink, fragrant flowers and dark green foliage.

Thunberg Bushclover

Lespedeza thunbergii

Botanical Pronunciation
less-pe-DEE-zuh thun-burg-EE-eye

Bloom Period and Seasonal Color
Clusters of rose-purple flowers in late summer

Mature Height × Spread
3 to 6 feet × 3 to 6 feet

Zones Hardy to Zone 5 and possibly to Zone 4 with protection

This delicate, graceful shrub offers masses of deep rosy-purple flower clusters that dangle from the tips of each branch. This plant is in the legume family so the odd-looking flowers look like miniature sweet pea flowers. The cascading growth habit and showy flowers droop to the ground, creating a beautiful fountain effect. The lacey, blue-green foliage adds a fine texture to the landscape, which is interesting even when the plant is not in flower. Its graceful, vase-shaped growth habit will reach mature size in one season as it is very fast growing, blooming on new growth. Thunberg bushclover actually looks like a perennial and thus works well with many fine-textured, sun-loving perennials that also bloom in late summer and early fall.

When, Where, and How to Plant

Thunberg bushclover will thrive in hot, dry conditions and full sun but will also perform very well in moist, well-drained soils and light shade. It is very tolerant of poor soils as long as they drain well; even rocky or sandy soils don't seem to slow them down too much. Although thunberg bushclover does not need soil with a lot of organic matter, if your soils are sandy, gravely, or heavy clay, adding some compost will help this plant over the long term. New plants bought in containers should be planted in mid-spring when the weather is warm and the chance of frost has passed. Spacing should be 3 to 4 feet apart.

Growing Tips

Avoid overfertilizing plants, which may cause long, spindly growth. Keep soil evenly moist.

Regional Advice and Care

For best flower production, thunberg bushclover should be pruned to the ground like a perennial in late winter or early spring to encourage a new flush of growth and flowers each growing season. Bushclover responds well to being treated as a "cut back" shrub, allowing it to be rejuvenated each year. This will keep the plants vigorous and looking good. Thunberg bushclover is relatively pest free and will thrive as long as it has adequate sunlight.

Companion Planting and Design

As a cut back shrub, thunberg bushclover is excellent in perennial borders, mixed shrub borders, or in groupings with other summer-blooming shrubs such as butterfly bush, spirea, and abelia. Its fine foliage texture and profuse flowers provide unique late-summer interest. Thunberg bushclover is a true performer in hot, dry areas with poor, infertile soils. It is especially useful in seashore conditions.

Try These

'Avalanche' is a striking variety with masses of pure white flowers that provides a nice contrast to the purple-flowering forms. 'Gibraltar' is similar to the species and also produces masses of deep rosy-purple flowers. 'Pink Cascade' is a pink-flowering form with a more compact growth habit. 'Spring Grove' is more floriferous than 'Gibraltar' and displays deeper rosy-purple flowers.

Viburnum

Viburnum spp.

Botanical Pronunciation
vye-BUR-num

Bloom Period and Seasonal Color
White or pink blooms in spring; fall color from yellow to reddish maroon

Mature Height × Spread
4 to 10 feet × 6 to 10 feet

Zones Most hardy to Zone 4 or 5

Viburnum is among the most versatile and beautiful flowering shrubs available. They have been cultivated for centuries but have increased in popularity over the past few decades. Viburnum is the total package, offering interesting foliage; fragrant and showy flowers; colorful red, yellow, or blue fruit; and incredible adaptability. Evergreen and deciduous types are available, making them four-season plants. Deciduous types display shades of reddish maroon leaves in fall. It would be easy for gardeners to landscape their home using various types of viburnums. Viburnum is eco-friendly, attracting a wide variety of pollinators and birds. Plant viburnum in groups because this will ensure good cross-pollination and fruit production.

When, Where, and How to Plant
Viburnum prefers moist, well-drained soil and full sun or partial shade. Adding compost to poor soil at planting time will help with establishment. Spring planting is preferred but viburnums can also be planted in early fall. Plants are usually sold in containers or as balled-and-burlapped plants. Spacing should be 4 to 6 feet apart depending on the species.

Growing Tips
One to 2 inches of wood chips aroud the base will help plants during times of drought. Keep soil evenly moist and if needed, use a well-balanced fertilizer in spring.

Regional Advice and Care
Viburnums are pest resistant and perform well with little attention once established. Certain species are susceptible to viburnum leaf beetle, which will defoliate entire plants, so monitor plants closely and check local nurseries for recommendations. Pruning in late winter to remove older, less productive stems will keep plants floriferous and dense. Modest pruning after flowering can be done to keep plants from growing too large.

Companion Planting and Design
Viburnums are compatible with spring- and summer-flowering shrubs, perennials, and ornamental grasses. They are ideal in mixed borders and are effective as informal hedges, foundation plants, and in woodland settings.

Try These
Korean spicebush viburnum (*Viburnum carlesii*) offers rounded, sweetly fragrant flowers that are pink in bud and pure white when fully open. Fuzzy, dark green leaves turn rich shades of red in fall. Linden viburnum (*V. dilatatum*) is known for its rounded, creamy white flowers, dark green foliage, red fruit, and reddish maroon fall foliage. Cardinal Candy™ offers large clusters of white flowers and bunches of glossy red fruit. 'Erie' displays 4- to 6-inch-wide flowers, lustrous green leaves, and showy red fruit. Both species are hardy to Zone 5 and 4 with protection. Of the evergreen types, burkwood viburnum (*V. × burkwoodii*) is wonderfully fragrant with showy white flowers and dark green, glossy leaves. 'Conoy' is semi-dwarf and hardy to Zone 4. Prague viburnum (*V. × pragense*) has leathery, glossy leaves and creamy white flowers in spring, adding wonderful bold texture to the landscape; it's hardy to Zone 5.

Virginia Sweetspire

Itea virginica

Botanical Pronunciation
eye-TEE-uh vur-JIN-ih-kuh

Bloom Period and Seasonal Color
White flower clusters in late spring/early summer; dark green leaves turn brilliant shades of yellow, orange, reddish purple, and scarlet in fall

Mature Height × Spread
3 to 5 feet × 5 to 7 feet or more

Zones Hardy to Zone 5

Virginia sweetspire is a lovely flowering shrub that is native from New Jersey to the southeastern United States. It is a durable, easy-to-grow shrub with the ability to thrive in wet soils. Its spreading, graceful growth habit creates thick colonies of dense branches. In June, long, dangling white flowers form at the ends of each branch. But what is most attractive about this native shrub is the intensely beautiful fall foliage color that ranges from yellow and orange to reddish purple. These rich colors brighten up the autumn landscape. Virginia sweetspire is especially effective in areas of the garden that have poor soil drainage or experience occasional flooding. It is one of those plants that once established will require very little maintenance and works well in informal plantings.

When, Where, and How to Plant

Virginia sweetspire is best in moist, rich acidic soils, which can either be well drained or not so well drained. Virginia sweetspire benefit from rich, organic soils so adding compost or manure when planting is a good idea. Full sun or partial shade is best for flowering and fall color. This shrub does not perform well in hot, dry conditions in exposed sites. Plants are usually sold in containers and can be planted in early spring. Spacing should be 3 to 4 feet apart to allow plants to spread, eventually forming thick colonies.

Growing Tips

Mulching new plantings with a thin layer of wood chips will help to retain moisture in the soil, which will help plants establish and reduce stress to plants in times of drought.

Regional Advice and Care

Leaf spots and insects such as flea beetles have been known to affect this plant but they're not typically a problem in plants that are sited correctly. Pruning can be done after flowering in early summer but is not usually needed as plants have a naturally graceful habit. Pruning back or thinning stems that sucker up from the base to reduce the overall spread of the plant can be done at this time.

Companion Planting and Design

Virginia sweetspire is ideal in mass plantings or small groupings, as foundation plantings, and along slopes where it will help with erosion. It is especially effective along streams or ponds or in areas of the garden that are poorly drained. Virginia sweetspire is a great companion to clethra, abelia, and other easy-to-grow summer-blooming shrubs.

Try These

'Henry's Garnet' is a well-known and excellent variety with 6-inch-long blooms and consistently brilliant reddish purple fall color. Little Henry® offers a compact habit to 3 to 4 feet tall and excellent reddish purple fall color. 'Merlot' is another dwarf selection with deep, rich reddish purple fall foliage color. 'Saturnalia' offers more of a striking yellow, orange, and red fall color that is very noticeable in the fall landscape.

Witch Hazel

Hamamelis × intermedia

Botanical Pronunciation
ham-uh-MEE-liss in-tur-MEE-dee-uh

Bloom Period and Seasonal Color
Frilly, straplike flower petals in shades of yellow, orange, or purplish red in late winter; dark green leaves turn brilliant shades of yellow, orange, and red in fall

Mature Height × Spread
12 to 15 feet × 12 to 15 feet

Zones Hardy to Zone 5

This species is a hybrid between the Chinese witch hazel with yellow flowers and the Japanese witch hazel with yellow-orange flowers. Witch hazel by design needs room to grow. They all possess a vase-shaped and often spreading growth habit that commands proper space. Unlike the native witch hazel, which blooms in fall, this hybrid witch hazel blooms in mid- to late winter, brightening up the landscape. Although witch hazel is considered an interesting plant for three seasons, it's all about the glorious flowers. In the cold of winter, rounded flower buds burst open to reveal strap like flowers that look like party poppers. This display can last for several months, followed by dark green, textured leaves that turn stunning shades of yellow, orange, and red in fall.

When, Where, and How to Plant
Witch hazel is rather easy to grow and tolerates a wide variety of soil conditions. Moist, well-drained soil is best and gardeners should beware of siting this plant in poor drainage. Witch hazels are adaptable but if you have rocky, sandy soil or heavy, clay soil, a generous amount of well-aged compost at planting will help new plantings for years to come. Full sun or partial shade is preferable. New plants are typically bought in spring in containers. Spacing is very important; take into consideration the proximity to other plants as well as the house, garage, walkway, and so forth. I would recommend spacing witch hazel at least 8 to 10 feet from any other major features of the garden.

Growing Tips
A 1- to 2-inch layer of mulch such as wood chips will help in times of drought. Keep soil evenly moist in summer.

Regional Advice and Care
Placement of witch hazel is so important because regular pruning should be avoided. Pruning to train the plants or to remove water sprouts from the base is acceptable but "shaping" is nearly impossible with witch hazel. In moist, cool springs a leaf disease known as witch hazel blight can cause browning of part or all of the leaves by midsummer. While there may be effective fungicides, you may want to try a non-chemical solution like siting plants in areas with good light and air circulation, and cleaning up diseased leaves in fall.

Companion Planting and Design
Witch hazel is truly a standalone plant that works well as a specimen. It can be used on a lawn or in a woodland garden as long as it has room.

Try These
'Angelly' has light yellow flowers and an upright, vase-shaped growth habit. 'Diane' has large, rich, brick red to orange flowers, and 'Jelena' has a coppery orange bloom that is stunning from late January until March. 'Arnold Promise' is an old variety introduced in 1928 and it is still a favorite. There are many more great varieties and interested gardeners should look at mail-order catalogues to select from a myriad of shapes, colors, and sizes.

SHADE TREES
FOR NEW YORK & NEW JERSEY

Shade trees can provide great value to the home landscape. These deciduous trees, which drop their leaves in fall, provide protection from wind, reduce harsh reflections, and provide habitat for wildlife, all the while providing privacy and beauty to your garden all summer long. In addition, trees help to cool the landscape by cooling the air around them through evapotranspiration and by protecting your home from the heat of the sun. This translates into a more pleasant home and garden and lower energy bills.

Shade trees are the largest plants in your landscape, usually towering over the rest of the garden. They provide height, structure, and soften the architectural features in a garden such as the house, garage, and shed. This section offers readers options when choosing shade trees as well as planting tips to ensure they will flourish and function as long-term inhabitants in your landscape.

Selecting Shade Trees for the Home Landscape

The notion of "right plant for the right place" is no more applicable than when deciding where to plant shade trees in your garden. Since shade trees have the potential to grow large, there is less room for error when siting them. There is nothing worse than planting a new maple or elm, only to find that within a few years it has outgrown its space and is now causing problems such as root competition, blocking needed views, or damaging hardscape features.

Besides ultimate size, there are other factors to consider when selecting shade trees including ornamental qualities, seasonal interest, whether these trees are compatible with the other plants you want to grow, and what site conditions you have to offer. While growth rate is a factor, it should not dictate where you place shade trees because ultimately these trees *will* reach their mature height and width, regardless of their growth rate. When it comes right down to it, the most important question you have to ask yourself is, do you have enough space and the right environment for shade trees? If the answer is *yes*, then let the planning begin.

Once you have determined which species or varieties of shade trees you want, it is time to go shopping. More so than any other plant you select from a nursery, a shade tree must meet certain criteria in order for you to make a responsible purchase. Mainly, you want to buy from a reputable nursery that stocks quality plant material. You should carefully inspect your potential trees to be sure the rootball is firm and a good size. Rootballs that are soft, broken, misshapened, or too small can spell doom for your new plant. Trees that are bare root or grown in containers are a bit easier to inspect for defects but the principles are the same. In addition to the rootball, check the main trunk and branches for abrasions or damage. If the damage is significant, you may want to take a pass. Last, make sure the leaves and canopy of the tree looks healthy and vigorous. Leaves that are weak, yellow, diseased, or badly damaged are signs of a stressed plant. When selecting shade trees, it is important to start off on the right foot with quality plant material.

General Care and Maintenance of Shade Trees

Like flowering trees and shrubs, shade trees need basic care to keep them healthy and productive. This includes training them at a young age to encourage a strong, main trunk, removing crossing or broken branches, and thinning out dead wood as it develops. Also, the preparation of the planting hole is very important because shade trees live in the soil you give them for the duration of their long lives. Follow the proper planting procedures outlined under "proper planting" on page 178 and be sure to keep your shade trees well watered for at least the first two growing seasons. With a little planning and proper care, you will be able to enjoy cool shade in your garden for many years to come.

Pin oaks (*Quercus palustris*) make excellent shade trees.

American Elm

Ulmus americana

Botanical Pronunciation
ULL-mus uh-mair-ih-KAY-nuh

Other Name White elm

Bloom Period and Seasonal Color
Bold, dark green, serrated leaves
during summer, graceful growth habit

Mature Height × Spread
60 to 80 feet × 40 to 60 feet

American elm was at one time one of the most popular and beloved native trees in America. Because of its beauty, picturesque vase-shaped weeping habit, durability, and versatility, American elms could be found by the thousands lining streets, providing shade to back yards, and gracing parks, golf courses, and public gardens. But starting in the 1970s, Dutch elm disease (DED) claimed many American elms, wiping them from most public and private landscapes. However, important research and breeding programs to develop disease-resistant cultivated varieties has created hope and excitement and thrust this popular tree back into the spotlight. Today, these easy-to-grow trees are once again gracing our large, expansive landscapes. For gardeners with limited space, American elm will get too large for your home garden but they can be planted and admired in larger settings that have the room to accommodate their size.

When, Where, and How to Plant

American elm is a fast-growing tree tolerating almost any type of soil as well as heat, drought, and pollution. American elm isn't picky but adding compost to poor soils at planting time will help them establish. American elm will even tolerate occasional flooding and seashore conditions. They thrive in moist, well-drained soil and full sun or partial shade. American elm should be planted in spring and are typically available as balled-and-burlapped trees at the local nursery. They need to be spaced a good distance from the house, garage, septic system, and other large trees. Spacing should be at least 20 to 30 feet.

Growing Tips

A 1- to 2-inch layer of mulch will benefit new plantings.

Regional Advice and Care

American elm is susceptible to many insects and diseases but DED and another disease known as elm yellows are the worst of them, although the latter is not seen as often. Damage from canker worms can partially or fully defoliate trees causing significant stress. While there are fungicide injections for DED and insecticide sprays that will control the worms, a licensed landscape professional should be consulted for those types of treatments. Pruning to train young trees is important mainly to remove excess growth, poor branching, and crossed branches.

Companion Planting and Design

American elm is one of the most spectacular specimens trees on the planet. It can be used as a lawn tree or to shade a patio. American elm also allows gardeners to grow grass underneath them, at least when they are younger, which is not always the case with European beech, maples, and other shade trees.

Try These

'Princeton' is one of the best for resistance to DED and is quite vigorous with large, leathery leaves. 'Valley Forge' has a classic vase-shape habit, dense canopy, and shows excellent resistance to DED. 'Jefferson' and 'Washington' also get good reviews for DED resistance.

European Beech

Fagus sylvatica

Botanical Pronunciation
FAY-gus sil-VAT-ih-kuh

Bloom Period and Seasonal Color
Glossy, dark green leaves in summer with golden yellow or bronze fall color; smooth, gray bark; majestic habit

Mature Height × Spread
50 to 60 feet × 35 to 45 feet or more

Zones Hardy to Zone 4

European beech is one of the most graceful and noble deciduous trees in both European and American gardens. For centuries, this elegant tree has been used as specimens, tall hedges, and to create allées on the great estates of the Gold Coast era. During this period from the late 1800s to the mid-1900s, beech trees were used in great numbers to craft large private estates and expansive public parks. Today, beech trees are as popular as ever and a wonderful addition to the landscape that can accommodate their large size. Many varieties are available to home gardeners including ones with purple, gold, and variegated leaves, weeping forms, and upright, slender growth habits. These long-lived trees will grace your landscape for generations, providing a great presence in the garden.

When, Where, and How to Plant
European beech requires well-drained, acidic, organic soil and full sun or partial shade. They do not tolerate poor soils and gardeners should not go to the trouble unless the soil is right for them. Be sure to incorporate a generous amount of compost into the soil at planting time. Beech can be purchased and planted in spring or fall as balled-and-burlapped or container-grown plants, although many growers feel spring is safer for success. Give beech trees plenty of room to grow since they look better when provided with ample room. Spacing should be at least 10 to 15 feet on smaller varieties and 20 to 30 feet on larger varieties.

Growing Tips
Adding a thin layer of crushed leaves or wood chips every spring or fall is essential to keep them thriving. A general-purpose, granular fertilizer in spring can be applied but you should take a soil sample every so often to be sure the trees need fertilizing. The soil needs to be kept moist, especially during hot, dry periods of summer.

Regional Advice and Care
European beech is susceptible to a wide variety of insects and diseases but the worst is a fungus known as bleeding canker, which attacks and damages the trunks of trees. Consult with a professional arborist to monitor and determine what plant health care program your trees might require including a pruning program.

Companion Planting and Design
European beech should be used as a single specimen in a sunny lawn area. It can be used in woodlands but large specimens will cast a lot of shade making it difficult to grow underneath them. Beech is usually grown with mountain laurel, rhododendron, dogwood, holly, and other acid-loving plants.

Try These
'Dawyck' grows very tall but only about 10 feet wide. 'Purpurea Pendula' is a dwarf, weeping variety with purple foliage all summer. 'Purple Fountains' is weeping but is taller and usually narrow. 'Tricolor' is a beautiful variegated with leaves splashed with combinations of pink, purple, and cream.

European Hornbeam

Carpinus betulus

Botanical Pronunciation
kar-PYE-nus BET-you-lus

Bloom Period and Seasonal Color
Catkins in spring; fruit clusters ripen to brown in fall

Mature Height × Spread
40 to 60 feet × 30 to 40 feet

Zones Hardy to Zone 5; to Zone 4 with protection

European hornbeam is a popular European native and a relative of birch. Hornbeam is a hardwood that is sometimes referred to as "ironwood" or "musclewood" because of the smooth, gray, sinuous, musclelike bark that is especially prominent on older specimens. Young trees are upright and pyramidal but as they mature they develop into wide-spreading, majestic trees with a rounded, broad growth habit. The lush, dark green leaves in summer turn yellowish green to yellow in fall. This tough tree can grow in many different landscape situations and tolerates a wide variety of environmental conditions including heat, drought, cold, and pollution. It is ideal as a specimen tree but can also tolerate excessive pruning and is typically used to form large hedges in Europe.

When, Where, and How to Plant
Hornbeam is really tough, tolerating sandy to clay soils and a wide range of soil pH. Although adaptable, incorporate compost to soils that are sandy or heavy clay-based. Ideally it should be grown in moist, well-drained soil and full sun but will also tolerate light shade. Hornbeam is very adaptable to poor soils, heat, drought, and pollution. Plants can be purchased in spring from a local nursery as container or balled-and-burlapped trees. Spacing depends on how you plan to use them. They can be planted 15 to 20 feet apart to grow as specimens or 3 to 4 feet apart to be grown as a hedge.

Growing Tips
Mulch new plantings to help them establish, especially in hot, dry areas. Even moisture in the soil is preferred. Fertilizer isn't necessary.

Regional Advice and Care
Hornbeam is rather pest free and requires little attention in that regard. Pruning is only necessary on a regular basis if hornbeam is being used as a hedge. In this case, the plant grows faster than normal and requires pruning once or twice a year.

Companion Planting and Design
Hornbeam is an excellent specimen tree near patios or in lawn areas. It is effective as a clipped hedge or tall screening plant. Hornbeam is an excellent companion to other birch relatives such as hophornbeam.

Try These
If you can't fit such a large tree in your garden, there are more upright and narrow cultivated varieties. 'Fastigiata' is distinctly upright and rounded making it ideal for gardens with limited space. This variety will grow 40 feet or more tall and half that wide. 'Frans Fontaine' is another upright variety with a tight, upright habit; it probably won't get as large as 'Fastigiata'. American hophornbeam (*Ostrya virginiana*) is a lovely deciduous tree with a dense, rounded habit and shaggy, grayish brown bark. The small, cigar-shaped flowers in groups of three are noticeable on the tips of the branches in winter. The papery fruit cluster resembles the fruit of hops, thus the name hophornbeam.

Ginkgo

Ginkgo biloba

Botanical Pronunciation
GINK-oh by-LOE-buh

Bloom Period and Seasonal Color
Unusual, fan-shaped leaves are golden yellow in fall; rough gray-brown bark offers winter interest

Mature Height × Spread
50 to 80 feet × 30 to 40 feet or more

Zones Hardy to Zone 4

Ginkgo is a very popular landscape tree and is also used as an edible and medicinal plant known to aid in reducing memory loss. Ginkgo is dioecious, with female and male flowers that are on separate trees, like holly. The female trees bear yellow, fleshy fruit which are quite odiferous, earning them the name "Stinko Ginkgo." For this reason, only the male trees are commercially available at local nurseries. Ginkgo is one of the exotic species that has adapted exceedingly well to the diverse climate of the United States, adapting to most landscape situations. As a young tree, ginkgo is a bit irregular and gawky but as it ages, it becomes magnificent and stately. For gardeners who have the room, ginkgo will provide shade and beauty throughout the seasons.

When, Where, and How to Plant

Ginkgo is extremely adaptable and will tolerate most soil types and pH except for poorly drained, waterlogged soil. Ideally, it should be planted in moist, well-drained soil and full sun or partial shade. When planting ginkgo, be sure to incorporate well-aged manure or compost into the planting hole. Ginkgo is readily available in nurseries, usually as balled-and-burlapped plants, and should be planted in spring. Spacing should be 20 to 40 feet from other large trees and the house or garage.

Growing Tips

Mulch new plants with 1 to 2 inches of wood chips to protect plants in times of drought. Even soil moisture is preferred but it can take dry periods. No fertilizer is needed.

Regional Advice and Care

Ginkgo is rather tolerant of heat, humidity, and drought and is also very resistant to insects and diseases. Pruning is not often needed regularly except for occasional dead wood removal. Pruning to shape ginkgo is nearly impossible since it takes on several distinct shapes as it matures.

Companion Planting and Design

Ginkgo really is a standalone tree and should be used as a specimen tree in a lawn area. It can also be incorporated into landscapes with mixed plantings such as flowering shrubs and perennials, but it will cast quite a bit of shade so the plants used with it should be tolerant of those conditions. The combination of green, fan-shaped leaves that turn brilliant yellow in fall, rough, textured bark, and diversity of growth habits makes this tree very desirable.

Try These

'Autumn Gold' offers a broad, conical growth habit and golden-yellow fall color. Princeton Sentry is an upright form with somewhat columnar growth habit for areas of the garden with limited space. There are many other varieties including weeping, dwarf, and variegated types, all which would be suited for the home garden. Spring Grove® is a beautiful dwarf form that reaches 6 feet high and 4 feet wide after 15 years.

Japanese Zelkova

Zelkova serrata

Botanical Pronunciation
ZELL-cove-uh sir-ATE-uh

Bloom Period and Seasonal Color
Dark green serrated leaves turn brilliant shades of orange and reddish maroon; exfoliating bark

Mature Height × Spread
35 to 45 feet × 20 to 30 feet

Zones Hardy to Zone 4

Japanese zelkova is a great example of an exotic species that has adapted well to the diverse landscapes of America. All too often it is assumed that exotic species, at some point, can become invasive. But this select tree defies that logic, growing in many different environments and adding beauty and function to the landscape. Zelkova is related to elm and is just as tough. It has a distinct upright, vase-shaped growth habit and exfoliating bark that is unmistakable in the winter landscape. It will tolerate almost any soil, grows fast, and is very resistant to pests, drought, heat, and cold. In some situations it is used as a replacement for elm because it doesn't grow as large. For lawns, streets, and patios, zelkova is a silver bullet in even the most challenging of landscapes.

When, Where, and How to Plant

Japanese zelkova prefers moist, well-drained soil and full sun or partial shade. However, it is incredibly tolerant of a wide variety is soil types, pH, and drainage issues, even tolerating occasional flooding. Even though Japanese zelkova requires little pampering, adding compost to heavy clay or sandy soils will keep trees happy. Japanese zelkova can be planted in spring or fall, although spring planting is preferred. Spacing should be between 15 to 20 feet.

Growing Tips

Supplemental fertilizer is usually not needed once established. Add a well-balanced, granular fertilizer in spring if needed. Adding a 1- to 2-inch mulch ring under new plantings will help them during stressful periods. Keep soil evenly moist for best growth but it tolerates dry periods as well.

Regional Advice and Care

Japanese zelkova is quite pest resistant even to the dreaded Dutch elm disease that plagues so many other elm relatives. Once trees are established they are virtually indestructible. Pruning when trees are young to encourage a strong, central trunk and good branching with no competing or crossing branches is about the only commitment trees need to succeed.

Companion Planting and Design

Japanese zelkova is ideal as a single specimen in a lawn or as a shade tree near a patio or driveway. It is an excellent street tree if your local municipality will allow them to be planted there. Because of their upright branching structure, zelkova will allow gardeners to grow plants underneath them such as grass or low-growing shrubs and shade-loving perennials such as hostas, hellebore, and heuchera. Zelkova offers that rare combination of a tree with four seasons of interest that is also easy to grow.

Try These

'Emerald Vase' is an upright tree with a strong vase-shaped growth habit and dark green foliage. 'Village Green' is also quite vigorous with more of a spreading habit.

Katsura Tree

Cercidiphyllum japonicum

Botanical Pronunciation
sur-sid-ih-FILL-um juh-PON-ih-kum

Bloom Period and Seasonal Color
Heart-shaped leaves emerge purple before maturing bluish green and changing to brilliant shades of yellow, orange, and reddish maroon

Mature Height × Spread
40 to 60 feet × 40 to 60 feet

Zones Hardy to Zone 4

Katsura tree is quite simply one of the most elegant, beautiful specimen shade trees you will ever encounter. From spring until late fall and even winter, this tree makes its presence known in the landscape. The reddish purple leaves unfurl in spring and develop into rounded, lustrous blue-green foliage. The fall color is nothing short of stunning with a combination of yellow, apricot, orange, and reddish maroon illuminating the landscape. As the leaves fall and dry on the ground, they emit a sweet fragrance that resembles burnt marshmallows. Although this lovely tree gets too large for the average residential landscape, there are several cultivated varieties that will offer the homeowner some options. Katsura tree is the quintessential specimen tree, offering shade all summer.

When, Where, and How to Plant

Katsura tree requires moist soil with plenty of organic matter; it's recommended to add compost when planting. It is very sensitive to drought and will partially defoliate during hot, dry summers. Full sun or partial shade is best for good foliage coloration in fall. Plants can be purchased in spring as balled-and-burlapped trees or in large containers and should be given plenty of water until they are established. Unless you are using a weeping or dwarf form of this tree, it will need at least 20 to 30 feet of space from other larger trees or structures.

Growing Tips

Mulching plants each spring helps moderate soil moisture and temperature. Katsura tree is quite surface-rooted so mulch will help to protect those roots from mowers and other machinery. Keep soil moist. Don't bother fertilizing.

Regional Advice and Care

Katsura tree is relatively pest free and will perform well as long as it is watered during times of drought. Regular pruning is not necessary except to thin out crossing or weak branches when it is young.

Companion Planting and Design

Katsura tree should be used as a single specimen or shade tree in a lawn area. It is ideal in gardens with moist conditions and near streams and ponds. It's a good companion plant for other moisture-lovers such as clethra, Virginia sweetspire, and river birch. Katsura tree should be placed a far enough distance from the septic system, drains, and any other underground infrastructure that roots could infiltrate.

Try These

'Pendulum' is a weeping form with a mounded, cascading habit growing to 15 to 25 feet tall with a comparable spread. 'Heronswood Globe' offers a rounded, dwarf habit to 15 feet tall. These dwarf or semi-dwarf forms are ideal for the gardener who wants this magnificent tree species for their garden but has limited space to offer. 'Red Fox' is a variety with reddish maroon leaves in spring that fade to green as the summer heat arrives.

Littleleaf Linden

Tilia cordata

Botanical Pronunciation
TILL-ee-uh core-DAY-tuh

Other Name Lime tree

Bloom Period and Seasonal Color
Inconspicuous, greenish white flowers in early summer; glossy, dark green leaves in summer

Mature Height × Spread
50 to 60 feet × 30 to 40 feet

Zones Hardy to Zone 4

Littleleaf linden is a well-known shade tree often found in lawns and lining streets in suburban and urban landscapes. Although in recent years it has taken a back seat to more mainstream trees such as American elm and ginkgo, linden still has great merit in the landscape. Littleleaf linden is a desirable species because it has a dense, pyramidal growth habit that can be used in a variety of landscape situations. Like most lindens, littleleaf linden is an easy-to-grow, adaptable tree that will require little to no maintenance once established. The leaves are smaller and more delicate than many other species of linden. Lindens are very attractive to bees and other pollinators and for those who keep honeybees, the sweet nectar of lindens also makes sweet honey.

When, Where, and How to Plant

Littleleaf linden is quite tolerant of soils, light exposure, and harsh conditions. They prefer moist, well-drained soil and full sun but will also grow in partial shade and sandy or clay soils. Although adaptable, adding compost to planting hole in poor soils will benefit new plantings significantly. Littleleaf linden can be purchased in spring as B&B trees. Spacing should be 15 to 20 feet from structures and other large trees.

Growing Tips

An application of a general-purpose, granular fertilizer will benefit plants in spring. Adding a light layer of wood chips after planting will help protect surface roots in times of drought and extreme cold. Soil should be kept evenly moist for best growth.

Regional Advice and Care

Littleleaf linden is susceptible to quite a few pests but none that are usually life threatening. Aphids, scale, and Japanese beetles can be troublesome but large, established trees do not usually need to be treated. On smaller specimens, check with your local arborist or nursery for recommendations. Pruning young trees to establish a strong, central trunk and to remove crossed or competing branches will help develop a structurally sound tree. On older specimens, sucker growth from the base is often an issue and this vegetation should be removed in midsummer.

Companion Planting and Design

Littleleaf linden is effective in groupings or as an allée lining a roadway, if you have the room; otherwise, it makes a nice specimen in a lawn. Lindens can be messy so planting too close to the house, patio, or driveway is not recommended. Littleleaf linden can be very effectively used with other deciduous trees such as elm, oak, and maple, as long as you have the room.

Try These

'Greenspire' is an excellent cultivar with emerald-green, glossy foliage and a tight, rounded growth habit. A cultivated variety of another species, 'Redmond' (*Tilia americana*) offers larger, dark green leaves and an upright, tightly pyramidal growth habit.

Maple

Acer spp.

Botanical Pronunciation
AY-sur

Bloom Period and Seasonal Color
Maples bloom in spring but are valued for their summer foliage, fall color, and winter bark interest

Mature Height × Spread
Up to 75 feet × 50 feet

Zones See "Try These"

There are over 200 species of maples that grow throughout the world, many of which are well adapted to grow on the East Coast of the United States. Maples are among the most identifiable trees in the landscape, growing just about everywhere. As a child, I remember the winged fruit known as samaras, floating through the air like mini helicopters. Maples are probably most beautiful in fall when their leaves change to brilliant shades of yellow, orange, and red. Beautiful majestic trees such as sugar maple (*Acer saccharum*), red maple (*A. rubrum*), and Japanese maple (*A. palmatum*) make up the majority of the maples found today in the landscape. But there are several other species mentioned here that don't get as large and grow much more slowly. Any of these maples that you choose should be used in a lawn setting or as a single specimen. It is important to *avoid* planting Norway maple (*A. platanoides*) since it is quite invasive.

When, Where, and How to Plant

Maples prefer moist, well-drained soil and full sun or partial shade. Maples benefit from organic matter in the soil. Sugar maple, paperbark maple, and striped maple are especially sensitive to heat, drought, and pollution. Red maple and trident maple tolerate less than optimum growing conditions without too many issues. Maples can be planted as balled-and-burlapped trees or in containers. Spring planting is ideal but fall planting is okay as long as it is early. Maples should be planted as single specimens or in small groups if you have the room, at least 20 feet or more depending on the species.

Growing Tips

Add a light layer of mulch applied once a year. Maples do not need regular fertilizer applications and this should only be done if there is a specific deficiency in the soil. Maples thrive in soils with even moisture.

Regional Advice and Care

Maples are susceptible to a wide range of insects and disease such as leaf spots, scale, aphids, and verticillium wilt. If you see a problem, be sure to take a sample of the plant to your local nursery or agricultural Extension office for positive identification and recommended treatment. Often, removing infected leaves or stems or, in serious cases, removing the diseased tree and planting a totally different species will solve any future problems. When you're pruning off diseased branches, always remember to sanitize your tools before pruning other trees.

Companion Planting and Design

Maples are ideal as single specimens in a lawn or patio or in a woodland garden. It's difficult to grow grass under a maple so forget it and just use mulch or a durable, shade-loving groundcover.

Try These

Japanese maple (*A. palmatum*) is the most cultivated maple today. This elegant tree is quite adaptable with delicate green or maroon, palm-shaped leaves and red fall color. Japanese maple typically grows 20 to 25 feet tall and wide but it can get larger. 'Sango Kaku' is a variety with pinkish red

plated bark make this a four-season tree. Trident maple is extremely adaptable and will tolerate less than ideal conditions. Trident maple can grow up to 35 feet tall with less of a spread. Hardy to Zone 5.

Paperbark maple (*A. griseum*) offers cinnamon to reddish brown bark that peels off like paper and is most noticeable in fall and winter. The dark green, trifoliate leaves turn brilliant shades of red in fall. This elegant tree is a slow grower but it will eventually reach 20 to 30 feet tall. This maple is a bit sensitive so be sure to plant it in good soil and adequate sunlight. Hardy to Zone 5.

Striped maple or moosewood (*A. pensylvanicum*) is a native tree with smooth, green bark highlighted by white stripes and dark green leaves that turn brilliant shades of yellow in autumn. It is most suited in a shaded garden but will also grow in full sun as long as it is well watered and mulched. For best performance, plant in moist, acidic soil with plenty of organic matter. 'White Tigress' is a fast-growing hybrid with pronounced white stripes on its stems and twigs.

Sugar maple (*A. saccharum*) is a native that is used to make maple syrup. Mature trees can become quite large and display yellow or orange fall color and rough, gray-brown bark. Sugar maple gets quite large and must be sited in large open areas where they have plenty of room. They do not tolerate hot, dry polluted conditions and require moist well-drained soil and full sun. Legacy® is a good variety that is drought tolerant and offers stunning fall color. Hardy to Zone 4.

Red maple (*A. rubrum*) is also a native that grows quite large but it is a bit more tolerant of a variety of growing conditions. It will handle both dry and wet soil conditions and full sun, partial shade, or full shade. The bright red fall color is most vibrant in full sun. October Glory® and Red Sunset® are still the best for vigor and fall color but several hybrids with silver maple resulting in *A. × freemanii*, including Autumn Blaze®, are worth trying as they have good vigor, drought tolerance, and excellent red fall color.

stems in winter and var. *dissectum* or the cut leaf type offers a mounded, graceful habit and finely cut foliage. Hardy to Zone 5.

Trident maple (*A. buergerianum*) is a less popular maple whose unusual three-lobed, glossy leaves, orange to reddish maroon fall color, and rough

Oak

Quercus spp.

Botanical Pronunciation
KWUR-kus

Bloom Period and Seasonal Color
Dark green leaves change to brilliant shades
of yellow, red, bronze, and orange in fall;
textured bark

Mature Height × Spread
50 to 80 feet × 50 to 80 feet but quite variable

Zones Varies by species

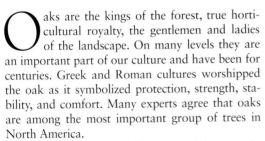

Oaks are the kings of the forest, true horticultural royalty, the gentlemen and ladies of the landscape. On many levels they are an important part of our culture and have been for centuries. Greek and Roman cultures worshipped the oak as it symbolized protection, strength, stability, and comfort. Many experts agree that oaks are among the most important group of trees in North America.

Oaks are also unrivaled in terms of their importance to the environment, providing habitat and food for a wide range of animals and insects and gracing our natural and cultivated landscapes with their beauty. Acorns provide a high protein food source for a wide variety of mammals. In the garden and the natural woodland, oaks provide the overhead canopy that so many plants and animals rely on for protection.

There is no denying that oaks are very diverse, comprised of about 450 species growing throughout the world. In general, oaks are slow-growing, hardwood, deciduous trees thriving in a woodland setting. In the fall landscape, it's hard not to admire oak trees as they display a rich assortment of yellow, orange, bronze, red, and brown. During winter, oaks provide structure to an otherwise barren landscape.

The following is a sampling of several of the most commonly found oak species in New York and New Jersey. White oak (*Quercus alba*), scarlet oak (*Q. coccinea*), pin oak (*Q. palustris*), and red oak (*Q. rubra*) are four well-known species that offer unique ornamental value and function in the landscape.

Of these four species, all develop into tall trees with the ability to get quite large, even in the residential landscape. The white oak group possesses white or gray, flaking rough bark while the red oak group offers gray or brown rough bark with patches of smooth areas.

White oak and red oak offer a spreading, broad canopy that consumes the landscape with its grandeur. Pin oak has a tight, pyramidal habit when young that eventually develops into an upright tree with an oval canopy and strong central trunk. Scarlet oak gets its name from the intensely colored, scarlet red fall foliage that seems to light the landscape on fire.

Oaks make great specimens, groupings, and lawn trees, but they *must* be given their space otherwise they can become more of a liability than an asset. Oaks are best suited for large sites such as parks, public gardens, golf courses, and university campuses, but home gardeners who have oaks on their property or have the room to plant new ones, consider yourself lucky. A landscape graced with the presence of oak trees is one of the great joys of gardening!

When, Where, and How to Plant

The species of oaks mentioned here prefer moist, well-drained, acidic soil that is rich in organic matter. Although oaks tolerate lawn underneath their canopy, I highly recommended you consider putting a mulch ring around your tree at least out to the drip line, if it is feasible. Rather than ripping up the lawn, mowing the grass very short and putting a layer of newspaper (newsprint, not glossy paper)

Growing Tips

Oaks greatly benefit from organic matter in the soil and many gardeners use oak leaves to make compost. If you do this, you can use this compost to incorporate into the soil of new trees or as a top dressing on the soil surface of existing trees. But only apply a very light layer (1 inch or less) near existing trees so their root system is not covered too much. A soil test before you plant a new oak is wise to ensure that you are working with acidic soil, as oaks prefer this over more alkaline soils. Oaks prefer soil with even moisture.

Regional Advice and Care

Oaks do not respond well to overpruning and removing live branches should be kept to a minimum. Dead or broken branches can be removed in winter when they are easier to detect. Proper pruning cuts should be made so that the tree heals those wounds properly. This information can be found in the "Pruning" section on page 180.

Companion Planting and Design

Oak is a specimen tree that should be incorporated into the overall plan for your garden. They should not be ignored or overlooked but brought into the design of the landscape as focal points. Oaks typically provide the shade and shelter that shade-loving flowering shrubs, broadleaved evergreens, and perennials need to survive. Oaks are excellent companions to rhododendron, azalea, holly, camellia, hosta, daylily, and many other landscape plants.

Try These

Here are a few "landscape-friendly" varieties of oak that require less space. Green Pillar® is a columnar variety of pin oak that grows 50 feet tall but only 15 feet wide. Pin oak and scarlet oak are hardy to Zone 4. Several English oak hybrids offer upright, narrow habits and lustrous, dark green foliage including Crimson Spire™, Kindred Spirit®, Regal Prince®, and Skyrocket®. It is incredibly important to continue to plant hardwood species such as oaks in our natural and cultivated landscapes where appropriate. Today, too much attention is paid to color and the short-term "wow" in the garden and less to the long-term viability of our landscapes and the environment as a whole.

down with a 2-inch layer of crushed leaves or wood chips will benefit oak trees greatly. Oaks prefer full sun or partial shade but will adapt to full shade as well. Oaks can be purchased as bare-root seedlings, container plants, or as balled-and-burlapped specimens that should be planted in spring. Oaks need their space and they should be sited at least 30 to 40 feet from the house, garage, septic system, and any other important infrastructure.

River Birch

Betula nigra

Botanical Pronunciation
BET-you-luh NYE-gruh

Other Name Red birch

Bloom Period and Seasonal Color
Dark, glossy green leaves turn yellow in fall;
flaking cream to cinnamon-brown bark is
interesting year-round

Mature Height × Spread
40 to 70 feet × 40 to 60 feet

Birch is a very identifiable tree in the landscape with striking bark, that is interesting all year. Many birch species are best suited for cold, northern climates and with global warming more of an issue than ever, adaptability of birch is important. Of all the native species of birch, river birch (*Betula nigra*) is the most durable and pest free. It is well adapted for wet soils but will thrive in well-drained soils as well. There is variation among this species with bark color, but most often this species has a creamy to cinnamon-brown, flaking bark that peels in sheets. A well-known variety called Heritage® offers lighter, creamy white bark with salmon tones that is spectacular, but it's not pure white like most birch.

When, Where, and How to Plant
River birch performs well in moist, well-drained, acidic soil but will grow well in poorly drained soils too. Adding compost to heavy clay or sandy soils is beneficial. Site in full sun or partial shade. They tolerate heat, humidity, and drought but in very dry conditions, the leaves on the interior of a plant will often fall prematurely. In high pH soils, the leaves will turn yellow and become chlorotic. Plants are easy to transplant and can be purchased in large containers or as balled and burlapped in spring. River birch gets quite large so give it ample room, at least 20 to 30 feet from any other large trees or structures.

Growing Tips
Mulch new plantings until they establish. Soil needs to be moist but it's remarkably adaptable. This species is not picky about fertilizer.

Regional Advice and Care
Many species of birch are susceptible to damaging insects such as bronze birch borer and leaf miners but that's not usually the case with this species. It is rock solid when it comes to diseases and insect infestations. With the exception of some pruning to remove crossed branches or to train this tree at a young age, its maintenance is minimal.

Companion Planting and Design
Birches can be trained as single stem trees or as a clump, which usually has three or more main trunks. River birch can be used as a single specimen lawn tree, along streams and ponds, and are also fast-growing shade trees. River birch works well with other shade-loving plants such as clethra, Virginia sweetspire, hosta, and heuchera.

Try These
Heritage® is by far the most accepted and popular of all of the cultivars available. Its vigor and creamy to cinnamon-brown bark is hard to beat. Dura-Heat® is another good selection that does not get as large as Heritage®. Fox Valley® is a true dwarf growing to 12 feet by 12 feet over twenty years. Paper birch (*B. papyrifera*) is another native birch with pure white bark that peels off like sheets of paper. Although not as tough, it works well in the Northeast.

BROADLEAVED EVERGREENS AND CONIFERS

FOR NEW YORK & NEW JERSEY

Evergreens always have foliage, retaining their leaves throughout the year. Actually, evergreens do have a "fall," dropping their older leaves and retaining their younger foliage. Just look around in autumn and you will see pines, hollies, and even rhododendrons shedding older foliage on the inner part of the plants. In the winter, evergreens come to the forefront and are most noticeable in the bare landscape once deciduous plants have shed their foliage. Evergreens are the staple that provides structure, color, and a variety of textures. In addition, evergreens provide protection and habitat for wildlife, especially conifers, which are a favorite of many bird species.

Selecting Evergreens for the Home Landscape

Evergreens come in many shapes and sizes and serve different landscape functions. There are two main categories: narrow-leaved or needled evergreens such as pine, spruce and juniper and broadleaved evergreens such as holly, rhododendron, mountain laurel, and pieris.

Selecting evergreens for the home garden can be challenging *and* rewarding. Evergreens provide a great presence in the landscape while offering a variety of practical functions. Evergreens can divide or enclose a garden as formal and informal hedges or tall screens or can be used as a single specimen or as foundation plantings to soften structures. But proper siting of evergreens is important in order to ensure their success. For example, placing certain broadleaved evergreens on a southern exposure can cause them to be more susceptible to winter damage known as sunscald. Or putting certain conifers in too much shade will result in open, leggy plants that lose their vigor over time.

General Care and Maintenance of Evergreens

Evergreens, more so than any other plant group, have specific requirements that must be met in order to thrive. Because they retain their foliage all year, evergreens are more vulnerable to fluctuations in temperature, moisture, and light. This vulnerability can affect the rest of the garden. For example, when a large tree in the back yard is lost after a bad storm, that leaves a huge void. That means more heat and exposure

A house surrounded by evergreens with snow on the ground is a lovely sight.

to plants that were once in shade and soil that will dry out quicker than before. Or a windy site can present added challenges to evergreens that have to adapt to these sometimes brutal conditions. A sudden or even gradual change in environmental conditions can negatively affect your prized evergreens and their performance.

There are several ways to protect and nurture evergreens. In fall as the cool weather and shorter days arrive plants begin to go into dormancy. Before you turn off the irrigation system or water spigots, water the entire garden thoroughly. Adequate moisture in the soil going into winter will be especially beneficial to evergreens. In addition, adding a light layer of mulch in fall will moderate soil moisture and temperature, reducing the likelihood of major fluctuations. With new plantings, or in areas where wind and exposure are an issue in winter, there are several ways to protect evergreens. Products known as anti-desiccants can be sprayed on the leaves in late fall. These products create a protective film on the leaves to protect them from drying out and from sunscald. (It is important to read the product label carefully before applying them.) Anti-desiccants should *not* be used on evergreens with colored leaves such as Colorado blue spruce and blue Atlas cedar. On smaller plants, a physical barrier can be used, such as wrapping your plants with burlap and twine. This wrapping is a low-cost, effective way to protect valuable shrubs but must be removed by early spring.

Whether it's the soft, fine texture of a white pine or the bold, thick foliage of camellias, evergreens have an undeniable presence in the landscape. When properly incorporated into an overall garden scheme with deciduous trees and shrubs, groundcovers, perennials and other garden plants, they can create a four-season landscape. Evergreens are always interesting and with a little care and planning will add exceptional beauty, interest, and function to the garden.

Arborvitae

Thuja spp.

Botanical Pronunciation THOO-yuh

Bloom Period and Seasonal Color
Medium to dark green, flat, scalelike, aromatic foliage and grayish brown bark

Mature Height × Spread
40 to 60 feet × 15 to 25 feet but usually smaller in cultivated landscapes

Zones Western arborvitae is hardy to Zone 5 but also 4 with some protection

Arborvitae, also called white cedar, is a well-known evergreen that has been used in residential landscapes for many years and is valued for its fast growth rate, adaptability, and uniform habit. American arborvitae (*Thuja occidentalis*) is a very common and somewhat overused evergreen used as informal hedges, tall screens, and in foundation plantings. Its West Coast cousin, western arborvitae (*T. plicata*), is a lesser-known species but is superior in some respects. For example, American arborvitae is more prone to deer browsing and storm damage from ice and snow than western arborvitae. With the loss of Canadian hemlock (*Tsuga canadensis*) as a viable landscape plant due to insect problems, western arborvitae has become one of the main evergreens of choice to replace them. The western arborvitae is also a superior choice over Leyland cypress.

When, Where, and How to Plant
Arborvitae is quite adaptable, tolerating sandy, well-drained soils and heavy, clay soils. They prefer well-drained, moist, organic soils so add compost to sandy or clay-based soils. Full sun or partial shade is acceptable but western arborvitae specifically is very shade tolerant. Arborvitae should be planted in spring and can be purchased as container or balled-and-burlapped plants. Spacing should be 6 to 8 feet or more.

Growing Tips
Adding granular fertilizer is only necessary if there is a nutrient deficiency. One to 2 inches of wood chips or pine straw will benefit both new and established plantings. Keep soil evenly moist, especially until plants are established.

Regional Advice and Care
Arborvitae is susceptible to leaf miner, bagworm, and spider mites but this is mostly prevalent of American arborvitae. Arborvitae do not respond as well as yew and holly to severe pruning and should only be sheared or pruned within green leaves and stems, not to bare wood.

Companion Planting and Design
Arborvitae can be used as tall screens, foundation plantings, and as single specimens. Shrubby forms can be sheared into formal or informal hedges. Arborvitae is a great companion to falsecypress, yew, and other fine-textured evergreens.

Try These
'Emerald' also known as 'Smaragd', is a very popular cultivar of American arborvitae with emerald green, fine leaves and a tight, pyramidal growth habit growing 10 to 15 feet tall × 3 feet wide. Western arborvitae offers a more graceful, loose, pyramidal growth habit and dark green, glossy leaves that are coarser than American arborvitae. It is more pest resistant and tolerant of wind and snow than American arborvitae. It can grow 50 feet or more tall and 15 to 25 feet wide, making it an excellent replacement for spruce and hemlock. 'Atrovirens' is a vigorous grower with deep green foliage and a graceful, pyramidal habit. 'Green Giant' is a hybrid with a tight, pyramidal growth habit, growing 30 to 40 feet tall but staying very narrow. 'Virescens' has a narrow, conical habit in deep green foliage making it suitable for a garden with limited space.

Arizona Cypress

Cupressus arizonica

Botanical Pronunciation
koo-PRESS-us ar-ih-ZAWN-ick-uh

Bloom Period and Seasonal Color
Thin, blue-green foliage, interesting round cones, and reddish brown, exfoliating bark

Mature Height × Spread
30 to 40 feet × 20 to 25 feet

Zones Hardy to Zone 7

Arizona cypress is a Southwestern native with an upright growth habit and unusual, blue-green foliage that is long and slender. Arizona cypress is a close relative to juniper and has a similar appearance and cultural requirements. This plant is well known for its remarkable heat, drought, and humidity tolerance. It thrives in almost any soil as long as it is well drained. Arizona cypress is ideal in hot, exposed sites and is especially useful at the seashore. With so much emphasis these days on global climate change and the potential for damaging storms and flooding near the shore, Arizona cypress is an excellent choice for the exposed landscape. Arizona cypress is also moderately deer resistant.

When, Where, and How to Plant
Arizona cypress is a carefree, easy-to-grow plant that thrives in hot, dry conditions. It will grow in heavy clay or sandy, rocky soils but will also grow well in rich garden loam. It is important that whatever soil Arizona cypress is growing in is well drained. This plant is also well adapted for exposed, windy sites. Full sun is best but this plant will also grow in partial shade as long as there is good air circulation. Plants are usually sold in containers and can also be sold as B&B plants but be sure the rootball is firm and not soft. Spacing should be 6 to 8 feet apart.

Growing Tips
In poor soils, adding compost will help plants establish and help retain soil moisture in times of drought. Mulching new plants will help during the heat and drought of summer. Once plants are established, soil can be kept on the dry side.

Regional Advice and Care
Arizona cypress is pest and disease resistant and as long as it has adequate sun and drainage, it will perform well and look good. Pruning to encourage dense growth can be done in the early summer and be sure not to prune too late in the growing season.

Companion Planting and Design
Arizona cypress is very suitable as a tall screen or hedge and in windy sites can be used as a windbreak. Arizona cypress is very effective in seashore conditions as well. They can be used as a single specimen and will stand out as a focal point in a mixed border. Arizona cypress will even adapt to being grown in large containers where they can be used on a patio.

Try These
Arizona cypress offers several striking cultivated varieties with bright blue foliage. 'Blue Ice' is a vigorous grower with silvery blue foliage, mahogany-red stems, and a strongly conical growth habit. 'Carolina Sapphire' is similar to 'Blue Ice' with striking blue foliage but it has a more open growth habit. 'Golden Pyramid' and 'Sulphurea' are two varieties with showy golden-yellow foliage.

Camellia

Camellia spp.

Botanical Pronunciation KUH-meel-e-uh

Bloom Period and Seasonal Color
Single, semi-double, and double flowers of white, pink, red, and bi-color types; thick, glossy leaves

Mature Height × Spread
8 to 12 feet × 6 to 10 feet

Zones Hardy to Zone 6 and are best in protected areas

Camellias are relatives of the tea plant and have been cultivated for centuries. They are native to Asia and became very popular in Europe before being imported to America in the late 1800s. The tea plant (*Camellia sinensis*) is very valuable as it is used to make one of the most popular beverages in the world but it is not an ornamental plant. However, Japanese camellia (*C. japonica*) and sasanqua camellia (*C. sasanqua*) are both ornamental and functional in the landscape. Historically, these two species were only grown in greenhouses in New York and New Jersey because they were not believed to be winter hardy. But today, many new selections and hybrids have been developed and will grow outdoors in Zones 6 and 7.

When, Where, and How to Plant
Camellia thrives in well-drained, acidic, organic soil. Camellia tolerates heavy, clay soils but well-aged compost should be used at planting. Camellias perform best in part shade and need mulch and even moisture in more sun. Camellias are typically sold as container plants and should be planted in the spring. Planting in fall is risky because they do not have enough time to establish. Spacing on camellias is 3 to 5 feet apart, depending on the species and variety.

Growing Tips
Adding a light layer of wood chips or pine straw to camellia plantings, whether new or established, is important to their success. Granular fertilizers are not typically needed unless there is a nutrient deficiency in the soil, so take a soil sample before

planting. Camellia prefer consistent moisture in the soil and do not like to dry out.

Regional Advice and Care
Camellias are pest and disease resistant and rather low maintenance once established. Success is found in proper siting and initial planting. Keep camellias away from a southern exposure in the garden, as that tends to burn plants in winter. As long as camellias are properly planted in the right soil and protected from harsh light exposure, they will do just fine. Prune right after flowering has finished in early summer. Do not shear plants, as that tends to ruin their natural shape and reduce flowering.

Companion Planting and Design
Camellias are very effective in a shade garden along with holly, azalea, hosta, and other shade-loving plants. They are also effective in foundation plantings, groupings, and mixed borders and as a single specimen.

Try These
Two groups of camellias are available that are worth trying. The April series includes 'April Kiss', 'April Blush', 'April Remembered', 'April Rose', and 'April Tryst'; selections of Japanese camellia that are hardy and colorful. Hybrids of sasanqua camellia known as the Winter series are equally as diverse and beautiful, but instead of blooming in spring, they bloom in fall and early winter. The Winter series includes 'Winter's Charm', 'Winter's Rose', 'Winter's Star', and 'Snow Flurry'.

Drooping Leucothoe

Leucothoe fontanesiana

Botanical Pronunciation
loo-KOTH-oh-ee fon-taynz-ee-AY-nuh

Bloom Period and Seasonal Color
White, urn-shaped flowers in spring; glossy, dark green pointed leaves

Mature Height × Spread
3 to 6 feet × 3 to 6 feet

Zones Hardy to Zone 5; to Zone 4 with protection

Drooping leucothoe is a native evergreen shrub that is not used often enough in the home garden. It is related to rhododendrons and azaleas and is ideal for a shaded garden with good soil and even moisture. It is called drooping leucothoe because it displays graceful branches and a spreading growth habit. The clusters of dangling urn-shaped flowers in spring look similar to pieris (andromeda) flowers. Even when not in flower this shrub is interesting with lustrous, dark green leaves that are smooth and pointed. As cold weather arrives in early winter, the leaves often turn a striking bronze to purple color. This durable plant is quite shade tolerant, the flowers are beneficial to pollinators, and it has also shown good deer resistance. Because of its graceful habit, leucothoe should be used in informal plantings.

When, Where, and How to Plant
As a relative of rhododendron, drooping leucothoe prefers moist, acidic, well-drained soils with plenty of organic matter so add compost to the planting hole. Do not plant leucothoe in dry, rocky soils or poorly drained soils. This plant preforms best when sited in a cool, shaded area of the garden; it will even tolerate dense shade. Leucothoe can be grown in full sun but it must be mulched and watered regularly. Leucothoe should be planted in spring from containers and spaced 3 to 5 feet apart in odd numbered groupings.

Growing Tips
Add a light layer of wood chips or pine straw on the soil surface. Apply a low-nitrogen fertilizer is spring and keep soil evenly moist.

Regional Advice and Care
Leucothoe is low maintenance once established although leaf spot can be a problem so avoid overhead watering in deep shade and areas with poor air circulation. Selective or rejuvenation pruning can be done in early spring and that will sacrifice one year of flowers. Removing the oldest stems every few years will keep older plants vigorous and compact.

Companion Planting and Design
Leucothoe is best suited for a shade garden with moist conditions. It is an excellent companion to rhododendron, aucuba, camellia, viburnum, dogwood, hosta, and other shade lovers. It can be used as a low screen or informal hedge but should be left natural and not sheared regularly as that will ruin its graceful appearance.

Try These
'Girard's Rainbow' is variegated with irregular, swirled combinations of green, white, and pink in the leaf. 'Scarletta' offers stunning, glossy scarlet-red new growth that matures to deep green and turns brilliant burgundy red in winter. Another species known as dog hobble (*L. axillaris*) is gaining in popularity and offers additional cultivated varieties. It differs from drooping leucothoe mainly by its smaller leaves and overall size.

Gold Dust Plant

Aucuba japonica

Botanical Pronunciation
UH-coo-bah jah-pon-ick-KUH

Bloom Period and Seasonal Color
Lustrous, dark green or variegated leaves with speckles, splotches, and streaks of gold

Mature Height × Spread
6 to 10 feet × 6 to 8 feet

Zones Hardy to Zone 7

Gold dust plant got its name because it looks very similar to a houseplant with the same name that is only suitable for tropical climates. Although the species has green leaves, the variegated types are far more popular, thus the name gold dust plant. Its broad, glossy leaves with gold accents and dense, rounded habit are very effective in a shade garden, providing a colorful accent and bold texture. Gold dust plant is "dioecious," meaning, like a holly, male and female flowers are borne on separate plants. So female plants that are pollinated by male plants will display a glossy red berry in fall and winter. Besides being colorful, gold dust plant is remarkably adaptable, tolerating intense shade and even clay soils.

When, Where, and How to Plant
Gold dust plant prefers moist, acidic, well-drained soil with generous amounts of organic matter. Gold dust plant can tolerate clay soils but incorporate compost or manure at planting. It is one of those broadleaved evergreens that is well adapted to shade and should not be placed in full sun. Avoid very dry soils and hot, exposed locations. Gold dust is best planted in spring from containers bought at a local nursery. Spacing should be 3 to 5 feet apart.

Growing Tips
Gold dust plant benefits from a 1- to 2-inch layer of wood chips or pine straw mulch to keep their roots cool in the summer. Gold dust plant requires evenly moist soil with no major fluctuations.

Regional Advice and Care
Gold dust plant is rather pest free and requires little maintenance. In too much sun plants will get sunscald so ideally they should be placed on an eastern exposure with afternoon shade. Once plants establish, regular pruning is not usually necessary and should only be done to cut back leggy plants or to remove dead branches. Shearing into tightly growing hedges is possible but should be done only if necessary, as it will alter their natural, broad shape.

Companion Planting and Design
Gold dust plant is an excellent companion plant to rhododendron, holly, camellia, and evergreen viburnum. It is one of the useful plants that can be used as a single specimen or in groupings. Gold dust plant can really brighten up a dark, shady area of the garden with its brightly colored foliage.

Try These
The straight species of aucuba has lush, dark green leaves that are beautiful. 'Serratifolia' offers dark green foliage, serrated along the edges. 'Variegata' has green leaves with gold speckles and is still the most common variety found in the garden. 'Mr. Goldstrike' has a similar pattern but is more striking with more gold than green on the leaves. 'Picturata' is a unique variety with dark green leaves with bright gold centers.

Heavenly Bamboo

Nandina domestica

Botanical Pronunciation
nan-DYE-nuh doe-MESS-tih-kuh

Bloom Period and Seasonal Color White
flowers in late spring/early summer, followed by red
berries; coppery to purplish red leaves mature to a
blue green, developing a reddish color in winter

Mature Height × Spread
6 to 8 feet × 4 to 6 feet but cultivated varieties
are often smaller

Zones Hardy to Zone 6

Although the common name of this plant is heavenly bamboo, it is not related to the invasive bamboo plants known to be problematic in many landscapes. Heavenly bamboo is a native of China and a relative to barberry, which are known for their impressive durability in the landscape. Heavenly bamboo has several ornamental qualities including lacey, fine foliage; clusters of white flowers; and red berries that last the entire fall and winter seasons. Birds will not usually eat the berries because they are hard and waxy. The upright, thin stems form dense clumps of thick growth. In the winter the thin, glossy leaves will be tinted red, especially in full sun. Heavenly bamboo is versatile, growing in many conditions, even dry soils and dense shade.

When, Where, and How to Plant
For best results, heavenly bamboo should be planted in full sun or part shade and moist, well-drained soil. They will tolerate both sandy and heavy clay soils and varying soil pH as well. Heavenly bamboo *is* very tough, but to start plants off right, incorporate compost in sandy and heavy clay soils. In too much shade, plants will become leggy and will lose their lower branches. Plants are usually available in spring in containers and should be spaced 2 to 4 feet apart, depending in the variety chosen. In harsh winters, plants may lose their foliage.

Growing Tips
Mulching is not necessary once it's established but mulch will help during times of heat and drought stress. Fertilizer applications are not usually necessary unless there is a specific nutrient deficiency in the soil. Heavenly bamboo prefers even soil moisture until it's established.

Regional Advice and Care
Heavenly bamboo does not typically need regular pruning unless you are using it as a hedge or screen. Removing older stems and leaving young, vigorous ones can selectively prune older plants. Pruning should be performed in late winter or early spring, while the shrub is still dormant. Like other members of the barberry family, heavenly bamboo is quite tolerant of insects, disease, drought, heat, and humidity.

Companion Planting and Design
Heavenly bamboo can be used as a foundation planting, hedge, and screen or in a mixed border. Because of its upright habit, strong stems, and its fine foliage, it makes a great accent plant and can be used with other fine-textured plants.

Try These
'Atropurpurea Nana' is an upright grower to 2 feet tall with yellowish green leaves highlighted with reddish purple coloration that eventually turn red in winter. 'Harbour Dwarf' is another compact form that is quite graceful as it matures with green leaves that are tinged with red in winter. 'Woods Dwarf' offers exceptional red foliage color in winter and a dense, low, mounded habit. There are several yellow-fruited forms that go under different trade names.

Hinoki False Cypress

Chamaecyparis obtusa

Botanical Pronunciation
CAMY-sigh-pur-is ob-TWO-suh

Bloom Period and Seasonal Color
Emerald-green, scalelike leaves; reddish brown, flaking bark on older specimens

Mature Height × Spread
50 to 75 feet × 10 to 20 feet or more

Hinoki false cypress is a very elegant, choice conifer that looks similar to arborvitae in texture, but offers more ornamental qualities in the landscape. In fact, although false cypress, arborvitae, and junipers are all related, Hinoki false cypress is considered the Ferrari of the three. Its circular, wavy growth pattern gives this evergreen a very graceful appearance. False cypress is very slow growing and does not require much pruning or primping. As specimens get older, they develop into broad, majestic specimens that have an unmistakable presence in the landscape. As the plant matures, it displays a reddish brown bark that sheds off in sheets. Hinoki false cypress is excellent as a specimen, in containers, and mixed with other conifers. It has also been reported to have moderately good deer resistance.

When, Where, and How to Plant
Hinoki false cypress requires moist, well-drained garden soil. It will not tolerate heavy, clay soils which are poorly drained or very sandy, dry soils. Hinoki false cypress benefits from organic soils so be sure to incorporate a generous amount of compost when planting. Full sun or partial shade is acceptable but dense shade is not recommended as it causes plants to look open and weak. Hinoki false cypress is also not suited for windy, exposed sites. New plantings are available in the spring as B&B plants or in containers. Spacing largely depends on if you are planting the straight species or a dwarf variety. In general, space Hinoki false cypress 15 to 20 feet from other large trees or the house. Smaller varieties can be planted much closer.

Growing Tips
Ideally, in addition to being planted in rich garden loam, it should be given even moisture throughout the growing season. Adding a light layer of wood chips will keep roots cool and retain soil moisture. Use a general-purpose fertilizer in spring on new plantings.

Regional Advice and Care
Hinoki false cypress is not plagued by diseases and insects but at the same time it's very sensitive. If soil type, drainage, or light conditions are not right, stressed plants could be more susceptible to root rot and other problems. Pruning should be kept to an absolute minimum, as it will ruin their graceful habit and cause stress.

Companion Planting and Design
Hinoki false cypress is a magnificent specimen and will only get better with age. It is also effective in containers for the patio and smaller-growing varieties can be used in rock gardens, foundation plantings, and a mixed planting with other dwarf plants.

Try These
'Crippsii' is an upright grower with bright gold foliage and is used as an accent plant. 'Nana Gracilis' and 'Nana' are two popular dwarf varieties that are very slow growing and only grow to 6 feet tall. 'Split Rock' offers striking blue foliage on the newest growth.

Holly

Ilex spp.

Botanical Pronunciation EYE-lex

Bloom Period and Seasonal Color Male and female flowers are not showy but female plants have red, yellow, or black fruit in fall and winter (depending on the species) as well as lustrous, evergreen leaves and a dense growth habit

Mature Height × Spread
5 to 40 feet × 8 to 20 feet depending on species

Holly is one of the most diverse and versatile evergreens in the world. It ranges from spreading shrubs with smooth leaves to large trees with more traditional spiny leaves. There are quite a few species that thrive in New York and New Jersey, functioning as foundation plantings, formal and informal hedges, and specimens. Holly is dioecious; female plants exhibit showy fruit from late summer until late winter. Holly is adaptable to a wide range of landscape conditions, from sunny and dry to shady and moist. While there are some diseases and insects that will attack holly, none are usually serious enough to cause significant issues. Holly is important to wildlife, providing shelter and habitat and edible, high protein fruit. Some species are resistant to deer browsing.

When, Where, and How to Plant
Holly prefers moist, acidic, well-drained soil and full sun or partial shade. However, many species are tolerant of sandy or clay soils and dense shade. Certain species are even adapted for hot, dry seashore conditions. Incorporate compost into soils that are very sandy. Plant in spring, although fall planting is acceptable as long as it is early (September). Spacing depends on the species but in general, it should be 3 to 5 feet for shrubby types and 15 to 20 feet or more for tree types.

Growing Tips
A general-purpose, granular fertilizer applied in spring will benefit new plantings in poor soils. A 1- to 2-inch layer of mulch is recommended in hot, exposed locations. Keep soil evenly moist until established.

Regional Advice and Care
Holly tolerates pruning extremely well and severe pruning should be done in early spring. Plants can be pruned back to bare stems and will regenerate most of the time as long as they are healthy. If light shearing is needed, do that in early summer.

Companion Planting and Design
Japanese holly (*Ilex crenata*) grows to Zone 5 and offers a dense, shrubby habit and small, smooth leaves similar to boxwood. Inkberry holly (*I. glabra*) has smooth, linear leaves and grows to Zone 4. Both Japanese and inkberry holly have small black berries in the fall. Meserveae holly (*I. × meserveae*) is a hybrid with dark green, spiny leaves and red berries growing to Zone 4. Winterberry holly (*I. verticillata*) is a deciduous holly with smooth leaves that drop in fall. The red or yellow fruit is stunning in early winter before birds strip them clean. All of these species can function in groups, foundation plantings, or as a single specimen. Plant a male pollinator of the same or related species in close proximity to female plants for consistent fruiting.

Try These
'Dragon Lady' has a pyramidal growth habit, dark green, spiny leaves, and red fruit. 'Mary Nell' has exceptionally glossy leaves and reddish orange berries. 'Red Sprite' is a dwarf, large-fruited variety of the deciduous winterberry holly that warms up the winter landscape.

Japanese Cryptomeria

Cryptomeria japonica

Botanical Pronunciation
CRIPT-toe-mary-uh jah-PON-ih-kah

Bloom Period and Seasonal Color
Small, dark green needles arranged along thin, long stems and an upright, pyramidal growth habit

Mature Height × Spread
40 to 50 feet × 20 to 30 feet

Zones Hardy to Zone 5

Japanese cryptomeria is also known as Japanese cedar but it's actually related to juniper and arborvitae and is not a true cedar. This needled evergreen is very fast growing and tough, adapting to a wide variety of landscape situations. It has been a popular landscape plant in the southern United States and is now becoming more available in the Northeast as well. With the loss of Canadian hemlocks to insects and the overuse of Colorado blue spruce and arborvitae, Japanese cryptomeria has become a good alternative. Although it's green in summer, often the leaves will turn a bronze color in winter (although some varieties will not turn colors). There are also several dwarf selections for gardens with limited space.

When, Where, and How to Plant

Japanese cryptomeria is very adaptable, tolerating poor soils, heat, drought, wind, and ice. It can grow in heavy clay soils, sandy soils, or well-drained garden loam. Although Japanese cryptomeria is adaptable to soils, adding compost or well-aged manure when planting is recommended in poor soils, especially sandy or rocky soils. Full sun or partial shade is best for growth but this plant is very tolerant of dense shade. Plants can be purchased in spring as B&B plants or container plants. Spacing should be 10 to 15 feet apart but can be slightly closer if you are creating a tight screen.

Growing Tips

Mulch with 1 to 2 inches of wood chips or pine straw. Soil should be kept evenly moist although cryptomeria is very drought tolerant once established. Use a general-purpose fertilizer in spring.

Regional Advice and Care

Japanese cryptomeria is very resistant to pests and diseases. It is also tolerant of heat, humidity, and drought once established. Pruning is necessary when plants are older as often the interior growth will turn brown and die. Shearing to keep plants as a dense screen can be done in the summer. In addition, older plants can be limbed up to expose the beautiful reddish brown, flaking bark.

Companion Planting and Design

Japanese cryptomeria is an excellent specimen in a lawn but can also work as a tall screen, blocking out unsightly views. Dwarf selections can also be used as foundation plantings and in mixed borders with Hinoki false cypress and other conifers.

Try These

'Black Dragon' is a semi-dwarf selection with very dark green foliage reaching 10 feet tall. 'Globosa Nana' is another dwarf selection with a rounded, mushroom-like habit. 'Yoshino' is a fast-growing variety with emerald-green foliage that does not turn bronze in winter.

Japanese Pieris

Pieris japonica

Botanical Pronunciation
pee-AIR-iss jah-PON-ih-kah

Bloom Period and Seasonal Color
White or pink, urn-shaped flowers in early spring; dark green, glossy foliage

Mature Height × Spread
3 to 6 feet × 3 to 6 feet but can get larger

Zones Hardy to Zone 4

Japanese pieris is a well-known flowering evergreen that is commonly used in foundation plantings and woodland gardens. It is related to rhododendron and likes the same growing conditions. Japanese pieris is often incorrectly referred to as "andromeda" but that name belongs to an entirely different plant group. The long, dangling clusters of white, and sometimes pink, urn-shaped flowers in April are quite a welcome sight after a long, cold winter. It is important to site Japanese pieris in shade as too much sun causes stressed plants to be more susceptible to insects and other problems. Japanese pieris is a great companion to many other rhododendron relatives such as mountain laurel and leucothoe as well as holly and camellia. And Japanese pieris is a highly deer-resistant plant.

When, Where, and How to Plant
Japanese pieris requires moist, acidic, well-drained soil with plenty of organic matter. Because Japanese pieris thrives in organic soil, adding compost or manure when planting is recommended. It should be planted in partial shade and will also perform fairly well in full shade. Planting in full sun will often result in yellowish leaves with tiny stippling from an insect known as lace bug. Plants are usually purchased in containers and planted in spring. Spacing on most varieties should be 3 to 5 feet apart.

Growing Tips
A 1- to 2-inch layer of pine straw or wood chips once a year is recommended. Japanese pieris requires consistent moisture and should be fertilized with a low-nitrogen, well-balanced fertilizer in spring.

Regional Advice and Care
Japanese pieris is susceptible to several pests including lace bug, mites, and root rot. Make sure plants are in a cool, shaded area of the garden with plenty of air circulation and that the soil is well drained. There are insecticidal oils and soaps that can be an effective control of insects and mites but check with your local nurseries or garden centers for exact recommendations.

Companion Planting and Design
Japanese pieris is best when it's grouped in a shade garden with azaleas, rhododendrons, leucothoe, camellias, and other broadleaved evergreens. It can be used as a foundation planting, informal screen, or specimen plant. Pieris is one of the few broadleaved evergreens that will work in areas where deer are prevalent.

Try These
'Cavatine' is a low-growing form to 2 to 3 feet tall and wide with long-lasting white flowers. 'Dorothy Wyckoff' offers dark red flower buds that open to pale pink flowers. 'Flamingo' offers several interesting attributes with striking new bronze-red foliage, purple flower buds, and rose-red flowers. 'Valley Valentine' displays rich, deep maroon flower buds and deep rose-colored flowers. 'Variegata' has white flowers and creamy white leaf margins giving the foliage a two-tone effect all year.

Mountain Laurel

Kalmia latifolia

Botanical Pronunciation
CAL-me-uh lat-if-owe-lee-UH

Bloom Period and Seasonal Color
Star-shaped flower buds open to bell-shaped flowers ranging from white to pink, rose, and bicolored in late spring; lustrous dark green leaves and rough, reddish brown bark when mature

Mature Height × Spread
8 to 15 feet × 8 to 15 feet

Zones Hardy to Zone 4

Mountain laurel is a native shrub growing in woodlands across the East Coast and Midwest. It's a valuable ornamental for the cultivated garden as a companion plant to rhododendron, holly, and camellia. The rounded clusters of white and pink flowers in late May are spectacular. Individual, star-shaped flower buds burst open to reveal delicate, bell-shaped flowers. Extensive breeding since the 1960s by Dr. Richard Jaynes has produced many exceptional cultivars with compact growth habits and a wide range of flower colors from white to deep rosy pink and striking, two-tone color combinations. Mountain laurel can be used effectively in groupings and mixed borders in a shady part of the garden and older specimens are exceptionally handsome when limbed up to expose rough bark.

When, Where, and How to Plant
Mountain laurel prefers moist, well-drained, acidic soil and full sun or partial shade. They thrive in a surface layer of organic soil with a very well-drained subsoil beneath. Compost can be added when planting but do not overdo it, as mountain laurel prefers a light soil. Mountain laurel is especially fond of slopes where water drains well. Plants situated in poorly drained, heavy clay soils will not perform well and often succumb to root rot. If grown in full sun keep plants well watered and mulched. Plant in spring from containers or B&B and space 3 to 5 feet apart.

Growing Tips
Mulching is very important and should be done once a year in spring or fall. An application of granular fertilizer is only necessary if there is a nutrient deficiency or plants are yellow or look weak.

Regional Advice and Care
Mountain laurel is quite tolerant of pruning and like holly can be pruned back severely in early spring to rejuvenate older, overgrown plants. This requires plants to be cut down to about 12 inches. New growth will emerge from hidden growth buds present along the stems, known as latent buds. This drastic pruning results in a more compact, vigorous plant that will flower heavily in a year or two. If only modest pruning is needed to shape plants, do that after flowering and remove dead flowers at this time.

Companion Planting and Design
Mountain laurel is an ideal woodland shrub for partial shade and can also be used in groupings, foundation plantings, informal hedges, or screens. It is a great companion to other shade lovers such as rhododendron relatives, dogwood, holly, and shade-loving perennials.

Try These
'Carousel' displays striking, bright purplish cinnamon coloration on the inside of the flowers. 'Minuet' offers a dwarf growth habit; thin, glossy leaves; and pink flower buds that open to creamy white flowers with deep maroon bands. 'Peppermint' has two-tone flowers that are striped with a combination of white and red. 'Raspberry Glow' offers rich, deep red flower buds that open to raspberry-pink flowers.

Northern Bayberry

Myrica pensylvanica

Botanical Pronunciation
mur-EYE-kuh pen-sil-VAIN-ih-kuh

Other Name Candleberry

Bloom Period and Seasonal Color
Inconspicuous flowers but fruit are grayish white, clustered along the stems in fall and winter and lustrous, deep green leaves most of the year

Mature Height × Spread
5 to 10 feet × 5 to 10 feet

Northern bayberry (also found as *Morella pensylvanica*) is another dioecious plant, with female plants bearing dense clusters of waxy, grayish white berries in fall. The berries are aromatic and are used to scent candles, thus its name of "candleberry." This tough native plant grows in a wide variety of environments from shady, moist areas to hot, dry, sandy soils at the seashore. The long, slender, lustrous leaves hold on for most of the year but usually completely drop during severe winters. Birds will feed on the berries, which offer a high protein food source and are usually gone by winter. Northern bayberry is typically used in natural settings in groupings and mass plantings but can also be used in a cultivated garden as a hedge or screening plant.

When, Where, and How to Plant
Northern bayberry grows in just about any soil but a yellowing of the leaves called chlorosis will occur in high pH soils. Northern bayberry is especially adapted to sandy soils but will also tolerate heavy, clay soils. Full sun or partial shade is best but bayberry can also tolerate significant shade, although it becomes leggy in those conditions. Northern bayberry is resistant to salt spray and pollution and is incredibly drought tolerant once established. Plants can be purchased in spring in containers and typically are slow to establish. Once the heat of summer arrives, northern bayberry will grow steadily. Spacing should be 3 to 5 feet apart.

Growing Tips
Mulching new plantings with wood chips until they are established is recommended. Aluminum sulfate or iron treatments may be necessary in high pH soils to reduce the chance for chlorosis. Northern bayberry prefers moist soils until established and then can take drier conditions.

Regional Advice and Care
Northern bayberry is a pest-free plant with few issues. Selective or rejuvenation pruning to reduce overall size can be done in late winter and shearing can be done in midsummer to keep plants dense and uniform. Neglecting regular pruning for too long can cause its growth habit to become open and irregular over time. Northern bayberry is very cold hardy and can grow in even the coldest areas of New York and New Jersey.

Companion Planting and Design
Northern bayberry is ideal in a natural setting in informal groupings or mass plantings. It can also be used as a formal or informal hedge or foundation plantings. Northern bayberry is an excellent companion plant to holly, clethra, serviceberry, and other eco-friendly natives. In hot, dry, exposed sites near the seashore there is no better shrub.

Try These
Bobbee™ is a compact grower to 6 feet with a mounded habit and dark green foliage. 'Wildwood' is an exceptionally cold hardy and vigorous form with good foliage and pest resistance.

Pine

Pinus spp.

Botanical Pronunciation
PYE-nus

Bloom Period and Seasonal Color
Thin green needles, dense, pyramidal to broad growth habit, and textured bark

Mature Height × Spread
25 to 60 feet × 25 to 40 feet but varieties mentioned are smaller in size

There are many species of pine that will grow in New York and New Jersey and I offer a few worthwhile ones to consider. While eastern white pine (*Pinus strobus*) is still the most popular in the Northeast, there are several other lesser-known species that will add interest and function to the landscape. These include the lacebark pine (*P. bungeana*), which not only has dark green needles but also offers multi-colored, exfoliating bark for year-round interest. Two relatives of the native white pine, Japanese white pine (*P. parviflora*) and Himalayan pine (*P. wallichiana*), offer soft blue-green foliage that adds elegant character and unique color and fine texture to the garden. These choice selections are ideal specimens that are a nice diversion from the norm.

When, Where, and How to Plant

In general, the pines covered here are sensitive to hot, dry conditions and windy sites. They prefer a protected site with well-drained, moist, acidic soil with plenty of organic matter. Full sun or partial shade is also preferred, as too much shade will cause plants to be open and irregular. New plants can be purchased as B&B or in containers in the spring and spacing should be at least 15 to 20 feet apart.

Growing Tips

When planting, add a generous amount of compost to the soil, especially those soils that are sandy or clay based. Mulching once a year with pine straw or fine wood chips will benefit both new and established plantings.

Regional Advice and Care

Pines are susceptible to a wide range of insects and diseases although the species mentioned here are fairly easy to grow. Keep a close eye on any signs of insect or disease issues and bring samples to your local nursery or agricultural Extension office for positive identification.

Companion Planting and Design

Pines are excellent specimen trees for a lawn or shade garden. They are also great companion plants to other shade lovers such as geranium, hosta, ferns, rhododendron, holly, and more.

Try These

The lacebark pine (*P. bungeana*) is an elegant pine with dark, glossy green needles and exquisite multicolored, exfoliating bark displaying shades of green, tan, brown, and cream. Young, shrubby plants will reach 30 to 50 feet tall and 20 to 30 feet wide. Hardy to Zone 4, but needs a sheltered location. Japanese white pine (*P. parviflora*) is an irregularly growing, semi-dwarf pine with short, blue-green needles and a spreading habit that is quite picturesque. Mature specimens can grow 25 to 50 feet tall with a similar spread but there are several dwarf selections including 'Adcock's Dwarf'. Hardy to Zone 4. Himalayan pine (*P. wallichiana*) has graceful branches and long, soft, drooping needles. It can grow to 30 to 50 feet tall. 'Zebrina' is a striking selection with bands of creamy yellow variegation on blue-green foliage. Hardy to Zone 5.

Plum Yew

Cephalotaxus harringtonia

Botanical Pronunciation
SEF-halo-tax-us har-ING-tone-e-uh

Bloom Period and Seasonal Color
Dark green, needled foliage and various growth habits including spreading, upright, and shrubby

Mature Height × Spread
2 to 10 feet × 5 to 10 feet

Zones Hardy to Zone 5

Plum yew looks very similar to a very popular evergreen shrub, yew (*Taxus*), which can be found as specimen trees, clipped hedges, and low-growing foundation plantings throughout the world. But plum yew offers gardeners a few options that common yew cannot. First, plum yew is more durable, pest resistant, drought and heat tolerant, and most importantly, deer resistant. It is a noticeably slower grower but also typically requires much less maintenance than yew. Plum yews will tolerate almost any soil type as long as it is well drained and will even grow near the seashore. Several choice varieties allow gardeners to choose low-growing, prostrate forms; upright, columnar types; and mid-level, shrubby growth habits that can be used just like yews but are much more durable.

When, Where, and How to Plant
Plum yew will grow in full sun and partial shade, and will even tolerate dense shade. It grows in rich, garden soil but will tolerate heavy, clay soils or rocky, gravely soils. While plum yew grows rather well in adverse conditions, it prefers good garden soil with plenty of organic matter. When planting, add a generous amount of compost to the soil. Plum yew will stand up quite well to heat, humidity, drought, pollution, and salt spray. New plants can be purchased from local nurseries and garden centers in containers and should be planted in spring. Larger plants are also available as B&B plants and rootballs should be handled with care. Spacing depends on the variety but in general should be 3 to 5 feet on the upright varieties, and 5 to 7 feet on the spreading varieties.

Growing Tips
Add a light layer of wood chips to keep plants moist during heat and drought. Soil should be kept evenly moist but can dry out as well.

Regional Advice and Care
Plum yew is relatively pest free compared to common yew. In fact, with the exception of poorly drained soils, not much else seems to bother plum yew. Plum yew grows slower than yew so regular pruning is not typically needed. If needed, hand pruning or shearing can be done in early to midsummer.

Companion Planting and Design
Plum yew can be used the same way you would use common yew: as informal and formal hedges, foundation plantings, groupings, and as a single specimen. Some of the lower-growing varieties can also be used on hillsides and slopes as erosion control. Plum yew is a good selection where deer are present.

Try These
'Duke Gardens' is the most popular variety with a dense, upright and spreading habit that can reach 3 feet or more in height by 5 feet or more in width. 'Fastigiata' is a strongly upright, columnar grower able to reach 10 feet tall. 'Prostrata' is a ground-hugging variety that is ideal in open areas, under trees, and on slopes.

Spreading Euonymus

Euonymus kiautschovicus

Botanical Pronunciation
yew-on-UH-mus kye-UH-cho-vi-cus

Bloom Period and Seasonal Color Greenish white flowers in summer; pink fruit capsules with red seed in fall; lustrous, dark green leaves

Mature Height × Spread
8 to 10 feet × 8 to 10 feet

Zones Hardy to Zone 5

Euonymus is a relative of bittersweet, which is known for its adaptability and showy fruit with some species being invasive. Spreading euonymus is an evergreen shrub with lustrous, dark green leaves and a rounded, spreading habit that is not invasive. In the summer, greenish white, fragrant flowers attract bees and other pollinators. Once fertilized, interesting pink fruit capsules will open to red seeds and the combination is attractive. Spreading euonymus is both adaptable and useful in the landscape. It will tolerate a wide range of environmental conditions and offer gardeners options as a formal or informal hedge or screen. While various insects and diseases plague many species of euonymus, this particular species tends to be lower maintenance. From a shady woodland garden to a hot, dry seashore condition, spreading euonymus offers versatility.

When, Where, and How to Plant
Spreading euonymus will tolerate most soil including dry, gravelly soil and heavy clay soil. It should not be planted in poorly drained soil although it will tolerate occasional flooding. Full sun or part shade is best for growth although it will even tolerate dense shade. New plantings can be purchased and planted in spring or fall in containers. Spacing should be 3 to 5 feet apart.

Growing Tips
Spreading euonymus is not picky but adding compost to poor soils will benefit new plantings.

Mulching new plantings and even established plants in hot, dry conditions is also beneficial. Spreading euonymus prefers even moisture but will tolerate dry soils once established. Regular fertilizer applications are not needed but adding a general-purpose, low-nitrogen fertilizer in spring is beneficial.

Regional Advice and Care
Euonymus is susceptible to pests such a crown gall, aphids, and scale. Go to your local nursery or agricultural Extension office for recommendations on treatment. Of all of the evergreen species of euonymus, spreading euonymus tends to be the least susceptible to these problems though. In sun, spreading euonymus will have dense, spreading habit but can become quite open and leggy in shade. Summer pruning or shearing will keep growth habit dense and neat. Unusual growths called crown gall can be pruned off to reduce the risk of spread.

Companion Planting and Design
Spreading euonymus is best as informal or formal hedges. It also works well in foundation plantings and is often used to define spaces and block unsightly views. It is similar in texture to rhododendron, holly, and viburnum and works well in combination with these and other trees and shrubs.

Try These
'Manhattan' is a popular variety with a vigorous, dense growth habit and offers good pest resistance. 'Manhattan' can grow 4 to 6 feet in height and spread.

Spruce

Picea spp.

Botanical Pronunciation PYE-see-uh

Bloom Period and Seasonal Color
Sharp, dark green needles, conical habit, graceful branches, and drooping cones

Mature Height × Spread
50 to 60 feet × 20 to 30 feet but varieties mentioned are much smaller

Zones Hardy to Zone 4

For years, the residential landscape has been home to Colorado blue spruce and Norway spruce, two lovely species that just get too big. In fact, most species of spruce are not suited for the average residential landscape because of their eventual enormous size. However, the few species and their cultivated varieties noted here are suited for a garden with limited space. Spruces in general are slow- to medium-growing, fine-textured evergreens with an upright, graceful habit. Spruce does not like hot, dry, windy locations but are drought tolerant once established. They are shade tolerant and do not need full sun to thrive. Spruces are excellent specimen trees, and the dwarf selections mentioned are also excellent foundation plantings and in combination with other dwarf conifers.

When, Where, and How to Plant
Spruces prefer full sun and well-drained, acidic, moist soils. In poor soils, incorporate compost when planting. Spruces tolerate partial shade and sandy soils as long as adequate moisture is provided until established. Spruces can be planted in spring, purchased in containers, or B&B. Spacing depends on species and cultivars and can range from 15 to 20 feet on larger-growing types to 3 to 4 feet on smaller varieties.

Growing Tips
Mulch the surface with 1 to 2 inches of wood chips or pine straw. Keep plants well watered for the first two growing seasons until established.

Regional Advice and Care
Spruce is susceptible to a range of insects such as mites and spruce gall aphid. With mites, good air circulation and washing leaves with cold water will help.

Companion Planting and Design
Use spruce as a specimen plant in a lawn, as a tall screen, foundation planting, and in a mixed border with other conifers or narrow-leaved evergreens.

Try These
Norway spruce (*Picea abies*) gets too large for the home garden but 'Nidiformis' has a tight, spreading habit, which is why this evergreen's common name is bird's nest spruce. 'Pendula' is a weeping form with an upright main trunk and cascading side branches. Serbian spruce (*Picea omorika*) is a tall, narrow conifer growing to 50 feet tall but only 20 feet wide. 'Nana' is a dwarf variety growing 8 to 10 feet tall with a conical or rounded growth habit. 'Pendula' is a slender, tall variety with weeping side branches; it's hardy to Zone 4. Oriental spruce (*Picea orientalis*) is the best of the best with small, delicate, dark green needles and a pyramidal growth habit with graceful, sweeping side branches. The male flowers in spring are carmine red. 'Bergman's Gem' is a beautiful compact form reaching 3 to 6 feet tall and wide. 'Gowdy' is a compact variety with a dense, narrow growth habit reaching 8 to 10 feet. 'Skylands' has striking bright golden-yellow needles that add a nice accent to a bland landscape.

White Fir

Abies concolor

Botanical Pronunciation
AYE-bees con-Col-or

Other Name Concolor fir

Bloom Period and Seasonal Color
Long, soft, silvery blue-green, flat needles

Mature Height × Spread 50 to 75 feet × 20
to 30 feet but more typically 30 to 50 feet × 15
to 20 feet in Northeast

Zones Hardy to Zone 4

Firs are needled evergreens well known as cut trees sold at the holidays. Most species display dark green foliage highlighted by two white lines on the undersides. But white fir is quite different, with soft, silvery blue foliage similar to blue spruce. This West Coast native is more durable, pest resistant, and able to tolerate heat and drought than blue spruce. While there is some variation to the degree of striking foliage depending on light and other factors, white fir is quite unique. Although white fir can get large, it is typically slower growing and does not reach the size here that it can in its native climate. White fir is very effective as an accent plant against dark green foliage plants and as a tall screen.

When, Where, and How to Plant

White fir is more adaptable to heat and drought than the average fir. White fir thrives in moist, well-drained, acidic soil with organic matter so adding compost at planting time is beneficial. Full sun is best for foliage coloration but partial shade is acceptable. Too much shade will produce leggy plants that lose much of their striking foliage color. White fir, like many conifers, is best if planted in spring. They are available as B&B plants or in containers. If used as a screen or informal hedge, spacing should be 12 to 15 feet apart.

Growing Tips

It will tolerate drier soils but mulch and regular watering during drought will be needed in these situations. Mulch new plantings, especially in hot, dry locations with poor soil.

Regional Advice and Care

White fir is quite pest and disease resistant as long as they are given well-drained soil and plenty of light and air circulation. Pruning is not generally needed regularly unless you are pruning to keep a tight, dense form or training plants as a screen.

Companion Planting and Design

White fir is aromatic and long lasting outdoors so it is useful as cut greens for the Christmas holiday. In addition, white fir is an excellent specimen tree on the lawn or in groupings to block unsightly views. I believe white fir is unique enough that it looks best when used independently of other plants although it works well in combination with other conifers.

Try These

'Candicans' is one of the bluest forms, with unusually large, powder blue needles. 'Compacta' is a dwarf, slow-growing form with striking blue foliage growing only to 6 feet tall in ten years. 'Dwarf Globe' is a very compact form only growing to 3 feet tall. 'Gable's Weeping' has an irregular, weeping habit that forms dense mounds of growth.

Yew

Taxus spp.

Botanical Pronunciation TACKS-us

Bloom Period and Seasonal Color Dark green, needlelike foliage; some species have striking reddish brown, exfoliating bark

Mature Height × Spread 2 to 3 feet up to 20 plus feet × 5 to 20 plus feet depending on species and cultivar

Zones Japanese and intermediate yews: hardy to Zone 4; English yew: hardy to Zone 5

Yews are popular and sometimes overused evergreens that serve many functions in the landscape. They offer dark, needlelike foliage; dense growth habit; red, fleshy covered seeds (not edible); and peeling reddish brown bark in some species. Yews come in many shapes and sizes and can take on many forms in the landscape. They are highly tolerant of regular shearing, making them ideal as hedges and screens. The three species of yews that are most available in commerce are English yew (*Taxus baccata*), Japanese yew (*T. cuspidata*), and *T. × media*, an intermediate hybrid between the two species. Yews are very useful but do have limitations as they require good drainage and are not resistant to deer. A good alternative to *Taxus* is plum yew (*Cephalotaxus*).

When, Where, and How to Plant
Yews require good drainage and are best suited for sandy or loamy, acidic soils. Full sun or partial shade is best but yews are very tolerant of dense shade. Yews should be planted in spring and can be purchased in containers or as B&B plants. Spacing depends on species and cultivar and should be 3 to 4 feet on smaller types and at least 10 to 15 feet on larger types.

Growing Tips
Add compost to planting hole, especially in sandy and clay soils. Mulching once a year will keep roots cool and soil moisture even throughout the year. Adding granular fertilizer is not usually necessary unless there is a nutrient deficiency.

Regional Advice and Care
Yews are very prone to scale, black vine weevil, and mealybug. In poorly drained soils, root rots will outright kill plants. Yews are remarkably tolerant of pruning and can be sheared into tight, formal hedges or trained into large, upright trees. Like holly, yews have latent buds and healthy specimens can be pruned back to bare stems in late winter and rejuvenated. Shearing or maintenance pruning to control size can be done during the early or mid-summer months.

Companion Planting and Design
Yews can function as formal or informal hedges, tall screens, foundation plantings, or individual specimens. I believe yews look their best as natural specimens without manipulation from well-intentioned gardeners armed with pruning shears.

Try These
English yew has long, flat, dark green leaves and showy, reddish brown, peeling bark as it ages. 'Repandens' is a popular, elegant shrub with a mounded, somewhat weeping habit. Mature specimens typically reach 2 to 4 feet tall and two to three times the width. 'Nana' is a variety of *T. cuspidata* that is slower growing with a dense, shrubby habit reaching at least 6 to 8 feet tall with a wider spread. 'Nana Aurescens' reaches 2 to 3 feet in height with bright, golden yellow new growth. 'Hicksii' and 'Hatfieldii' are cultivars of *T. × media* used as specimens, foundation planting, or formal and informal hedges.

GROUNDCOVERS AND VINES

FOR NEW YORK & NEW JERSEY

Groundcovers and vines can be a great way to enhance the horizontal and vertical lines of the landscape. Instead of a boring, high-maintenance lawn, groundcovers can add beauty and interest while reducing maintenance. Groundcovers are ideal in hard-to-mow areas and are also effective on slopes to reduce erosion. Vines can be trained to grow up fences, posts, and arbors and even in other plants like trees and shrubs. They soften structures and screen unpleasant views, maximize limited spaces, and can even be interesting in winter. The groundcovers and vines listed in this section are non-invasive, durable plants that will complement other horticultural and architectural features in your garden.

Selecting Groundcovers and Vines for the Home Landscape

One of the main advantages of planting groundcovers instead of lawns is the unique and diverse interest they provide.

Well-behaved pachysandra (*Pachysandra terminalis*) is an excellent groundcover to line a walkway.

Unlike lawns, groundcovers can protect tree roots and the main stems of trees and shrubs by shielding them from mowers and weed trimmers. Groundcovers also tend to retain moisture around tree roots and keep the ground cool.

Groundcovers and vines must be adaptable, growing in shady areas among larger plants. This could mean limited area for roots to grow and soil that may dry out faster. Think about the aesthetic that you are trying to create and how these plants can accomplish that goal while functioning properly.

One issue with groundcovers is that grass and weeds will grow through them, which looks unsightly and requires tedious care to remove. Today, groundcovers are being selected for their ability to suppress weeds. Andy Senesac from Cornell University Cooperative Extension shared information with me on weed suppressive groundcovers several years ago. These groundcovers provide thick vegetation and in some cases, ornamental flowers. Find more at http://ccesuffolk. org/gardening/horticulture-factsheets/ tree-shrub-groundcover-vine-selection.

Vines, such as this *Campsis radicans*, may need strong supports.

The trend these days with vines is improved flowers and foliage and adaptability to a wide range of growing conditions. These vines require some maintenance such as pruning but give far more than they require. Today, many interesting vines can offer seasonal interest, requiring limited maintenance, unlike Asian wisteria and climbing roses.

General Care and Maintenance of Groundcovers and Vines

Properly preparing the soil and aftercare are essential to establishing groundcovers and vines. But once established, most of the selections offered are relatively self-sufficient. The time and effort spent on site selection, planting, and establishment will pay off in the long run.

When planting groundcovers under existing trees, take special care to disrupt the root system as little as possible. Gently removing weeds by hand or with a hand-held cultivator can accomplish this. Avoid adding additional soil, which will damage tree roots. If you want to replace a lawn with groundcovers, turn the soil over or eliminate the grass by using a non-selective herbicide. Be sure to read the label directions before applying these products. Once you have a level area with soft, friable soil, the planting can begin. In large, open areas, small pots can be used, but in areas under existing trees or shrubs, smaller plants such as plugs or cell packs can be used to limit soil disruption.

Adding a light layer of mulch such as fine wood chips or pine straw will keep soil moist and reduce weed competition until plants get established. Also, add a slow-release, low-nitrogen fertilizer after planting. Regular watering to ensure your new groundcovers do not dry out is *essential*. Water plants the first two years after planting.

With vines, proper placement in an area large enough for the vine to expand is important. It is also important to know how vines attach themselves to objects they are growing on. Some vines are twining, wrapping around structures, while others have appendages that stick to surfaces. Knowing these details will enable you to pick the right plant for the right structure. Pruning is vital to the success of vines, and this is covered under "Regional Advice and Care."

American Wisteria

Wisteria frutescens

Botanical Pronunciation
wiss-TEER-ee-uh froo-TESS-enz

Bloom Period and Seasonal Color
Hanging clusters of fragrant, lilac-purple flowers in spring and early summer; dark green leaves

Mature Height × Spread
20 to 30 feet × 4 to 8 feet

Zones Hardy to Zone 5

American wisteria is a southern native that is a great alternative to the high-maintenance Asian wisterias that can become invasive in the garden. Although American wisteria blooms are not quite as large as the Chinese and Japanese wisteria in full bloom, it is still very impressive. The tight, cone-shaped drooping flower clusters reach 4 to 6 inches long when they're fully open. American wisteria is a vigorous, twining vine that is ideal for an arbor or trellis. It can get large so whatever structure it is allowed to grow upon should be well built and able to withstand some weight. American wisteria is relatively deer resistant and when browsed by deer, it will usually bounce back rather quickly.

When, Where, and How to Plant
American wisteria is very adaptable, but for best flowering grow it in full sun. It thrives in moist, well-drained, acidic soil with plenty of organic matter. Incorporate a generous amount of compost or well-aged manure into the planting hole. Young plants can be purchased in containers in spring and will need time to establish, often not flowering well until after their first growing season. Spacing should be 8 to 10 feet to give this plant some room to spread out.

Growing Tips
Add a low-nitrogen, slow-release fertilizer in spring to encourage growth and flowers. American

wisteria is quite drought tolerant but even soil moisture is preferred.

Regional Advice and Care
American wisteria is an easy-to-grow, pest-free plant that is not as high maintenance as most wisterias can be. Since this plant flowers on new growth, a hard pruning to reduce the overall size can be done in winter and will encourage flowering the following spring. Main stems can be cut to three or four buds. Pruning to train plants or control size can be done after flowering to keep plants tidy. Established plants will send out runners on the ground which should be pruned back regularly in summer.

Companion Planting and Design
American wisteria is a standalone plant that is ideal for an archway or arbor that it can climb on. On fences and trelliswork it needs to be pruned regularly to keep it manageable. It is *not* meant for small posts or structures that it will outgrow quickly, such as a mailbox post.

Try These
'Amethyst Falls' is the most popular and available cultivated variety; it has showy lavender blue flowers. 'Nivea' is a white-flowering form and 'Peter's Pink' is a pink-flowering variety. A naturally occurring variety, *W.* var. *macrostachya*, is similar but more cold hardy, growing into Zone 4. 'Blue Moon' offers beautiful blue flowers that can reach 6 to 12 inches long in early summer.

Barrenwort

Epimedium spp.

Botanical Pronunciation
ep-ih-MEE-dee-um

Other Name Fairy wings

Bloom Period and Seasonal Color
Flowers in yellow, pink, and many variations
except blue; lustrous, evergreen foliage

Mature Height × Spread
6 to 18 inches × 12 to 18 inches

Zones Hardy to Zone 5

Barrenwort is as beautiful as it is tough. This relative of barberry has smooth, lush compound leaves that often start off with a reddish tint before changing to dark green. This low-growing, clumping plant retains it foliage most of the year. In spring, delicate pink or yellow flowers emerge and look similar to columbine flowers as they unfurl. Barrenwort can tolerate dry shade and is especially resistant to pests and deer browsing. This underutilized groundcover is useful in a shaded woodland garden and is effective in a mass planting. Many new selections have been introduced recently but this plant is still a challenge to find in a local nursery. However, it is worth the effort to seek this plant out from local or mail-order sources.

When, Where, and How to Plant
Barrenwort is a rugged, adaptable plant tolerating root competition from trees and even dry shade. Ideally it prefers moist, well-drained soil and partial shade with protection from the afternoon sun. The more sun it is given, the more risk of damage from exposure. Deep shade will be tolerated as well but that may sacrifice flowering. Plants are available in spring and should be spaced 12 to 18 inches apart.

Growing Tips
In poor soils add compost and a light layer of fine-textured mulch to the surface of the soil. This will also help plants in dry soil conditions and in times of drought. Barrenwort prefers even moisture but will tolerate periods of dry conditions as well.

Regional Advice and Care
Barrenwort is very resistant to disease and insects but will get damaged in exposed sites. Keep them well watered and mulched under the shade of large trees. If plants get beat up from a long, hard winter, they can be cut back in late winter and will rejuvenate, but only do that if necessary. Large clumps can be divided in late winter or early spring or fall.

Companion Planting and Design
Because of the combination of lustrous, evergreen foliage and delicate flowers, barrenwort is a four-season plant. Barrenwort are ideal companions to other favorite shade-loving plants such as hellebore, hosta, heuchera, and astilbe. This versatile plant can be used in many landscape situations and is most effective in a mass planting.

Try These
'Rose Queen' (*Epimedium grandiflorum*) offers rosy-pink flowers and new crimson leaves that change to green in summer. Many catalogues list 'Rose Queen' as growing in Zone 4 so give it a try. 'Frohnleiten' (*E. × perralchicum*), a German selection, is one of the most beloved selections with bright yellow flowers unfurling through the purple-tinged new foliage. 'Sulphureum' (*E. × versicolor*) has delicate flowers that are pale yellow in the outer part of the flower and bright yellow in the center. This is just a sampling of many great selections available today. The sky is the limit with barrenwort!

Black-Eyed Susan Vine

Thunbergia alata

Botanical Pronunciation
thun-BURG-ee-uh uh-LATE-uh

Bloom Period and Seasonal Color
Orange-yellow flowers with a dark purple to black center summer and fall

Mature Length × Width 3 to 8 feet × 3 to 6 feet

Zones Annual

This is actually an annual vine but it offers stunning, bright yellow-orange flowers with a dark center; its leaves are triangular. Although it is not related to the perennial black-eyed Susan, it has the same color combination as that flower, which is where it gets its name. This easy-to-grow vine can grow on a post, trellis, or fence and also can be used to make colorful hanging baskets. In a large container with other annuals, it will spill over the sides, cascading to the ground. With variations in flower color due to ongoing breeding and selection, black-eyed Susan vine isn't only yellow anymore. It can be found in white, peach, red, and rose. Although it will only last one growing season, black-eyed Susan vine is well worth the effort.

When, Where, and How to Plant

Black-eyed Susan vine thrives in moist, well-drained soil with plenty of organic matter. Because black-eyed Susan vine prefers organic matter, incorporate a generous amount of compost to the planting bed or container they are growing in. Full sun or partial shade is acceptable and this vine also prefers protection from afternoon sun. Plants can be purchased in mid-spring and planted in groups of three to give plantings more structure. Spacing can be 8 to 12 inches apart or more depending on the type of growing environment you are planting them in.

Growing Tips

In flowerbeds, be sure to lightly mulch new plantings. A granular, general-purpose fertilizer to start plants off in the spring is also recommended. Keep plants well watered in times of drought.

Regional Advice and Care

Black-eyed Susan vine is easy to grow and once it gets going, it doesn't need too much. Prune to train as needed. Besides small plants purchased in spring, sow seed indoors six to eight weeks before the last frost in your area. Or cuttings can be made from existing plants and easily rooted. Plants in containers can be brought into a warm, sunny room in the house and overwintered.

Companion Planting and Design

Black-eyed Susan vine is excellent for climbing up a structure or used in a hanging basket. It can be combined with other annuals in a mixed container to add summer color. In a container, support this vine with a small trellis or other structure and this twining plant will climb its way up.

Try These

African Sunset series offers a variety of colors including apricot, peach, pink, salmon, red, and ivory with a dark center. Sunny series is another good series with varieties including 'Sunny Lemon Star' and 'Sunny Orange', two variations with yellow and orange flowers. The Superstar mix offers some of the larger flowers of this species. Clock vine (*Thunbergia grandiflora*) is a late bloomer that often won't bloom until fall but the rough, lustrous leaves and large, sky blue flowers with a yellow throat are outstanding.

Carolina Jessamine

Gelsemium sempervirens

Botanical Pronunciation
jell-SEEM-ee-um sem-PUR-vur-enz

Bloom Period and Seasonal Color
Golden yellow flowers in spring; dark green leaves

Mature Length × Width
10 to 20 feet × 3 to 6 feet

Zones Hardy to Zone 6

Carolina jessamine is a southern native that is slowly gaining in popularity in northern gardens. Southern New York and northern New Jersey are its northern cold hardiness limits and it's a worthwhile addition to the garden with the right growing conditions. Carolina jessamine has a profusion of golden-yellow, trumpet-shaped flowers that are showy and fragrant. They will attract pollinators and hummingbirds to the garden. It will flower sporadically for several months and even into the fall if conditions are right. The dark green, glossy leaves are either evergreen or semi-evergreen, depending on the severity of the winter. This twining vine is ideal for a fence, latticework, or a sturdy post and if it's not trained to grow on a structure, it will creep along the ground until it finds something to support it. Note: Leaves and flowers are poisonous so keep this plant away from pets and children.

When, Where, and How to Plant

Carolina jessamine is quite tough and although it thrives in moist, well-drained soil, it will tolerate less-than-optimum soil conditions that are sandy or clay based. Because Carolina jessamine thrives in rich, organic soil with a good amount of organic matter, add well-aged compost to the planting hole. Full sun is preferred for best flower production but partial shade is also acceptable. Plants will tolerate a wide range of soil pH including acidic and slightly alkaline. Keep it out of exposed areas where strong winter winds are prevalent. Plants can be purchased in containers in spring and planted when the soil temperatures warm up. Spacing should be 2 to 4 feet apart.

Growing Tips

Adding 1 to 2 inches of wood chips, pine straw, or shredded leaves as mulch will also benefit plants. Keep soil evenly moist and use a well-balanced, low-nitrogen fertilizer in spring.

Regional Advice and Care

Carolina jessamine is a tough, easy-to-grow vine with no serious insect or disease problems. Pruning to train this plant and to neaten it up if it gets too large can be done after flowering in midsummer. It's hardy to Zone 6 and should receive protection in those areas; planting on an eastern exposure with morning sunlight and afternoon shade will help.

Companion Planting and Design

Carolina jessamine works well when trained on a fence, arbor, or trelliswork. It is a nice vine to grow on an archway or on a wall. It works well with other spring-blooming, sun-loving shrubs and perennials.

Try These

'Lemon Drop' is a more compact, shrubby form with lighter yellow flowers than the species. 'Margarita' is a form that is more cold-hardy than the species and has slightly larger yellow flowers. 'Pride of Augusta' is a double flowering form that adds a rather unique aesthetic to the landscape.

Clematis

Clematis spp.

Botanical Pronunciation KLEM-uh-tiss

Bloom Period and Seasonal Color
Spring-, summer-, and fall-blooming species
and hybrids offer white, pink, purple, yellow, and
many other variations

Mature Length
5 to 20 feet depending on type

Zones See "Regional Advice and Care"

Clematis is a very popular flowering vine that has been used in the garden for centuries. With over 300 species and many hybrids, it's not hard to understand why this is such a diverse group of garden favorites. With very active plant societies and faithful growers, clematis is still one of the most cultivated plants available today. I know avid gardeners who have dedicated their entire gardens in honor of this plant group. There are three distinct categories of clematis including spring bloomers, repeat bloomers, and summer/fall bloomers. All are quite different and offer something unique to the garden. Clematis is a great complement to annuals, perennials, and flowering shrubs.

When, Where, and How to Plant
Clematis prefers moist, organic, well-drained soil. Avoid heavy, soggy soils or hot, dry, exposed sites. Adding compost to the planting hole is beneficial. If grown in full sun, clematis benefit from some light afternoon shade and they should be kept well watered. Plants are grown in containers and should be planted in spring. Spacing varies but should be 3 to 5 feet apart.

Growing Tips
Clematis grows best when their roots are kept cool so a light layer of mulch is very important. A general-purpose granular, slow-release fertilizer applied in spring is beneficial but should not be high in nitrogen. Clematis prefer even moisture with no major fluctuations in the soil.

Regional Advice and Care
Clematis can be subject to many pests including leaf spots, stem rot, mildew, mites, whiteflies, and scale, so siting and aftercare is important. Pruning is dependent on what species and hybrid you are working with. For spring-flowering types, which have one major flush of flowers in spring and bloom on the previous seasons' growth, prune *after* flowering. This would be true of *Clematis montana* (Zone 5) and its cultivars. For repeat bloomers including large-flowering hybrids such as 'Nelly Moser', prune lightly in late winter and again after the first flush of flowers in late spring or early summer. Summer and fall bloomers such as *C. × jackmanii* (Zone 4) can be pruned down to about a foot in early spring and then they grow vigorously and bloom. Another approach is to prune severely every few years.

Companion Planting and Design
Clematis can be grown in containers or in combination with herbaceous plants and flowering shrubs. It is ideal on a fence, lamppost, or even among small trees.

Try These
Jackman clematis (*C. × jackmanii*) offers big, violet purple flowers in summer and is still one of the most popular clematis available. 'Nelly Moser' is a lovely pink flowering clematis with large blooms. The anemone clematis (*C. montana*) offers delicate white or pink flowers in profusion in spring and var. *rubens* is a rosy-red flowering form.

Climbing Hydrangea

Hydrangea anomala subsp. *petiolaris*

Botanical Pronunciation
hye-DRAIN-juh uh-NOM-uh-luh pet-ee-oh-LAIR-iss

Bloom Period and Seasonal Color
Pure white, lacecap flowers in early summer;
dark green foliage

Mature Length × Spread
Can grow 30 to 50 feet × 5 to 6 feet or more

While hydrangeas are among the most popular and beloved flowering shrubs in the world, they also are available as a vine. Climbing hydrangea is an exquisite climber that gets better with age. Although it's slow to establish, once it does it grows vigorously. The flush of fragrant, white lacecap-type flowers in early summer and rounded, dark green leaves are interesting all summer long. But as the leaves turn yellow and fall, the interesting stems and bark of this vine are revealed. The stems are covered with rootlike anchors that grab onto walls, arbors, and trees and as plants mature they exhibit rough, cinnamon-colored bark that is attractive while the plant is dormant. This is a long-lived plant that is only limited by how far it will climb by the size of the object it is growing on.

When, Where, and How to Plant
Climbing hydrangea does best in rich, well-drained soil with plenty of organic matter. It is not meant for hot, dry, exposed sites with poor soil. Climbing hydrangea will benefit from the addition of organic matter to the soil at planting time. It prefers full sun or partial shade and will perform best on an eastern exposure where it gets morning sunlight and afternoon shade. It suffers from transplant shock so new spring plantings should be purchased from a local garden centers in containers. Spacing should be 5 to 10 feet apart but usually one plant will suffice in a home garden.

Growing Tips
Well-aged compost or manure will work well and adding a light layer of mulch around new plantings will help keep plant roots cool in summer. Keep soil evenly moist and do not let it dry out. Fertilizer is not necessary on established plants but if needed, use a well-balanced fertilizer in spring.

Regional Advice and Care
Climbing hydrangea is fairly pest free although Japanese beetles will chew up the leaves. Beetles can be picked off by hand or check your local nurseries for recommendations on insecticides that will control them. Pruning right after flowering can be done to keep vines in check and trained to grow how you want them to grow. Severe pruning may affect flower production. But do not over-prune as it will ruin its natural habit and reduce flower production.

Companion Planting and Design
Climbing hydrangea is very much a standalone plant and can be a focal point in the garden. It needs a good support structure to grow on as it will get big and heavy over time. Climbing hydrangea will work well as a backdrop for other flowering plants such as shrubs and perennials.

Try These
'Firefly' is a variegated form with soft yellow leaf edges and dark green centers. I have seen this plant at Chanticleer Gardens in Pennsylvania and it was stunning. 'Kuga Variegated' offers a combination of pink, white, and green and is most interesting when first emerging in spring.

Common Periwinkle

Vinca minor

Botanical Pronunciation VINK-uh MY-nur

Bloom Period and Seasonal Color
Delicate lilac-blue to violet flowers in spring; dark, glossy green leaves

Mature Height × Spread
3 to 6 inches × 1½ feet or more

Zones Hardy to Zone 4

Common periwinkle is a popular ground-cover that spreads along the ground, forming low matted clumps of dark green leaves. The small, tubular flowers look similar to phlox flowers. Common periwinkle is quite tolerant of even dense shade but will also grow in full sun. It is ideal along slopes and embankments and is a great accent plant around rhododendron, azalea, holly, viburnum, and many other shade- and sun-loving flowering plants. Common periwinkle isn't as aggressive as Japanese pachysandra but can still grow vigorously and will need to be pulled away from the base of other plants over time. This hardy woody plant is closely related to the annual periwinkle, which has much larger flowers and leaves and is often used in hanging baskets and mixed borders.

When, Where, and How to Plant
Common periwinkle prefers moist, well-drained, acidic, organic soil so add compost to the soil when planting. This can be done by incorporating organic matter into the top 6 to 12 inches of the soil before planting. It likes partial shade and will also do admirably well in dense shade. It will grow in full sun but often turns yellowish green and is more susceptible to winter damage. Plants can be purchased is small pots or bare-root and planted 12 inches apart. Dividing large plantings every few years and transplanting it to other parts of the garden can be done in early spring.

Growing Tips
Gently adding a light layer of mulch such as shredded leaves, pine straw, or fine wood chips will help plants start off right.

Regional Advice and Care
Common periwinkle is subject to several diseases and you should consult with your local nursery or agricultural Extension office for recommendations on effective fungicides if needed. Pruning or thinning is only needed on established plantings that crowd out smaller perennials or shrubs.

Companion Planting and Design
Common periwinkle is best as a mass planting surrounding flowering shrubs, trees and perennials. It is also a good cover plant for flowering bulbs, which will grow through it and then die back after flowering. Common periwinkle is very effective on slopes as erosion control.

Try These
There are many cultivated varieties offering white, blue, burgundy, and rose-colored flowers as well as variegated foliage. Take your pick when you visit the nursery and see this plant in full bloom before deciding. 'Argenteovariegata' has green leaves with white edges and blue flowers, making this a striking combination. 'Atropurpurea' is an old variety with plum-purple flowers in spring. 'La Grave' is a larger-flowering variety with beautiful lavender-blue blooms.

Cotoneaster

Cotoneaster spp.

Botanical Pronunciation kuh-toe-nee-ASS-tur

Bloom Period and Seasonal Color
Small white or pink flowers in spring; red
fruit in late summer persisting into winter;
evergreen and deciduous foliage

Mature Height × Spread
1 to 3 feet × 5 to 8 feet

Zones See "Try These"

Cotoneaster, which is often wrongly pronounced "cotton-E-stur," was at one time
a very popular groundcover and shrub but
has lost some appeal over the past two decades.
But there are several species and varieties of low-
growing type cotoneasters that are still worthy of
inclusion in gardens. Cotoneasters have a lot to
offer with their ground-hugging, creeping, and cascading habits and delicate, fine texture. Small white
to pink flowers are hard to notice in spring but the
red, glossy fruit and reddish maroon fall and winter
foliage color is striking. Cotoneaster is able to adapt
to a wide variety of soil conditions, soil pH, and
light exposures. It is an excellent foundation planting or facer plant, growing in front of taller plants
along the edge of a border.

When, Where, and How to Plant
Cotoneaster will tolerate almost any soil but performs best in well-drained, acidic, loamy soil. Add
compost or manure in poor soils. Cotoneaster
adapts to light exposures, tolerating dense shade
but it grows best in full sun or partial shade. Plants
are usually grown in containers and sold in spring.
Spacing should be 3 to 5 feet apart, depending on
the species.

Growing Tips
Spread 1 to 2 inches of wood chips or pine straw
once a year around existing plants. Adding an
application of a well-balanced granular fertilizer in
spring will give plants a boost in poor soils. Keep
soil evenly moist but it can take drier conditions
once established.

Regional Advice and Care
Cotoneaster is susceptible to a wide variety of pest
such as aphids, lacebugs, fireblight, scale, and spider
mites so keep a close eye on any signs of trouble.
The insects can be treated so check with your local
garden center; removing infected branches typically
controls fireblight. These groundcover species of
cotoneaster do not need regular pruning as it can
ruin their graceful habit but if needed, pruning can
be done in late winter or after flowering in summer.

Companion Planting and Design
Cotoneaster is a great companion to both deciduous and evergreen shrubs and trees and can be used
in rock gardens, conifer gardens, foundation plantings, mixed borders, and even in containers.

Try These
Creeping cotoneaster (*C. adpressus*) is a low-
growing, delicate groundcover with dark green foliage, rosy-pink flowers, and red fruit. Its compact,
ground-hugging habit is beautiful. 'Tom Thumb'
and 'Little Gem' are two cultivated varieties worth
trying; hardy to Zone 4. Bearberry cotoneaster (*C.
dammeri*) is an evergreen groundcover with lustrous,
dark green leaves and red berries. 'Mooncreeper' is
an outstanding variety with a low, matted growth
habit and dark green foliage; hardy to Zone 5.
Rockspray cotoneaster (*C. horizontalis*) has cascading branches with dark green, glossy leaves that turn
brilliant shades of red before falling in autumn. Red
fruit ripen in later summer and persist through fall.
'Variegatus' is a slower-growing variegated form
that is ideal for rock gardens; hardy to Zone 5.

Crossvine

Bignonia capreolata

Botanical Pronunciation
big-NO-nee-uh kap-ree-uh-LAY-tuh

Bloom Period and Seasonal Color
Trumpet-shaped flowers are reddish orange on the outside and yellow orange on the inside in spring

Mature Length
Can climb up to 50 feet but usually less

Zones Hardy to Zone 6; possibly to Zone 5 with some protection

Crossvine is southern native with long, dark green leaves that are either semi-evergreen or evergreen depending on the severity of the winter. The clusters of showy reddish orange, trumpet-shaped, fragrant flowers in spring create a spectacular display. It will bloom for about a month and then sporadically through the summer. The flower colors are quite variable and several select cultivated varieties add to the diversity of this species. Their twining branches will cover trees, trellis, walls, fence posts, or anything else it can grab onto. The flowers are a great source of nectar to hummingbirds and butterflies. Some sources list it as deer resistant but there is only one way to find out. Crossvine gets its name from the cross-shaped stems and, although it looks similar to trumpet vine (*Campsis radicans*), it is much less aggressive.

When, Where, and How to Plant
Crossvine prefers moist, well-drained soil and full sun or partial shade. It will also grow in deep shade but will not flower as well. Because crossvine thrives in organic soil, in heavy clay or sandy soils add a generous amount of compost or well-aged manure. Crossvine will even take occasional flooding. Plants can be purchased in spring from a local or mail-order nurseries or garden centers in containers. One plant is sufficient to cover a large area but if needed, multiple plants can be spaced 10 feet apart.

Growing Tips
Mulching new plantings with wood chips is desirable, as crossvine does not like very dry situations.

Crossvine prefers even moisture and can be fertilized with a well-balanced, general-purpose fertilizer in spring.

Regional Advice and Care
Crossvine is quite carefree and is not bothered by diseases and insects. It will need regular pruning and training when it's young and follow-up pruning as it establishes to keep it vigorous and looking good. Pruning can be done after the majority of flowering has finished.

Companion Planting and Design
Crossvine is an excellent plant for a post or fence and can be used effectively in a woodland or among flowering shrubs and perennials. Choose plants with warm-colored flowers such as yellow, orange, and red to color coordinate with crossvine.

Try These
'Atrosanguinea' is quite a variation from the norm with dark red-purple flowers with yellow interiors. The evergreen leaves are narrower and longer than the species. 'Dragon Lady' is an exceptionally cold-hardy form with improved adaptability to adverse soil conditions and drought. It offers showy flowers that are reddish orange on the outside and orange inside. 'Jekyll' is a special variety with stunning flowers featuring rich orange color on the outside and yellow inside. 'Tangerine Beauty' is a very vigorous grower displaying a profusion of ruby-tangerine flowers.

Hellebore

Helleborus spp.

Botanical Pronunciation hell-EBB-er-iss

Other Name Lenten rose

Bloom Period and Seasonal Color
White, green, rose, purple, and many other color combinations in late winter and early spring; evergreen foliage

Mature Height × Spread
12 to 18 inches × 12 to 15 inches

Zones See "Try These"

Hellebores are among the hottest and most cultivated perennials available today. They consist of about twenty species and countless cultivars, all of which have unique ornamental qualities. Intense breeding of this plant has rendered countless new variations, which are constantly changing and improving with each coming gardening year. With the species covered here blooming in winter and early spring, hellebores keep the gardening season alive even during cold weather. As a result, other common names include Christmas rose and Lenten rose. Because they bloom in cool weather, often their flowering will continue for months. Their evergreen foliage is also rather handsome and durable. Hellebores are well adapted for shade, dry conditions, and poor soil. Some hellebores are poisonous and are also quite resistant to deer browsing and pests.

When, Where, and How to Plant
Although hellebores are adaptable and tolerant of adverse conditions, moist, well-drained, acidic soils are best for maximum performance. Hellebores will benefit from organic matter in the soil so incorporate compost when planting, especially in heavy clay or dry, sandy soils. They also prefer partial shade but can grow in full shade as well. New plants can be purchased in small containers in spring and should be spaced about 12 to 18 inches apart.

Growing Tips
A spring application of fertilizer will help plants grow rapidly and expand. Add a light layer of shredded leaves or pine straw to keep plants cool in the summer.

Regional Advice and Care
Hellebores are not particularly easy to propagate from seed although some species will self-seed. You may want to purchase small plants in spring from a local or mail order nursery to introduce new and exciting selections into the garden. Dividing larger clumps that have established can propagate existing plants. Hellebores are reliably hardy, low-maintenance plants with no significant pest or disease issues. Although evergreen, if foliage gets beat up after a long, hardy winter, cut plants back in spring and they will rejuvenate.

Companion Planting and Design
Hellebores are shade lovers and fit well into a woodland garden with rhododendron, camellias, hosta, barrenwort, and ferns. They are especially effective in large mass plantings and can also be used in containers.

Try These
There are too many cultivars of hellebores to mention but just doing a bit of research online of *Helleborus* × *hybridus* will offer a treasure trove of cultivars with a wide variety of flower and foliage colors and types. Most hybrids are hardy to Zone 4. Christmas rose (*H. niger*) has saucer-shaped white (sometimes pink) flowers in winter and early spring. Lenten rose (*H. orientalis*) is one of the most popular species and easiest to grow, with nodding flowers ranging from white to plum color and other color variations; it's hardy to Zone 4. Bearsfoot hellebore (*H. foetidus*) has light green, nodding flowers and finely dissected leaves; it's hardy to Zone 5.

Honeysuckle

Lonicera spp.

Botanical Pronunciation
luh-NISS-ur-uh

Bloom Period and Seasonal Color
Flowers are orange-red, pink, or yellow (depending on species) in late spring and early summer

Mature Height × Spread
10 to 20 feet × 3 to 6 feet

Zones See "Try These"

In addition to fragrant, flowering shrubs, some honeysuckle are available as vines and low growing shrubs as well. These colorful vines have gained in popularity and are most effective when trained on a lamppost, fence, or latticework. A low-growing, evergreen groundcover honeysuckle is available as well and is discussed below. Honeysuckles offer long, tubular flowers, which are frequently visited by hummingbirds, bees, and butterflies. The flowers on these vine-type honeysuckles are not usually as fragrant as some of their shrubby counterparts but are nevertheless just as beautiful and functional. Flower colors are variable but are typically bright and striking smooth, blue-green foliage. These twining vines are very effective when planted with flowering shrubs and perennials and can even be used in containers.

When, Where, and How to Plant
Honeysuckle vines are fast-growing, adaptable plants that prefer moist, well-drained, acidic or near neutral soil pH. Honeysuckles thrive in rich, organic soils so add compost to sandy or heavy clay soils. Full sun is best for flower production but partial shade is also acceptable. Honeysuckle should be planted from containers in spring and spaced 3 to 5 feet apart.

Growing Tips
A 1- to 2-inch layer of wood chips will keep plants happy during the long hot days of summer. Keep soil evenly moist.

Regional Advice and Care
Honeysuckles are relatively pest resistant although leaf spots and aphids can be problematic so keep a close eye on them during the summer months. Pruning to keep plants trained and under control should be done right after flowering in early summer. If it doesn't have a strong support structure, often honeysuckle will creep on the ground, causing tangled vegetation on the ground that has to be pruned.

Companion Planting and Design
Vine-type honeysuckles are excellent to cover a wall, fence, or arbor and will complement annuals, perennials, and shrubs in the summer landscape. I have seen them grown in large containers and moved around the garden with good results.

Try These
Goldflame honeysuckle (*Lonicera* × *heckrottii*) is a vigorous vine displaying carmine flower buds that open to showy creamy yellow inside and pink outside. The soft, blue-green foliage is evergreen to about 15 degrees Fahrenheit and will partially or fully drop if colder. Hardy to Zone 5 but will grow to Zone 4 with protection. Trumpet honeysuckle (*L. sempervirens*) is a southern native with flowers that are yellow-orange inside and orange-red on the outside. The new growth is tinged with reddish purple before maturing to bluish green. 'Flava' is an attractive pure yellow form with bright green foliage. Hardy to Zone 4 but will grow to Zone 3 with protection. A unique groundcover-type shrub honeysuckle called Privet honeysuckle (*L. pileata*) has lustrous, dark green leaves and a spreading, cascading growth habit to 2 to 3 feet tall. Hardy to Zone 6.

Japanese Skimmia

Skimmia japonica

Botanical Pronunciation
SKIMM-ee-uh juh-PON-ikuh

Bloom Period and Seasonal Color
Greenish white or reddish maroon flower buds open to creamy white flowers in spring; glossy red fruit in fall; dark green foliage

Mature Height × Spread
3 to 4 feet × 4 to 5 feet

Zones Hardy to Zone 7; to Zone 6 with protection

Skimmia is actually related to citrus even though it bears no resemblance except for its toughness and adaptability. This low-growing shrub forms thick mounds of aromatic foliage and is ideal in partial or dense shade. Since this plant is dioecious, only the female plants have the glossy red berries. However, the male plants have noticeably larger flower clusters and are quite attractive. The flower buds are typically a striking reddish maroon and are especially interesting in winter. The small, creamy white flowers are more fragrant on male plants and birds will eat the berries of the female plants. The flowers will attract a wide variety of pollinators to the garden. This plant works well in a woodland or in small groupings along the foundation of the house.

When, Where, and How to Plant
Skimmia prefers moist, well-drained, acidic soil that is high in organic matter. Therefore, add a generous amount of well-aged compost to the planting hole. Full sun will bleach the leaves so site them in partial or full shade. Once established skimmia is low maintenance and drought tolerant. Plants are typically sold in containers in the spring. Skimmia should be spaced 2 to 4 feet apart.

Growing Tips
Add 1 to 2 inches of pine straw, wood chips, or another fine mulch. If plants are yellow and seem weak, take a soil sample to check nutrient content of the soil. Sometimes in higher pH soils the leaves of skimmia will turn greenish yellow and may need nitrogen or iron. Add a well-balanced, granular fertilizer in spring if needed.

Regional Advice and Care
Skimmia are rather pest free although spider mites may be a problem. There are organic products that can be used so check your local nursery or agricultural Extension office for the latest recommendations. Pruning can be done in early to midsummer as older plants can get leggy and sparse. Trimming back the tips of the plants will encourage denser, bushy plants.

Companion Planting and Design
Skimmia is a great companion for sweetbox, evergreen viburnum, holly, camellia, and many other shade-loving shrubs. It can be used effectively in groupings, as an edging or facer plant, and in containers.

Try These
'Winter Bouquet' is a male plant offering striking, large clusters of red flower buds opening to small, fragrant flowers and a reliable pollinator to female plants. Reeves skimmia (*Skimmia reevesiana*) is a species with bisexual flowers meaning that it is self-pollinating. It is more open growing than Japanese skimmia and only grows 2 to 3 feet tall and wide.

Juniper

Juniperus spp.

Botanical Pronunciation joo-NIP-ur-us

Other Name Cedar

Bloom Period and Seasonal Color
Low, spreading habit and gray, blue, or green needlelike leaves. Female plants have gray berries

Mature Height × Spread
1 to 2 feet × 8 to 10 feet or more

Zones Hardy to Zone 4; *J. conferta* hardy to Zone 5

Junipers are well-known, often-used groundcovers, shrubs, and trees that are valued for their colorful evergreen foliage, variable growth habit, and durability. Juniper species specifically used as groundcovers are very effective on slopes, in foundation plantings, and mass plantings. They can cover large, open areas or smaller, more confined areas depending on the species and variety chosen. Like all junipers, these groundcovers thrive in hot, dry conditions and sandy, rocky soil. Once established, junipers are low maintenance, requiring little to no care with the exception of occasional pruning. Foliage colors vary from emerald green to blue and gold and function as accents in the landscape. Like holly and yew, juniper is dioecious, meaning they have female plants bearing fleshy cones.

When, Where, and How to Plant
Juniper requires well-drained soil and full sun—anything less is risky. Although they tolerate clay soils and partial shade, diseases will often prevail if the environment is too moist and shady. Juniper thrives in sandy loam soil and full exposure with plenty of air circulation. Juniper tolerates heat, humidity, salt spray, and pollution. Purchase plants in containers and space 3 to 5 feet apart depending on the species.

Growing Tips
Juniper does not usually require regular fertilizer but adding a modest amount of compost to a sandy or rocky soil is acceptable. Mulching new plantings will help them establish.

Regional Advice and Care
Juniper is susceptible to a wide range of pests including bagworm, spider mites, and a blight called phomopsis. Phomopsis can usually be minimized with plants sited in full sun with air circulation and proper watering. Water junipers only when needed; automatic irrigation systems can cause serious disease problems. Monitor insect problems closely and take appropriate action early to minimize damage. Pruning to remove dead or diseased stems or damaged branches after a long hard winter is important.

Companion Planting and Design
Groundcover junipers are excellent as edging or facer plants in the front of a sunny border, in mass plantings, rock gardens, and on slopes and embankments. They are excellent companions to other conifers such as falsecypress, arborvitae, and yew. Juniper is especially effective in seashore conditions.

Try These
Shore juniper (*J. conferta*) is a low, mounded, bushy juniper with green needle foliage and blackish blue fruit on female plants. 'Blue Pacific' is striking with blue-green foliage. Creeping juniper (*J. horizontalis*) has deep green foliage that often turns plum color in winter. Japanese garden juniper (*J. procumbens* 'Nana') is a compact, mat-forming juniper with bluish to gray-green foliage. This species is one of the nicest and low maintenance of the groundcover types. Russian arborvitae (*Microbiota decussata*) is a juniper relative with a low-growing, dense habit and emerald-green leaves that turn plum color in winter. It is excellent as a weed-suppressive groundcover.

Moss Phlox

Phlox subulata

Botanical Pronunciation
FLOCKS sub-you-LAY-tuh

Other Name Moss pink

Bloom Period and Seasonal Color
Masses of white, pink, blue, or purple flowers in early spring

Mature Height × Spread
4 to 6 inches × 1 to 1 ½ feet

   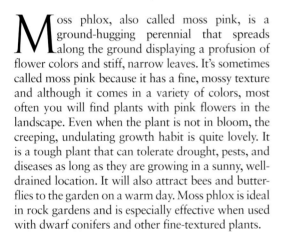

Moss phlox, also called moss pink, is a ground-hugging perennial that spreads along the ground displaying a profusion of flower colors and stiff, narrow leaves. It's sometimes called moss pink because it has a fine, mossy texture and although it comes in a variety of colors, most often you will find plants with pink flowers in the landscape. Even when the plant is not in bloom, the creeping, undulating growth habit is quite lovely. It is a tough plant that can tolerate drought, pests, and diseases as long as they are growing in a sunny, well-drained location. It will also attract bees and butterflies to the garden on a warm day. Moss phlox is ideal in rock gardens and is especially effective when used with dwarf conifers and other fine-textured plants.

When, Where, and How to Plant
Moss phlox prefers moist, well-drained soil and full sun but will tolerate drier, rocky soils and partial shade. Moss phlox has few requirements but if you have those growing conditions found in rocky, gravely soils, incorporate a generous amount of compost to the soil. Too much shade will cause plants to be sparse and unproductive. Plants can be purchased in small containers in spring and spaced about 12 inches apart.

Growing Tips
Add a 1- to 2-inch layer of wood chips or shredded leaves. Plants do not need regular fertilizer applications but if needed, add a low-nitrogen, well-balanced granular fertilizer in spring. Soil should be kept evenly moist.

Regional Advice and Care
Moss phlox is pest free with the exception of spider mites but that typically isn't a problem unless plants are growing in hot, dry locations. Spritzing plants with cold water a few times a day may help light infestations; otherwise, visit your local nursery or agricultural Extension office for treatment options. Pruning should be done after flowering to keep plants inbounds and dense. If plants are leggy or too large, cut them back as much as half without leaving them with bare stems and that will encourage dense plants that may rebloom the same season. Propagate plants by divisions in spring or fall.

Companion Planting and Design
Moss phlox is a nice accent plant to dwarf conifers, flowering shrubs, and sun-loving perennials. It is ideal in a rock garden, foundation planting, as an edging plant, or on a slope.

Try These
'Candy Stripe' is a nice bicolor with pink flowers edged with white. 'Drummond's Pink' has large, deep pink flowers with a red center that will dazzle the spring landscape. 'Emerald Blue' offers a blanket of deep blue flowers that is stunning in the early spring landscape. You can also try the Early Spring series, which come in a variety of colors. Creeping phlox (*Phlox stolonifera*) is similar but tends to be taller and tolerates more shade than moss phlox, giving gardeners another option for the woodland garden.

Pachysandra

Pachysandra spp.

Botanical Pronunciation pack-ih-SAN-druh

Other Name Spurge

Bloom Period and Seasonal Color
White flower spikes in early spring; handsome green foliage

Mature Height × Spread
6 to 12 inches × 1 to 2 feet

Zones See "Regional Advice and Care"

Pachysandra is a popular evergreen ground-cover that spreads freely throughout the garden. Although it can be aggressive, proper siting and maintenance can make this a useful and rewarding plant in the landscape. There are two distinct species of pachysandra, the native Allegheny pachysandra (*Pachysandra procumbens*) and the more common Japanese pachysandra (*P. terminalis*). These two look similar is some ways but are quite different in others. Allegheny pachysandra has mottled, green to blue-green foliage with no sheen while Japanese pachysandra has dark green, glossy leaves. Both have spikes of white flowers in spring although Allegheny pachysandra flowering is a bit more noticeable in the landscape. Both are ideal in partial or even full shade and have a reputation of being carefree and adaptable.

When, Where, and How to Plant
Pachysandra prefers moist, well-drained, acidic soil with a generous amount of organic matter. They are not meant for poorly drained soils, full sun, or high pH soils. Add a generous amount of compost or manure to the soil before planting pachysandra. I have seen Japanese pachysandra tolerate full sun but it often turns a yellowish green and is subject to more winter damage. Plants are usually purchased in spring in small pots or flats and should be planted 6 to 12 inches apart.

Growing Tips
A light application of a well-balanced, low-nitrogen granular fertilizer is recommended in sandy soils to give plants a boost in spring. Keep plants watered during drought and water in the morning so plants have a chance to dry up going into the evening hours.

Regional Advice and Care
Japanese pachysandra is susceptible to leaf blight, scale, and mites, but those problems are more common in plantings that are stressed. Boxwood blight can affect the health of pachysandra so do not over-water and monitor plants closely for signs of this disease, which appear as small brown lesions with yellow haloes around them. Fungicides are available at your local nursery if needed for certain diseases. Be careful not to prune pachysandra back too hard. This spreading plant does not like to be cut back to its bare stems. Allegheny pachysandra is hardy to Zone 5 but will grow to Zone 4 with protection. It will be semi-evergreen or deciduous in very cold climates. Japanese pachysandra is hardy to Zone 4.

Companion Planting and Design
Pachysandra is excellent in a woodland garden mixed with rhododendrons, azaleas, holly, camellia, hosta, and other shade lovers. Japanese pachysandra will need to be pulled away from the base of trees, shrubs, and perennials every year to reduce competition.

Try These
'Green Sheen' is an outstanding cultivated variety of Japanese pachysandra with a high gloss finish to its leaves. 'Silver Edge' is a nice variegated form that is slower growing but adds a nice accent to a shade garden.

Sweetbox

Sarcococca hookeriana var. *humilis*

Botanical Pronunciation sar-koe-KOCK-uh
hook-ur-ee-AY-nuh HEW-mih-liss

Other Name Himalayan sarcococca

Bloom Period and Seasonal Color
Inconspicuous but very fragrant flowers in early
spring; small, glossy, dark leaves

Mature Height × Spread 1 to 2 feet × 2 to 4 feet

Zones Hardy to Zone 6; will grow to Zone 5
with protection

Sweetbox is related to boxwood but is quite different in appearance. It has larger, more pointed leaves and sweetly fragrant flowers in early spring. The leaves hide the flowers and often-unsuspecting visitors to the garden will find themselves stopping dead in their tracks to find out where the intoxicating fragrance is coming from. Sweetbox is stonoliferous, meaning it spreads by small, underground stems that will send out roots and shoots. This colony of vegetation develops into a neat mass of foliage and is a very effective groundcover or low growing shrub. Sweetbox works well in a woodland garden or along the edge of a path so you can enjoy its fragrance. Sweetbox has shown good resistance to deer and is very shade tolerant as well.

When, Where, and How to Plant

Sweetbox prefers moist, well-drained, organic and acidic soil, and partial shade. Sweetbox does not like poor soils and in sandy soils it should be given generous amounts of compost when planting. Incorporating compost or manure into the soil before planting is recommended so the organic matter is evenly distributed throughout the planting area. It will tolerate full shade and full sun, but will often turn yellow with too much sun. Plants can be purchased in small containers in spring and should be spaced 12 to 18 inches apart. Eventually, new plants will spread and form a dense mat of foliage.

Growing Tips

One to 2 inches of wood chips, shredded leaves, or pine straw will help plants establish and prosper. Keep soil evenly moist, especially in the hot, dry summer months. Regular fertilizer applications are not usually needed but a low-nitrogen fertilizer in spring can be applied when needed.

Regional Advice and Care

Sweetbox is a carefree, easy-to-grow groundcover with few pest problems. The recent boxwood blight issue has revealed that sweetbox is susceptible to this disease, which causes browning, and death of plants quickly. Keep overhead watering to a minimum and closely monitor your plants. Pruning of sweetbox can be done after flowering to cut back or trim plants but that is not often needed with this low-maintenance plant.

Companion Planting and Design

Sweetbox is an excellent companion plant to skimmia, holly, camellia, and other broadleaved evergreens. It can be used as a facer plant, along the edge of a pathway, in a woodland garden, and as a foundation planting.

Try These

Two other species worth trying are *Sarcococca confusa* and *S. orientalis*. Both are small to medium shrubs with fine foliage, fragrant flowers, interesting fruit, and a durability that is a welcomed attribute to any gardener.

Sweet Woodruff

Galium odoratum

Botanical Pronunciation
gal-EE-um odor-AYE-tum

Other Name Bedstraw

Bloom Period and Seasonal Color
White flowers in spring; fine foliage

Mature Height × Spread
4 to 9 inches × 12 inches or more

Zones Hardy to Zone 4

Sweet woodruff is a low-growing, spreading perennial that is a native to the woodlands of Europe. The slender, creeping root system and the ability to self-seed will allow sweet woodruff to develop into larger masses of vegetation. The petite, white flowers in spring offer a sweet fragrance and the leaves smell like freshly mown hay when crushed. The green, lance-shaped, whorled leaves are sometimes used to flavor teas and fruit punch and are used for sachets and potpourris. Sweet woodruff is an ideal groundcover for a moist, partially shaded area of the garden near a path or at the edge of a flowerbed where it can be seen. It is especially effective with other shade-loving plants such as ferns, hellebores, barrenwort, and astilbe.

When, Where, and How to Plant

Sweet woodruff requires moist soil and will thrive in damp, shaded areas of the garden. It will suffer in dry, exposed sites and will often go dormant in the summer months if subjected to a serious drought. Sweet woodruff prefers rich, organic soil so add compost or well-aged manure to the soil before planting. Part or full shade is best to keep sweet woodruff looking good. Small plants in containers will quickly establish in spring and spacing can vary depending on the space you have available. General spacing of 10 to 12 inches apart is recommended.

Growing Tips

Keep plants well watered until established, at least for the first growing season. Even moisture should be maintained in the soil during the hot summer months. Regular fertilizer applications are not necessary but a low-nitrogen, granular fertilizer in spring can be applied if needed.

Regional Advice and Care

Sweet woodruff is quite easy to grow if you have the right growing conditions. It is not bothered by pest and disease and its only enemy is full, direct sunlight. Plants can be divided in spring or fall and spread around the garden. Sweet woodruff can be somewhat aggressive in the right situation and in open areas can be mowed with a mower at the highest setting.

Companion Planting and Design

Sweet woodruff is a wonderful groundcover to naturalize in a woodland or to grow under the dappled shade of trees. In spring, the white flowers resemble freshly fallen snow and are an effective combination with the delicate, aromatic leaves. It is a very nice companion plant to ferns, hellebores, hosta, and other shade-loving, moisture-seeking perennials.

Try These

Most species of *Galium* are considered weeds native to Europe and are typically removed from the garden. *G. odoratum* is the exception and an exceptional plant indeed.

Trumpet Vine

Campsis radicans

Botanical Pronunciation
KAMP-siss RAD-ih-kanz

Other Name Trumpetcreeper

Bloom Period and Seasonal Color
Large, trumpet-shaped orange to scarlet flowers
from early summer to early fall

Mature Length
30 to 40 feet or more

Zones Hardy to Zone 4

Trumpet vine is a fast-growing vine that creeps and clings to whatever it can get its hairlike rootlets in contact with. The long, compound leaves are dark green all summer with no significant fall coloration. To many this plant is considered invasive and a real garden thug! But with regular pruning and a large open space to climb, it can also brighten up the summer landscape. Whatever structure is used to support trumpet vine should be sturdy and long lasting, since trumpet vine develops thick, winding stems. Trumpet vine needs regular pruning and can be cut back hard to main stems in spring. The flowers are favorites to a variety of pollinators and hummingbirds. In addition to orange, other cultivated varieties offer yellow, apricot, and red.

When, Where, and How to Plant
Trumpet vine will grow in virtually any soil and light conditions from heavy clay to sandy, dry soils. Full sun is best for flower production although it will also flower fairly well in shade (though it won't flower reliably in full shade). Plants can be purchased in containers in spring, and one plant will be plenty for the average home garden.

Growing Tips
Plats become rampant in rich, garden soil, so no soil amendments or fertilizer applications are required. Trumpet vine is not picky but prefers even moisture in the soil.

Regional Advice and Care
Trumpet vine is susceptible to a variety of insects and diseases but none that will slow it down. Powdery mildew will develop on leaves late in the growing season but is generally more cosmetic than damaging. Pruning is the key to success with trumpet vine and a hard pruning while dormant in late winter will help to keep plants productive. For example, if growing on a fence, cut the trumpet vine level with the top of the fence so it cannot grow much above that. Trumpet vine will also colonize, sending out suckers, which need to be dug up and removed.

Companion Planting and Design
I have fond memories of trumpet vine growing on a fence at my childhood home. My father would brag about it and it would be the talk of the neighborhood every summer. Trumpet vine is a standalone plant that doesn't play nice with others and needs its own dedicated space.

Try These
'Apricot' offers beautiful apricot-yellow flowers while 'Flava' displays yellow to orange-yellow flowers. 'Tango' offers dark, glossy green leaves and coral red flowers. 'Mme Galen' is a variety of a hybrid trumpet vine with large, showy orange flowers. 'Morning Calm', a cultivated variety of C. *grandiflora*, has distinctly large, peach-colored flowers with a yellow center.

DEER-RESISTANT PLANTS

Deer can be devastating visitors to the garden, defoliating the landscape like a swarm of locusts. Your prized specimens can be ruined overnight and some plants such as pine, spruce, arborvitae, and juniper often do not recover. Mature trees can be transformed into lollipops with all of the bottom branches defoliated, leaving foliage only on the top half of the tree. Deer feeding on plants is referred to as "browsing." This browsing is most evident on evergreens and can be especially damaging during winter when plants are dormant. Although deer can potentially browse any plant, there are certain plants that tend to be less appealing to them under normal conditions. However, understand that "deer resistant" is a relative term, and *very few plants are truly safe if deer get really hungry.* There are many differing opinions among gardeners about what plants are truly deer resistant, with few people agreeing on a concise list. The severity of deer browsing depends on many factors such as weather, scarcity of food, what other food sources are available nearby, and the size of the deer population in a given area. In harsh winters where much of the landscape is under ice and snow and food is scarce, deer may forage on any plant material they can find.

While there are various deer repellents and elaborate fences on the market to protect your garden, there are some reliable deer-resistant plants that are less likely to be devoured by deer. Often published lists of deer-resistant plants are categorized by terms such as *rarely damaged* or *occasionally damaged*, to reflect the relative resistance plants have to deer browsing. There are several excellent lists from Dr. Mark Bridgen of Cornell University (www.gardening.cornell.edu/factsheets/deerdef) and Rutgers University Agricultural Experiment Station (http://njaes.rutgers.edu/deerresistance). Some of the plants I have observed as reliably resistant to deer are:

Annuals: Cleome, Lantana, Marigold (*Tagetes* spp.), Snapdragon (*Antirrhinum* spp.)

Perennials: Butterfly Weed (*Asclepias* spp.), Coreopsis, Nepeta, Black-Eyed Susan (*Rudbeckia* spp.)

Groundcovers: Epimedium, Hellebore (*Helleborus* spp.), Pachysandra, Skimmia

Bulbs: Allium, Daffodil (*Narcissus* spp.), Snowdrops (*Galanthus* spp.), Winter Aconite (*Eranthus hyemalis*)

Shrubs: Butterfly Bush (*Buddleja davidii*), Pieris, Japanese Plum Yew (*Cephalotaxus harringtonia*), Tree Peony (*Paeonia suffruticosa*)

Trees: American Holly (*Ilex opaca*), Bottlebrush Buckeye (*Aesculus parviflora*), River Birch (*Betula nigra*), Serviceberry (*Amelanchier* spp.)

*Many ornamental grasses and ferns are also deer resistant.

SEASHORE PLANTS

lants that are adapted to grow near or at the seashore must have certain qualities such as salt tolerance; the ability to withstand drying wind, heat, and drought; and the ability to withstand dry, sandy soils. These often-harsh conditions will severely damage or kill the average plant but the seashore is also home to a wide range of native species. In a home garden setting where you desire a more cultivated, less naturalistic look, there *are* non-invasive, exotic species that will also tolerate seashore conditions. While this environment creates some challenges not experienced inland, maritime landscapes can be just as rewarding and beautiful.

In addition to the typical growing conditions associated with seashore conditions, coastal areas of New York and New Jersey have been ravaged by natural disasters over the last few years. Hurricanes Irene and Sandy wreaked havoc on natural environments and residential areas along the Jersey shore, southern New York in New York City, and on Long Island. Wind damage, fresh and salt water flooding, and erosion have caused serious damage to landscapes, which have had to be totally rebuilt in some cases. But landscape professionals, researchers, and homeowners have learned a lot about which plants withstood these severe conditions and how to better protect these landscapes now. This list of plants offers some herbaceous and woody plants that are recommended for seashore conditions. Please note that there are different levels of exposure, with fewer species thriving closer to the harshest conditions and more species thriving with some protection from wind, salt spray, and flooding. These recommended plants function as specimen plantings, mass plantings, on slopes, or as foundation plantings.

Annuals: Cleome, Sweet Potato Vine (*Ipomoea* spp.), Lantana, Petunia, Marigold (*Tagetes* spp.), Salvia, Verbena

Perennials: Aster, Black-Eyed Susan (*Rudbeckia* spp.), Coreopsis, Daylily (*Hemerocallis* spp.), Iris, Nepeta, Ornamental Grasses, Sedum

Groundcovers and Vines: Trumpet Vine (*Campsis* spp.), Cotoneaster, Barrenwort (*Epimedium* spp.), Honeysuckle (*Lonicera* spp.), Juniper (*Juniperus* spp.), Russian Arborvitae (*Microbiota decussata*)

Shrubs: Bayberry (*Myrica pensylvanica*), Butterfly Bush (*Buddleja davidii*), Clethra, Winterberry and Inkberry Holly (*Ilex* spp.), Japanese Plum Yew (*Cephalotaxus harringtonia*), Landscape Rose (*Rosa* spp.)

Trees: Crabapple (*Malus* spp.), Crape Myrtle (*Lagerstroemia* spp.), American Elm (*Ulmus americana*), Heritage Birch (*Betula nigra*), Ornamental Cherry (*Prunus* spp.), Redbud (*Cercis canadensis*), Serviceberry (*Amelanchier* spp.)

POLLINATOR-FRIENDLY PLANTS

Beneficial insects such as butterflies and bees are an essential and rewarding part of gardening. These helpful insects pollinate our flowers, fruits, and vegetables and keep the garden healthy and viable. In general, pollinators have three basic requirements: a food source, water, and shelter. A well-designed, diverse garden with a wide variety of plant and flower types will provide all of these things necessary for pollinators to make your garden a home.

In the case of butterflies, remember they have several stages of their life cycle including a larval stage as a caterpillar. These caterpillars need the right food sources to develop into adult butterflies. For example, the Monarch butterfly feeds specifically on native milkweed species (*Asclepias* spp.), first with the leaves as a food source for the caterpillars and then as butterflies, feeding on the flower nectar. In addition, butterflies need full sun at least part of the day, flat rocks or other surfaces to sun themselves, shelter from the elements (such as strong winds and rain), and a source of water, which can be accomplished by putting out water dishes or a clean bird bath.

Bees also need habitat and food and water to survive in the garden. We often think about the importance of honeybees, a non-native species, but gardeners should also remember there are native bees, such as bumblebees, miner bees, and carpenter bees, that are just as important. The best way to support a healthy and diverse bee population is to introduce masses of native plants with overlapping bloom times; maintain some unmowed, natural areas for nesting and shelter; and provide a reliable water source, which can be used by both butterflies and bees. Check out this list of pollinator-friendly plants that should be incorporated into the garden.

Annuals: Wax Begonia, Cosmos, Dahlias, Lantana, Salvia, Verbena

Perennials: Aster, Black-Eyed Susan (*Rudbeckia* spp.), Butterfly Weed (*Asclepias* spp.), Catmint (*Nepeta* spp.) Coneflower (*Echinacea purpurea*), Coreopsis, Geranium, Lily, Sedum

Shrubs: Abelia, Butterfly Bush (*Buddleja davidii*), Clethra, Lilac (*Syringa* spp.), Rose, Viburnum

Trees: Crabapple (*Malus* spp.), Magnolia, Ornamental Cherry (*Prunus* spp.), Redbud (*Cercis* spp.), Serviceberry (*Amelanchier* spp.)

GARDEN KNOW-HOW

Proper Plant Maintenance

Properly maintaining your garden is the key to healthy and productive plants. With a diverse landscape that includes flowers, groundcovers, vines, trees, shrubs, and evergreens, specific care is needed for each plant type. That means that you need to be detailed oriented and pay close attention to what is going on in your garden on a regular basis. Soil preparation and enhancement, composting and mulching, proper watering techniques, sound planting techniques, and pruning of the landscape are all-important factors that must be implemented correctly. A well-designed and maintained garden will require time and patience but will result in a four-season garden that will reach its maximum potential.

Site Assessment

In order to properly maintain your garden, you must first do a thorough site assessment to determine the finer details of the garden environment. This requires you to take some soil samples and have them tested for nutrients and pH. A detailed analysis will provide helpful information on the types and current condition of your soil and what adjustments if any need to be made in order to grow plants successfully. Both Cornell University and Rutgers University can provide this service so check your local agricultural Extension office for details. There is great value in doing these types of tests every few years because it helps monitor soil conditions and what you need to be doing to keep the soil environment at an optimum level for plant growth. This is important both for existing and new plants that are introduced into the garden.

There are three main types of garden soil: sand, silt, and clay. Loam is soil that is composed of mostly sand and silt with some clay and generally contains nutrients and organic matter, allows for the infiltration of water and air, and is well drained. Loam is considered ideal for growing plants and is sometimes referred to as topsoil. Most plants recommended in this book will grow in well-drained, rich garden loam. But most soils aren't this ideal and require some amendments to make them more suitable for plant growth. Sandy soils that dry out quickly and heavy clay soils that retain water and compact easily are two prime examples of challenging soil environments that gardeners often face. But soil improvements must be thought out very carefully and are very dependent on the results of a soil sample and the type of soil you are gardening with. Too often gardeners are on autopilot, adding peat moss, bone meal, granular fertilizer, and other additives without knowing if or what the real issue is.

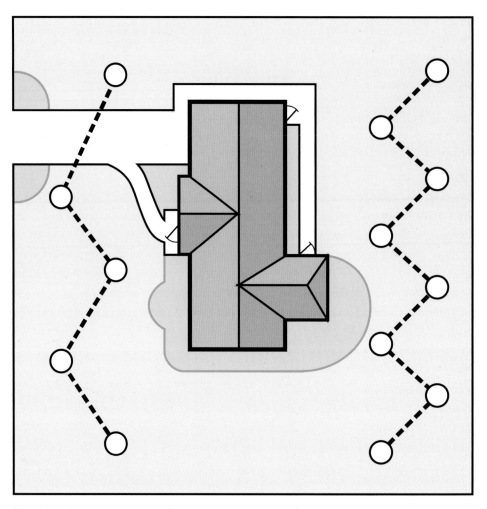

Sketch your home and landscape (you don't have to be great!) so you can perform a site assessment. Include the major hardscapes and softscapes, and take soil samples at various points.

Of all of the soil amendments available to gardeners today, I believe the most valuable is a well-aged compost. Compost is the derivative of organic waste such as leaves, grass clippings, wood chips, kitchen waste such as leafy vegetables, and so forth. The benefits of composting are far reaching and long-term. In sandy soils, compost increases the water-holding capacity of the soil. In clay soils, compost improves the consistency of the soil and makes in more friable (loose) and easy to work and easier for plant roots to penetrate. Compost adds nutrients and beneficial microorganisms that you cannot get in other soil amendments. We will talk more about compost and mulching below; it is an inexpensive and efficient way to help your garden grow.

Composting and Mulch

Composting is the recycling of organic materials to enhance soil biology, improve soil conditions, and encourage plant growth. Composting is a great way to reuse materials such as organic yard waste, leafy vegetable scraps, coffee grounds, and other materials to make a natural form of fertilizer for your plants. Composting is a complex

procedure that requires good raw materials to create the best possible finished product, also called "humus." Compost that has been aged properly will provide a safe and useable dose of nutrients and beneficial organisms that support plant health. It also helps to improve the soil structure and water-holding capacity of the soil.

A productive compost pile needs quality raw materials and oxygen and moisture to support the microorganisms necessary to break down organic material. A compost pile should be sited in an open area with plenty of air circulation and room to work the pile regularly. A compost pile *can* be sited in partial shade but be sure it's not located in too much shade where the overhead canopy of trees inhibits rainfall from reaching the pile.

Oxygen is very important in order to encourage microorganisms to consume the organic materials you have put into the compost. This can be accomplished by turning the pile regularly; once a week or several times a month during the growing season is a good frequency. The pile can be turned with a garden fork, pitch fork, or shovel. This turning process provides oxygen and aids the decomposition process.

Even moisture is another important component of proper composting. The compost pile should be moist, but not wet or soggy. If you have adequate rainfall

Build a compost pile by layering green materials and brown materials like you'd make a lasagna. Start with chopped up dried leaves (you can run over them with the lawn mower). Then add grass clippings or kitchen scraps and keep layering. The smaller the pieces you add to the pile, the faster they'll decompose.

Continuously add material to the compost pile—shredded newspapers, the stems of broccoli, last summer's dead annual flowers that you pulled up, even the Halloween pumpkin. Keep the pile "cooking" (a healthy pile will heat up) by using a pitchfork or garden fork to turn the pile and mix it up.

in spring and summer, adding water to your compost pile should not be necessary. But if there is a drought or the compost pile begins to dry out, water should be added as needed.

As the material in the compost pile decays, the pile will heat up. This heating cycle aids in the decomposition process while killing off harmful pests and weed seeds. A healthy combination of oxygen, moisture, and heat encourage beneficial fungi, bacteria, and other organisms such as worms to complete the transformation from raw materials to finished, useable compost. "Green" products such as herbaceous material, vegetable scraps from the kitchen, or grass clippings will be consumed by bacteria while "brown" products such as leaves and wood chips will be consumed by fungi. The compost pile will heat up to 130 to 140 degrees Fahrenheit before cooling off, which usually means the compost process is complete. Turn your compost pile regularly to ensure that it does not heat up too much, as compost piles reaching over 160 degrees Fahrenheit is not desirable.

Compost bins can be storebought or homemade. Prefabricated models come in many shapes and sizes and feature self-contained units that can be easily turned. A homemade compost bin can be constructed from wire fencing or wooden pallets. Start off with a compost bin that is 3 feet × 3 feet. This is a manageable size and you can always expand later once you have the process down to a science. It is also advisable to have two separate compost bins—one for an active pile that is in the process of being made into finished compost and the other for new materials. This allows the first compost pile to finish decomposing without being disturbed.

Mulch

Mulch is very important and is part of a composting program. Mulch can be shredded leaves, wood chips, pine straw, wood shavings, and any organic material that can be spread on the surface of the soil. Mulch is very beneficial as it regulates soil moisture and temperature, reducing the chance of fluctuations such as freezing and thawing. It also reduces weed growth and, as mulch decomposes, it adds organic matter and nutrients back to the soil. Mulch also reduces soil compaction over time because as it breaks down, soil organisms active along the surface will break up soil compaction a little at a time. Mulching should be done in the cool temperatures of spring or fall and never in the heat of summer or during the frigid temperatures of winter. I try to avoid mulching the garden when the soil is very moist or in muddy conditions.

Mulch should be applied at a depth of 1 to 2 inches, but never more than 3 inches. Avoid creating mounded mulch "volcanoes"; they not only look bad but they can seriously harm plants over time. Overmulched plantings will develop surface roots because it creates a low oxygen environment, forcing roots to the surface where there is air. This can eventually cause girdling roots, which will wrap around the main trunk of a tree or shrub or create a secondary root system. These abnormalities can and will shorten the life of your plants, even causing root rots and other problems. Too much mulch will also repel water rather than absorbing it.

As for quality and type of mulch, stay away from dyed or processed mulches for which you do not know the contents. A natural mulch that has been produced locally is a much better scenario. Buy your mulch from a local garden center or nursery that has a good reputation and offers a clean source of mulch, or talk to your local arborist about a delivery of wood chips, which can be aged and then used in the garden.

Fertilizing

A sound fertilizer program is also very important to keep your plants healthy and productive. Processed fertilizers can be used to supplement a composting program or aid in the correction of deficiencies found in the soil. There are many types of processed fertilizers, which can be fast-release or slow-release and chemical- or organic-based. Fast-release fertilizers tend to be cheaper and short-lived while slow-release fertilizers tend to be more expensive but have more of a residual effect.

There are many general-purpose fertilizer products on the market, such as 10-6-4 or 5-10-5. You want to look for a well-balanced fertilizer with the three main elements important for plant growth. These essential elements are nitrogen (N), phosphorus (as P_2O_5), and potassium (as K_2O). The percentage of these elements is printed on the bag of the fertilizer. A bag of 10-6-4 contains 10 percent nitrogen, 6 percent P_2O_5, and 4 percent K_2O. Therefore, in 40 pounds of 10-6-4, there are 4 pounds of nitrogen, 2.4 pounds of P_2O_5, and 1.6 pounds of K_2O. The amount needed of these elements depends on your soil test and what deficiencies, if any, are present.

Sometimes these well-balanced fertilizers may not be enough. Other micronutrients may be deficient in the soil, causing yellow or chlorotic plants and requiring you to supplement with over-the-counter products. Iron and magnesium are two good examples of such micronutrients. Iron chelate or iron sulfate are two forms of iron that can be added to iron-poor soils while Epsom salt is a good source of magnesium. Another important nutrient that is sometimes deficient in the soil and is important for plant growth is calcium. Lime and gypsum are two good sources of calcium for plants. If you have acidic soil and need to raise the soil pH, add granular or pelletized limestone over the course of a few growing seasons, which will alter soil pH gradually. Gypsum does not alter soil pH but will improve the structure of the soil.

Ready to Use

FERTIFEED
All Purpose Plant Food

12-4-8

FertiFeed Ready To Use All-Purpose Plant Food
Net Weight 4lb. 12oz. (2.15kg)

GUARANTEED ANALYSIS
Total Nitrogen (N)...12%
    12.0% Urea Nitrogen
Available Phosphate (P_2O_5)..4%
Soluable Potash (K2O)..8%
Manganese (Mn)...0.05%
    0.05% Chelated Manganese (Mn)
Zinc (Zn) 0.05%
    0.05% Chelated Zinc (Zn)
Inert Ingredients...76%

Information regarding the contents and levels of metals in this product is available on the Internet at http://www.regulatory-info-sc.com.

KEEP OUT OF REACH OF CHILDREN

A fertilizer label indicates the percentages of NPK (nitrogen, phosphorus, and potassium), as well as other minor nutrients and filler materials.

Whatever fertilizer you choose, make sure it is good quality and well balanced. Fertilizers are based on ratios, which determine the relative N, P, and K in the bag. For general gardening purposes, a ratio of 2:1:1 is usually sufficient. 10-6-4 is a good example of a 2:1:1 ratio. If you fertilize your lawn, a higher ratio of nitrogen can be applied in spring, if needed. An example would be 21-7-14 or 3:1:2 ratio. A soil test will tell you exactly what ratio and amount of nutrients you will need for your garden.

Organic fertilizers have become more popular over the years and are another good way to keep your plants vigorous. These organic products tend to be slower release than chemical fertilizers and take time to work. They are also less likely to damage plants than fast-release, chemical fertilizers, which can burn plants if applied too heavily. Ideally, a balanced fertilization program incorporates several different forms of fertilizer at certain times during the year. Organic, processed fertilizers include blood meal, bone meal, feather meal, fishmeal, and corn gluten meal. Corn gluten meal has become a popular product that provides an organic form of nitrogen and can also be used as a natural herbicide in a lawn.

The two best times to apply fertilizers in the garden are spring or fall. Spring is ideal because nutrients are often depleted from the soil after a long winter. But depending on specific plant needs, a fall application can be done as well. The main goal is not to apply fertilizers in the heat of summer as that can cause plant damage, especially with fast-release, chemical fertilizers. The application of lime to the soil should also be done in spring but should not be done at the same time as fertilizer applications, as the two often counteract each other. Spread lime applications a few weeks after any fertilizer applications in spring, and water both applications in thoroughly.

Proper Planting

Once you know your soil conditions, it is time to select and plant your new plants. To ensure success, it is imperative that you use proper planting techniques. It is not enough to simply dig a hole and place soil around the rootball of the plant. Special care must be taken to prepare the planting site to ensure easy establishment of the plant. There is something to be said for preparing a $50 planting hole for a $5 plant. Half of the success of plants is how and where they are planted and the other 50 percent is aftercare.

Purchase plants from a reputable nursery with quality plant material and a knowledgeable staff. You will benefit from this reliability and expertise in the long run. These reputable nurseries will employ educated staff that can help you choose appropriate plants for your garden and often will guarantee them for a certain period of time. Once you had made your purchases, there are several important steps that should be followed before actual planting occurs. Make sure you have selected a site in the garden that has the right conditions and appropriate space for your new plants.

Once this is done, the planting hole can be prepared. The size of the planting hole depends on the size of the rootball of your plant. Perennials, groundcovers, and vines are typically sold as bare-root or containerized plants. Planting areas for bulbs and

The planting hole should be three times wider than the rootball and just as deep.

Add fluffy soil and tamp down; add a light layer of mulch.

Water thoroughly after planting.

annuals should be prepared by turning the soil and creating a well-tilled area for the plants to grow in.

Shrubs and trees can be sold as bare-root, container, or balled-and-burlapped (B&B) plants. Burlap can be treated or natural and in either case, it should be removed as much as possible once the plant is set at the right height in the planting hole. Sometimes a wire basket will surround the rootball for extra support. Once again, wait until the plant is set in the hole before the majority of the wire basket is carefully removed. Also remove any wire, rope, or plastic that might be in and around the roots of your plant. The planting hole should be at least three times wider than the diameter of the rootball but should be slightly above the grade of the soil. The rootball should sit on firm ground that is not loose and fluffy. This allows the roots to establish in loose soil but will reduce the chance of settling. With trees, find the root flare or the widening area at the base, and make sure that is above the grade of the soil.

It is important that your plants are placed at the proper depth in the soil. Do some research and find out at what depth the particular plant should be. For example, some perennials need to be planted at a certain depth that you normally would not do for other plants, and bulbs need a specific planting depth to be successful. In the case of container or balled-and-burlapped plants, when in doubt, plant so that the top of the soil in a container is at the same level as the surface of the soil. Trees and shrubs that are planted too deep are doomed for failure and can develop troublesome surface roots that will "girdle" the plant.

Dig a wide planting hole and position a container-grown or balled-and-burlapped tree or shrub at the same level as the soil's surface.

Container-grown plants are handled slightly differently than balled-and-burlapped plants. Plants growing in containers are often pot-bound, with a large volume of roots that consume the container, forming a thick, meshlike appearance. This network of roots should be carefully teased out or sliced with a knife or garden cultivator to encourage roots to grow into the soil.

Certain plants such as some perennials, roses, and, of course, bulbs can be purchased and shipped as bare-root plants. This requires gardeners to take special care to make sure planting is done right away so roots do not dry out. Bulbs do not have to be planted right away but should be kept in a cool, dry place until you are ready to plant them.

Regardless of how your plants arrive, the planting procedure is similar. Once the planting hole has been prepared and the plant is at the appropriate depth, soil can be backfilled into the planting hole and lightly tamped down. Any excess soil, rocks, or debris can be removed and mulch can be added. Unless the soil is poor, use the existing soil, otherwise add compost as needed. With trees and shrubs, do not fertilize at time of planting unless soil is very deficient. It is better to wait a few months so the plants have time to grow new roots that can absorb the fertilizer. After planting and mulching is complete, water your new plantings thoroughly.

The best time to plant in New York and New Jersey is spring or fall while the temperatures are still cool and the soil is moist. Some plants such as flowering trees are better planted in spring while some gardeners plant their rhododendrons in either spring or early fall. Transplanting and dividing can also be done in spring and fall depending on the specific plant species, and some perennials and bulbs can even be transplanted in summer. Exact timing of planting is offered in more detail within each plant description in this book.

Pruning

A properly pruned landscape is healthy, productive, and aesthetically pleasing. Pruning should be done regularly to remove dead or diseased flowers, seedheads, or branches but not so much that it hinders the plant's ability to flower or fruit or destroys the plant's natural growth habit. It is important to know a few things about your plants before you prune them. What is the growth and flowering cycle of the plant? Does it flower on new growth or previous seasons' growth? What are you trying to accomplish by pruning the plant? Reduce its size? Create a screen or hedge? These are all important questions that you should know the answers to before starting a pruning project.

Obviously there is different types of pruning for a wide range of plants and not all plants are pruned the same. Trees and shrubs can be selectively pruned to increase growth and flower production. Shrubs can even be pruned severely to rejuvenate them and keep them at smaller sizes. Evergreens can be sheared or hand-pruned into more formal shapes to create a thick hedge or screen. Herbaceous plants, however, are pruned much differently and usually for a different reason. Herbaceous plants can be pruned to reduce size, deadhead, or cut them back for the season once they are going dormant. Whatever your motivations are, pruning is an important part of garden maintenance and should be done at the proper time of the year with sound techniques to ensure the plant will respond in a positive way.

Selective Pruning

Selective pruning is a method in which certain parts of the plant are selected and removed. For example, selective pruning may be necessary on a lilac that is not producing flowers because it is old and overgrown. The dead, weak, or oldest stems would be selectively removed and the younger more vigorous stems would remain. You may have to go back the next year or two to remove additional stems but within a few growing seasons, the plant should be vigorous and producing flowers again. Trees are usually selectively pruned only to remove deadwood or lower limbs to allow more sunlight to low-growing plants. A regular selective pruning program will benefit woody plants, keeping them productive and in scale. For best results, this selective pruning should be done in late winter or early spring while plants are dormant. For shrubs, the rule is if you are removing less than one-third of the growth at one time, pruning can be done in the growing season. For example, flowering shrubs that just need a light trimming, such as a hydrangea, can be pruned right after flowering in midsummer. If you need to cut the plant back severely, removing more than one-third, do that when the plant is dormant in late winter or early spring.

Prune out crossing branches in trees; they are weak and subject to breaking.

Rejuvenation Pruning

Rejuvenation pruning is much more severe involving cutting the entire plant low to the ground.

Rejuvenation pruning is typically done on shrubs that flower on new growth such as butterfly bush (*Buddleja davidii*). Rejuvenation pruning can also be done on shrubs that bloom on previous seasons' growth such as forsythia and viburnum, but these plants will skip one year of bloom. It can also be done on herbaceous plants such as perennials, bulbs and ornamental grasses once they are dormant. This type of pruning will encourage new growth from the base, or crown, of the plant. This drastic form of pruning is typically done in late winter or early spring on woody plants but can also be done on herbaceous plants whenever they turn yellow and go dormant.

Shearing

Shearing is a form of pruning that is done to maintain tight, formal shapes or to tidy up a loose, free-flowing plant. Hand-pruning shears or trimmers are usually used to prune off newest growth, which encourages a thick, dense plant. I typically do not recommend this type of pruning on shrubs unless it is for a specific reason, as shearing will create unnatural forms and can reduce flowering.

Deadheading

Deadheading is a type of pruning to remove dead or dying flowers. It is done to prevent plants from going to seed and to keep them tidy. This can be done anytime of the year.

Pruning Trees

Trees are pruned a bit differently than shrubs. Trees have larger limbs that require specific pruning techniques in order to remove them without damaging the tree. On limbs that are large enough to require a pruning saw (over 1 inch in diameter), the three-cut method is used.

The first cut is made by flipping your saw upside down and making the pruning cut on the underside of the branch, only partly through, about 1 to 2 feet from the larger limb or main trunk. This cut will reduce the chance of the next cut causing the branch to pinch your saw or tear the bark off the branch or main trunk. The second cut is made on the top of the branch farther out on the limb from the first cut. As the second cut is made, the weight of the branch will cause it to break as it reaches the first cut but stopping there.

With the majority of the weight lifted from the limb, the third and final cut can be made close to the main trunk or branch. It is important to locate the branch bark collar before making the final pruning cut. The branch bark collar is the swollen area where the branch meets the larger limb or trunk. Leaving the branch bark collar will ensure that the wound heals properly.

For smaller limbs that are 1 inch in diameter or less, hand-pruning shears or lopping shears can be used to prune or remove them. In general, younger trees require more pruning than older trees in order to train them, removing crossing or flimsy branches, and so forth. Do not remove too much healthy foliage on older, more established trees as it puts them under stress.

Watering

Proper watering is crucial to the success of your garden. New plantings require water to establish and established plantings benefit greatly from a consistent, proper watering schedule. Poor watering practices can cause all sorts of problems in the garden such as disease problems, weak or shallow root systems, and poor flowering. Too often we rely on an automatic irrigation system to water the garden with little control. These automated systems disperse water whether the garden needs it or not. In addition, remember that a typical garden has many different types of plants such as trees, shrubs, herbaceous plants, and lawn, all of which have unique water requirements. The light exposure can be different in the garden as well, with some areas in full sun and other areas in shade. Even varying soil types can be found on the same property. The point is that a well-drained, sandy loam soil in full sun is going to require more water than a clay loam soil in deep shade. This is why I believe that watering schedules should be tailored to these unique environments and plant types. This will save time, money, and water and create a lush, green oasis that you can enjoy.

In New York and New Jersey, the soils are rather varied with a wide range of soil types and pH. Summers can be hot and humid and spring and fall usually cool but sometimes dry. These factors are important to consider when setting up a watering schedule and here are a few valuable tips. As a general rule, long, infrequent watering is preferred over shorter, more frequent watering schedules. Specific watering amounts depend of soil type,

3 CUT METHOD

Branch Bark Collar

2nd Cut

1st Cut

Yes   No

No

3rd Cut

First cut is "undercut." Second cut is out farther than undercut. Remove what is left, leaving a branch collar. Proper cut will now heal properly.

specific plant needs, size of area to be irrigated, and so forth. However, long, deep watering allows the water to penetrate deep into the soil. This creates a deep root system and may actually *save* water because watering is being done less often and thus reduces waste. Watering for short periods of time only moistens the top few inches of the soil, creating shallow root systems in plants that are vulnerable to drought. Frequent

This illustration shows a comparison of root growing of a plant watered often, for short periods (to the left) vs. a plant watered for longer periods, less frequently (to the right). The root growth on the right is deeper and stronger.

watering also creates more disease problems since the foliage inevitably gets wet more often.

As an example of a more effective watering schedule, water the sunny areas of the garden for two hours once or twice a week. This will provide a deep watering, encouraging an extensive, deeper root system. This is preferred over watering for a half hour, five times a week. Of course, watering frequency is very dependent on weather patterns, soil types, and plant needs, so you will have to adjust the frequency of watering on those factors. You should consult with your local water authority on water restrictions in your area.

Unlike established plants, new plantings are more vulnerable and will need supplemental watering for the first two growing seasons until their established. This rule applies more to trees and shrubs as most herbaceous plants and bulbs will establish quicker.

There are many types of watering systems that can be used for a wide range of plants. For in-ground systems, rotary or mist heads will provide an even and deep watering. For aboveground systems, a simple impulse sprinkler or oscillating type may be used. In flowerbeds and tight areas where you want to be more selective on where the water goes, try drip irrigation or soaker hoses. They deliver low volumes of water more gradually and can be used with lower water volume and pressure. They are also effective if you do not want to get the foliage of your plants wet to avoid disease problems.

Integrated Pest Management

Integrated pest management, or IPM, is a very important part of the overall maintenance of a garden. IPM works hand-in-hand with the idea of creating a sustainable, eco-friendly landscape with the need for fewer chemicals. IPM involves incorporating different forms of pest control to effectively and efficiently control harmful pest populations. These forms of control include biological, cultural, physical, or mechanical, as well as proper plant selection. It does include the use of pesticides *when needed* but usually only as a last resort. By employing these alternative, non-chemical controls, pesticides are needed less often. For IPM to be successful, gardeners must monitor their landscape carefully and determine acceptable thresholds before some form of action is needed.

Biological controls include the use of beneficial insects and other organisms such as lady beetles and praying mantises. Beneficial insects can be attracted to the garden using certain types of plants and creating habitat for them. In addition, several garden supply companies sell beneficial insects for release into the garden. Be sure to research and try to release only insect species that are native to your area. Beneficial insects should be released in the evening when it is cool so the insects do not migrate to your neighbor's garden prematurely.

Physical and mechanical controls require gardeners to physically remove pests from the garden. For example, pests such as scale or mealybugs can be physically removed by wiping off your plants with a cotton swab and rubbing alcohol. Or a spider mite infestation can be kept under control by spraying them with a strong stream of water from the garden hose. Although these methods can be time consuming, they are also very safe to plants and the environment. Mechanical control involves some type of machinery or mechanical device to control pests. Running a small-motorized cultivator or tiller in your vegetable or cut flower garden to keep weeds under control is a form of mechanical control.

Using sound cultural practices can be an effective way to control pests to create a healthy environment for plants and not a breeding ground for pests and diseases. Crop rotation for annual flowers or vegetable crops is a good way to reduce the likelihood of pests festering in one area. Another example is using a small-motorized shredder to mulch up diseased leaves or branches, allowing you to compost them and reduce infected parts of the plant from spreading to healthy areas. Remember that a healthy, stress-free plant is usually not as susceptible to pest and disease problems.

One the most important aspects of IPM is using the right plant in the right place and selecting superior species and cultivated varieties that are more pest resistant. Hundreds of new, superior varieties of landscape plants and agricultural crops are being developed each year to the benefit of gardeners and farmers. Plant breeding programs from universities and horticultural companies continue to yield excellent plants and helpful information to educate the interested consumer.

I should repeat to make it very clear that IPM does *not* mean that pesticides are never used. It simply means you try to use pesticides as a last resort and, if needed, try to use the safest and most effective products available. IPM encourages alternatives to pesticides whenever possible and the responsible use of them when necessary. Good examples of lower-toxicity pesticides are horticultural oils and soaps, which are effective on a wide variety of pests but break down quickly in the environment so there is little residual effect. Check with your local agricultural Extension service or horticultural professional and read the label before applying any pesticides.

To effectively implement a sound IPM program, it is important to monitor your landscape regularly and take the appropriate action based on the specific issue. If a particular pest population on a plant is low and causing not harm, little action may be needed. Once the issue escalates to a level where the plant will be damaged, appropriate action may need to be taken. IPM helps gardeners make educated decisions while protecting the health and beauty of the garden.

MAIL-ORDER NURSERIES

- Brent & Becky's Bulbs, 7463 Heath Trail, Gloucester, VA 23061 (www.brentandbeckysbulbs.com)
- Broken Arrow Nursery, 13 Broken Arrow Road, Hamden, CT 06518 (www.brokenarrownursery.com)
- Camellia Forest Nursery, 9701 Carrie Road, Chapel Hill, NC 27516 (www.camforest.com)
- Completely Clematis, 217 Argilla Road, Ipswich, MA 01938 (www.clematisnursery.com)
- Fairweather Gardens, PO Box 330, Greenwich, NJ 08323 (www.fairweathergardens.com)
- Fancy Fronds, PO Box 1090, Gold Bar, WA 98251 (www.fancyfrondsnursery.com)
- Forest Farm, 990 Tetherow Road, Williams, OR 97544 (www.forestfarm.com)
- Gardener's Supply Company, Burlington, VT, 1-888-833-1412 (www.gardeners.com)
- Gossler Farms, 1200 Weaver Road, Springfield, OR 97478 (https://secure.gosslerfarms.com/home.php)
- Greer Gardens, 1280 Good Pasture Island Road, Eugene, OR 97401 (www.greergardens.com)
- Joycreek Nursery, 20300 NW Watson Road, Scappoose, OR 97056 (www.joycreek.com)
- Klehm's Song Sparrow, 13101 E. Rye Road, Avalon, WI 53505 (www.songsparrow.com)
- Kurt Bluemel, Inc. 2740 Greene Lane, Baldwin, MD 21013 (www.kurtbluemel.com)
- Niche Gardens, 1111 Dawson Road, Chapel Hill, NC 27516 (www.nichegardens.com)
- Plant Delights, 9241 Sauls Road, Raleigh, NC 27603 (www.plantdel.com)
- Rare Find Nursery, 957 Patterson Road, Jackson, NJ 08527 (www.rarefindnursery.com)
- Swan Island Dahlias, 995 NW 22nd Ave, Canby, OR 97013 (www.dahlias.com)
- Woodlanders, 1128 Colleton Ave, Aiken SC 29801 (www.woodlanders.net)

Public Gardens of New York and New Jersey
- Bailey Arboretum (www.baileyarboretum.org/)
- Bayard Cutting Arboretum (www.bayardcuttingarboretum.com)
- Brooklyn Botanic Garden (http://bbg.org)
- Clark Botanical Garden (http://clarkbotanic.org)
- Cornell Plantations (www.cornellplantations.org)
- C.W. Post Arboretum (www.liu.edu/arboretum)
- The Frelinghuysen Arboretum (www.arboretumfriends.org)
- Hofstra Arboretum (www.hofstra.edu/Community/Arbor/index.html)
- Landis Arboretum (www.landisarboretum.org)
- Mohonk Mountain House and Gardens (www.mohonk.com)
- New Jersey Botanical Garden (www.njbg.org)
- New York Botanical Garden (http://nybg.org)
- Old Westbury Gardens (www.oldwestburygardens.org)
- Planting Fields Arboretum State Historic Park (www.plantingfields.org)
- Queens Botanical Garden (www.queensbotanical.org)
- Sonnenberg Gardens (www.sonnenberg.org)
- Reeves-Reed Arboretum (www.reeves-reedarboretum.org)
- The Rutgers Gardens (http://rutgersgardens.rutgers.edu/default.asp)
- Wave Hill, Bronx (www.wavehill.org)
- Willowwood Arboretum (http://willowwoodarboretum.org)

GLOSSARY

Accent: Accent plantings are plants with striking foliage, flowers, fruit, or bark that add interest to the garden.

Acidic soil: Soil that has a pH less than 7.0. Most plants prefer slightly acidic soil with a pH between 6.0 to 7.0.

Alkaline soil: Soil with a pH that is greater than 7.0.

Allée: A typically formal landscape feature that consists of a walkway or roadway that is lined with trees or shrubs.

Annual: A plant that completes its life cycle in one growing season. It germinates, grows, flowers, sets seeds, and dies within one year.

Balled and burlapped (B&B): A tree or shrubs whose roots are wrapped in burlap and twine after it is dug. Burlap protects plant roots and prepares the plant for shipping, sale, and transplanting. Burlap can be natural or treated to reduce deterioration.

Bare root: Trees, shrubs, or perennials that have been grown and soil removed, exposing their roots. Plants are bare-root prior to sales and shipping, which is a method used by mail order nurseries.

Beneficial insects: Insects and their larvae that prey on pests in their adult and their immature stages. Lady beetles, praying mantises, spiders, and parasitic wasps are examples of beneficial insects.

Bract: A modified, usually colorful leaf that resembles a flower petal, located just below or surrounding a true flower. Dogwood is a good example of a plant with colorful bracts.

Catkin: A hanging or upright flower cluster on certain plants, most notably plants in the birch and willow family.

Co-dominant stems: Two or more main stems that are about the same size and emerge from the same location on a tree

Compost: A rich, organic material comprised of humus (plant and animal matter) that has decomposed, used to improve soil conditions.

Compound leaves: A leaf made up of several or many parts called leaflets joined on a single stem.

Corm: A modified bulblike stem. Crocus is a good example of a corm.

Conifer: A plant bearing cones such as pines, spruce, and fir.

Crown: A growing point on a plant where the stems and roots meet, located just below the soil surface.

Cultivated variety: Also called a cultivar, this is a variation of a species that is produced through breeding or selection. Cultivated varieties are most often of garden origin and need to be asexually propagated.

Cut-back shrub: A shrub that is severely pruned annually or every few years in early spring to promote new, vigorous vegetative growth and/or flowers.

Deadhead: A pruning process where dead or fading flowers are removed to improve appearance, prevent seed production, and encourage additional flowers.

Deciduous: Plants that shed their leaves at the end of the growing season and regain them at the beginning of the next growing season in spring.

Desiccation: Drying of foliage, usually due to drought, wind, or harsh winter conditions.

Dioecious: Male and female flowers borne to separate plants with the female plants often bearing ornamental fruit. Holly is an example of a dioecious plant.

Dividing: Splitting apart of perennials and bulbs to create several smaller rooted plants. This practice is useful in propagation, controlling a plant's size, and stimulating an overgrown plant.

Dormancy: A period, usually in winter, in which plants temporarily cease active growth and rest.

Established: A point at which a new plant has recovered from transplant shock and begins to grow by producing new leaves and roots.

Evapotranspiration: Plant transpiration plus evaporation from land and water, which will have a cooling effect on the landscape.

Evergreen: Evergreens are plants that retain their leaves year-round.

Facer or edging plant: These terms refer to low growing plants that grow in front of taller plants. Theses plants are an effective way to give a flower border definition and form.

Foundation plantings: Plantings used near or around the foundation of a house, building or structure. The purpose of foundation plantings is to soften harsh architectural lines, textures, or colors and create seasonal interest in a highly visible area of the living space.

Frond: A leaf of a fern.

Germinate: A plant's first stage of growth, a sprout or seedling.

Groundcover: A low-growing, creeping plant that covers the grounds as it grows.

Groupings: Strategically placed shrubs placed in small groups to accomplish a harmonious planting. If room is limited and a large quantity of shrubs is not necessary, a smaller grouping will maintain harmony on a smaller scale. Groupings in odd numbers such as 3, 5, or 7 can result in a less formal look.

Hardscape: A structural, non-plant part of a landscape such as a house, walls, shed, masonry, pools, etc.

Hedge: Typically medium- to fast-growing, dense shrubs pruned as formal or informal plantings to define a garden space, screen an unsightly view, or create formality in the garden.

Herbaceous: A plant that has fleshy, non-woody stems that die back after frost, typically perennials and annuals.

Humus: A naturally complex organic material made up of plant matter or animal manure.

Hybrid: A plant that is produced by crossing two or more different species, varieties, or genera, usually indicated with an "x" in the name.

Inflorescence: A cluster of flowers occurring at the tip of a branch.

Loam: A nutrient-rich soil comprised of sand, silt, clay, and organic matter offering good water-holding capacity and drainage to support plant growth.

Mass plantings: The use of one type of plant in significant quantities to create harmony and maximize the effect these flowering plants can have in the landscape. Mass plantings are meant to create a natural rhythm that is pleasing to the eye and is often more attractive than one shrub planted as an individual.

Mixed border: A mixture of shrubs, trees, and herbaceous plants, including annuals, perennials, and bulbs that offer multiple seasons of interest.

Mulch: A layer of material, usually organic, applied to the soil surface to suppress weeds, retain soil moisture, moderate soil temperature, and add organic matter to the soil. Wood chips, pine straw, and leaves are all good examples of mulch.

Mycorrhizae: A beneficial soil-borne fungus that forms a symbiotic relationship with plants. These fungi live in and around roots and help plants absorb needed nutrients and water from the soil.

Naturalize: To plant seed, bulbs, or plants in a random, informal manner as they would appear in nature.

Nectar: The sweet fluid produced by flowers to attract pollinators.

Organic matter: Any material that is derived from plants, usually used to make compost.

Perennial: A flowering herbaceous plant that lives over two or more growing seasons. Many of these plants will die back to the ground after frost, go dormant, and regenerate from the roots in spring.

Rhizome: A swollen stem structure, similar to a bulb, that lies horizontally in the soil. Roots emerge from the lower surface and stems emerge from a growing point at or near tip. Bearded iris grows from rhizomes.

Rootbound (potbound): A condition in which a plant has been confined to a container long enough that its roots are forced to intertwine and wrap around themselves, forming a thick mat. When planting a rootbound plant, the roots should be gently teased with a cultivator, knife, or with your fingers.

Root flare: The swollen area at the base of a tree or large shrub where bark tissue begins to differentiate and roots begin to form just before entering the soil. The root flare should never be covered by mulch or silt and should always be visible.

Screening: Shrubs used as screening plants function as a physical and visual barrier in the landscape. Their purpose is to hide a specific view, create privacy, or even act as a buffer to wind or noise. Evergreens or densely branched upright shrubs should be selected for this purpose.

Self-seeding: A tendency by some plants to sow their seeds freely, which creates many new seedlings that may or may not be desired,

Semi-evergreen: A plant that tends to lose some of its foliage in the winter, and can be deciduous in a harsh winter or fully evergreen in a mild one.

Shearing: A pruning technique performed with a hedge trimmer or hand-held shear that cuts the tips of branches uniformly, causing dense growth. This method is used to create formal hedges and topiary.

Slow-release fertilizer: Fertilizer that is water insoluble and releases its nutrients when initiated by soil temperature, moisture, and/or related microbial activity. This fertilizer is typically granular and can be organic or synthetic. Compost is a natural form of slow-release fertilizer.

Soil pH: A measure of the alkalinity or acidity of the soil. The pH is measured by a scale from 1 to 14, with 1 being the most acidic and 14 being the most alkaline. A pH reading of 7 is considered neutral.

Specimen planting: Typically refers to one individual plant that is attractive and noticeable enough to stand alone in the landscape. These strategically placed plants are considered focal points or main attractions in the garden. A specimen is a striking, noticeable plant growing where it can be clearly seen.

Stamen: A pollen-producing reproductive organ of a flower.

Sucker: A new shoot emerging from underground plant roots, which only produce leaves and no flowers. Water sprouts are similar but emerge from above ground stems and branches.

Tuber: A thick, underground stem used to store energy and reproduce. Dahlias grow from tubers.

Turf: A uniform layer of grass, usually manicured, also called a lawn.

Variegated foliage: Leaves striped, edged, or marked with a color different from the primary color of the leaf. Variegation can be creamy white, gold, and other showy colors.

Well-balanced fertilizer: Also known as a complete fertilizer, a powdered, liquid, or granular form of fertilizer that has a balanced proportion of all three major nutrients: nitrogen (N), phosphorus (P2O5), and potassium (K2).

BIBLIOGRAPHY

Alliums for the Flower Garden. Gardener's Supply Company website. 2015.
http://www.gardeners.com/how-to/growing-alliums/7371.html

American Dahlia Society website. 2015. http://www.dahlia.org/

American Hemerocallis Society website. 2015. http://www.daylilies.org/

American Iris Society website. 2015. http://www.irises.org/index.html

Anderson, R. Zinnia. University of Kentucky Extension Service. HortFact-51.14.06.

Angelonia. University of Florida website. 2015. http://gardeningsolutions.ifas.ufl.edu/giam/
plants_and_grasses/flowering_plants/angelonia.html

Armitage, M. Allan. Herbaceous Perennial Plants: A Treatise on Their Identification, Culture
and Garden Attributes. Varsity Press, 1989.

Armitage, M. Allan. Armitage's Greatest Perennials and Annuals App. 2015.

Autumn Crocus, Colchicum spp. The Wisconsin Master Gardener Program website. 2015.
http://wimastergardener.org/?q=Colchicum

Bachman, G.R. Senorita Rosalita, Sparkler Cleomes are Good in Gardens. Mississippi State
University website. 2015. http://msucares.com/news/print/sgnews/sg13/sg20130408.html

Bandana Lantana- Warm season bedding plant. Spring. 2013. LSU Agcenter.com website. 2015.
http://www.lsuagcenter.com/en/our_offices/research_stations/Hammond/Features/super_plants/
spring-2013/Bandana-Lantana--Warmseason-Bedding-Plant.htm

Bearce, B.C. Marigolds. West Virginia University Extension Service website. 2015.
http://www.wvu.edu/~agexten/hortcult/flowers/marigold.htm

Bender, S. Colorful Coleus. Southern Living website. 2015.
http://www.southernliving.com/home-garden/gardens/colorful-coleus

Bluestone Perennials website. 2015. http://www.bluestoneperennials.com/

Botanical Latin Pronunciation Guide. Overplanted website. 2015.
http://overplanted.com/resources/latin.php#A

Camellia 'Polar Ice', 'Snow Flurry', 'Winter's Hope', 'Winter's Rose', 'Winter's Star', and
'Winter's Charm'. The United States National Arboretum website. 2015.
http://www.usna.usda.gov/Newintro/camelli1.html

Coleus. Organic Gardening website. 2015.
http://www.organicgardening.com/learn-and-grow/coleus

Dirig, Robert. Klass, Carolyn. Schroer, Trish. Gardening to Attract Butterflies. Cornell
University Cooperative Extension. Rockland County, 2007.

Dirr, A. Michael. Manual of Woody Landscape Plants. Fifth Edition. Stipes Publishing,
Champaign, New York, 2009.

Farm Management for Native Bees: A Guide for Delaware. Delaware Department of
Agriculture, 2007.

Fine Gardening Magazine Plant Guide. Fine Gardening website. 2015. http://www.finegardening.com/Plantguide/

Geraniums Fact Sheet. The National Gardening Bureau article. Northern gardening website. 2015. http://www.northerngardening.com/NGB_articles/geranium.htm

History of Tulips. Holland.com website. 2015. http://www.holland.com/us/tourism.htm

Home Gardening. Cornell Home Gardening website.2014. http://www.gardening.cornell.edu/homegardening/

Hort Answers. University of Illinois website. 2015.

Hybrid Geraniums: Calliope vs. Caliente. Horticulture Magazine website. 2015. http://www.hortmag.com/weekly-tips/qa/hybrid-geraniums-calliope-vs-caliente

Jauron, R. Selecting and Planting Petunias. Horticulture & Home Pest. Iowa State University website. 2015. http://www.ipm.iastate.edu/ipm/hortnews/1999/2-19-1999/petunias.html

Landscape Plants Rated by Deer Resistance. Rutgers University Agricultural Experiment Station website. 2015. http://njaes.rutgers.edu/deerresistance/

Meyers, M. Michigan: Getting Started Garden Guide. First Edition. Cool Springs Press. 2013.

Missouri Botanical Garden Plant Finder. Missouri Botanic Garden website. 2015. www.missouribotanicalgarden.org/gardens-gardening/your-garden/plant-finder.aspx

Monrovia Nurseries plant catalogue website. 2015. http://www.monrovia.com/plant-catalog/?msg=notactive

New Jersey Tea. Illinois Wild Flowers website. 2015. http://www.illinoiswildflowers.info/prairie/plantx/nj_teax.htm

North Carolina State University Extension website, 2014. www.ces.ncsu.edu

North Creek Nursery website. 2015. http://www.northcreeknurseries.com/

Ottesen, C. Ornamental Alliums. The American Gardener. September/October 2014.

Peony's Envy website. 2015. http://peonysenvy.com/peonycare.html#growth

Perry, L. Dr. Japanese Painted Fern. University of Vermont Extension website. 2015. http://www.bluestoneperennials.com/

Plant Hardiness Zone Map. United States Department of Agriculture website. 2013. http://www.usna.usda.gov/Hardzone/ushzmap.html

Plant Trials Database website. 2014. http://www.planttrials.org/TrialGardens

Rakow, D. and Weir, R. Pruning: An Illustrated Guide to Pruning Ornamental Trees and Shrubs. Third Edition. Cornell University. 1996.

Reich, L. Pruning Clematis. Fine Gardening website . 2015. http://www.finegardening.com/pruning-clematis

Salvia Fact Sheet. The National Gardening Bureau. Northern Gardening website. 2015. http://www.northerngardening.com/NGB_articles/salvia.htm

Selecting and Planting Petunias. Horticulture and Home Pest News. Iowa State University website. 2105. http://www.ipm.iastate.edu/ipm/hortnews/1999/2-19-1999/petunias.html

Simeone, V. Great Flowering Landscape Shrubs. First Edition. Ball Publishing. 2005.

Simeone, V. Grow More With Less: Sustainable Garden Methods. First Edition. Cool Springs Press. 2013.

Simeone, V. Wonders of the Winter Landscape. First Edition. Ball Publishing. 2005.

Snodsmith, R. New York Gardeners Guide. Second Edition. Cool Springs Press. 2004.

The Trial Gardens at UGA website. 2014. http://ugatrial.hort.uga.edu/.

Tsontakis -Bradley, Irene, Eshenaur, Brian, Senesac, Andy, Weston, Leslie. Weed Suppressive Ground Covers. Cornell University: New York State Integrated Pest Management Program. 2007. http://nysipm.cornell.edu/factsheets/n_gh/groundcovers.pdf

Trees and Vegetation. EPA website. 2015. http://www.epa.gov/heatisland/mitigation/trees.htm

Turf Grass Seed and Seed Mixtures. Penn State University website. 2015. http://plantscience.psu.edu/research/centers/turf/extension/factsheets/seed

University of Connecticut Ornamental Horticulture website. 2014. www.hort.uconn.edu.

Wikipedia website, 2014. http://en.wikipedia.org

PHOTO CREDITS

André Viette: pp. 56, 155

Candace Edwards: pp. 175 (both), 179 (all)

Bill Kersey: pp. 17, 174, 180, 181, 184

Dave MacKenzie: p. 80

George Weigel: p. 167

Gloria Simeone: p. 183

Heather Claus: p. 177

JC Raulston Arboretum at NC State University: pp. 49, 63, 96, 121, 143, 147, 160, 169

Jerry Pavia: pp. 6, 23, 32, 39, 50, 60, 73, 77, 79, 81, 88, 92, 114, 125, 126, 129, 149, 152, 161, 168

Katie Elzer-Peters: p. 136

Liz Ball: pp. 51, 100, 101, 120, 157

Proven Winners® ColorChoice®: pp. 103, 105, 113

Neil Soderstrom: p. 75

Shawna Coronado: p. 57

Shutterstock: pp. 10, 18, 22, 24, 28, 35, 36, 37, 52, 68, 70, 72, 89, 131, 158

Susan Weigel: cover

Tom Eltzroth: pp. 20, 27, 29, 31, 34, 40, 41, 44, 45, 47, 48, 53, 55, 58, 59, 62, 69, 71, 76, 82, 83, 90, 98, 99, 117, 119, 124, 127, 132, 134, 137, 138, 141, 144, 150, 153, 154, 159, 164, 165, 166

Vincent A. Simeone: pp. 8, 9, 11, 12, 13, 14 (both), 15, 19, 21, 25, 26, 30, 33, 38, 42, 43, 46, 54, 61, 64, 65, 66, 67, 74, 78, 85, 86, 87, 91, 93, 94, 95, 97, 102, 104, 106, 107, 108, 109, 110, 111, 112, 115, 118 122, 123, 128, 133, 135, 139, 140, 142, 145, 146, 148, 151, 156, 162, 163

INDEX

moss phlox, 165

moss pink, 165

moss verbena, 32

mountain hydrangea, 97–98

mountain laurel, 92, 119, 142

mountain stewartia, 101

mountain sweet, 91

Muhlenbergia capillaris, 79

mulch

    evergreens and, 131

    groundcovers and vines, 151

    microclimates and, 13

    tips for, 176–177

    trees and shrubs, 85

Myrica pensylvanica, 143, 171

Nandina domestica, 137

Narcissus spp., 65, 170

Nassella tenuissima, 79

native plants, 16

nepeta, 47, 170, 171, 172

Nepeta × *faassenii*, 47, 172

New England aster, 39

New Guinea impatiens, 27

New Jersey tea, 91

New York aster, 39

nitrogen, 177

Northern bayberry, 143

Norway spruce, 147

oak, 127–128

oakleaf hydrangea, 97

oak sedge, 81

Oehme, Wolfgang, 74

Okame cherry, 106

old-fashioned weigela, 105

onion, giant, 62

orange coneflower, 44

Oriental lily, 70

Oriental spruce, 147

ornamental flowering cherry, 106, 171, 172

ornamental grasses

    American history of, 74

    care of, 75

    deer resistance and, 170

    as seashore plants, 171

    selecting, 74–75

Orton, Elwin, 94

Osmunda cinnamomea, 50

ostrich fern, 50

Ostrya virginiana, 120

pachysandra, 166, 170

Pachysandra procumbens, 166

Pachysandra spp., 166

Pachysandra terminalis, 166

Paeonia spp., 56

Paeonia suffruticosa, 170

panic grass, 82

panicle hydrangea, 97–98

Panicum virgatum, 74, 82

paperbark maple, 125–126

paper birch, 129

Pelargonium spp., 23

Pennisetum spp., 74

peony, 56

perennial rye grass, 83

perennials

    care of, 37

    deer resistant, 170

    double digging, 37

    pollinator-friendly, 172

    for the seashore, 171

    selecting, 36–37

recycling, 10

red birch, 129

red buckeye, 86

redbud, 93, 171, 172

red maple, 125–126

red oak, 127–128

Reeves skimmia, 163

rhizomes. *See* bulbs

rhododendron, 85, 92, 94, 100, 107, 119, 128, 135, 136, 141, 142, 144, 146, 161, 166

Rhododendron spp., 107

river birch, 123, 129, 170, 171

rockspray cotoneaster, 159

Rosa spp., 102

roses

  as companion plants, 95, 98

  landscape rose, 102, 171

  for pollinators, 172

Rudbeckia fulgida, 44, 170, 171, 172

Rudbeckia hirta 'Herbstsonne', 44

Russian arborvitae, 164, 171

Rutgers Gardens, 7

Rutgers University Agricultural Experiment Station, 170

saffron crocus, 68

sage, 29

salvia, 29, 47, 171, 172

Salvia farinacea, 29

Salvia splendens, 29

Salvia spp., 29

sand, 173

Sarcococca confusa, 167

Sarcococca hookeriana var. humilis, 167

Sarcococca orientalis, 167

sasanqua camellia, 134

scarlet oak, 127–128

scarlet sage, 29

Schizachyrium scoparium, 74, 78

Scilla siberica, 73

seashore plants, 171

sedge, 80, 81

sedum, 39, 41, 53, 171, 172

Sedum × 'Autumn Joy', 41

selection of plants

  annuals, 18

  bulbs, 60–61

  for deer resistance, 170

  perennials, 36–37

  pollinator-friendly, 172

  for the seashore, 171

Senesac, Andy, 151

Serbian spruce, 147

serviceberry, 108, 143, 170, 171, 172

shadblow serviceberry, 108

shadbush, 108

shade trees

  care of, 117

  selecting, 116–117

Shadow, Don, 94

shasta daisy, 42

shearing, 182

shore juniper, 164

shrubs

  care of, 85

  deer resistant, 170

  pollinator-friendly, 172

  for the seashore, 171

  selecting, 84

shrub verbena, 24

MEET
VINCENT A. SIMEONE

Vincent A. Simeone has specialized expertise in woody plant identification, culture, use, and selection of superior varieties. He received an AAS degree in ornamental horticulture from SUNY Farmingdale/New York, and a BS in ornamental horticulture from the University of Georgia. Vincent obtained a masters degree in Public Administration from C.W. Post Long Island University. He is an experienced lecturer, instructor, and horticultural consultant. He has spoken to many groups nationwide and has appeared on several garden shows including *Martha Stewart Living* and HGTV. Annually, Vincent presents an average of fifty horticultural lectures, workshops, and tours to garden clubs, plant societies, professional landscape, nursery, and arboricultural trade associations, and academic institutions. Vincent has taught horticulture classes at The New York Botanical Garden since 1999.

Vincent is a proud member of many organizations including The American Public Garden Association, New York Hortus Club, New York State Arborists Assoc., Long Island Arboricultural Assoc., Long Island Holly Society, American Rhododendron Society, Nassau Suffolk Landscape Gardeners Association, and the Long Island Nursery and Landscape Association. Vincent serves as chairman of the Gold Medal Plant Award Committee, which selects and promotes superior species and varieties of plants for professionals and homeowners alike.

For more than twenty years Vincent has worked in public horticulture at Planting Fields Arboretum State Historic Park in New York, where he is the director. He has written and contributed to various gardening articles for magazines and newspapers including the Long Island-based newspaper Newsday. In 2010, Vincent contributed to a first-ever textbook on public garden management. Also in 2010, Vincent was named Man of the Year by the Long Island Nursery and Landscape Association. He was awarded the Centurion Award by SUNY Farmingdale as one of the top 100 alumni over the past century. He received the distinguished arborist award from the New York State Arborists Association. Simeone is the author of five books: *Grow More With Less: Sustainable Garden Methods* (Cool Springs Press), *Great Flowering Landscape Shrubs*, *Great Flowering Landscape Trees*, *Great Landscape Evergreens*, and *The Wonders of the Winter Landscape*. In 2015, he received the Distinguished Arborist Award from the New York State Arborists Association.